OSCAR SNUBS

FROM CITY LIGHTS TO MAESTRO

OTHER WORKS BY

LAURENCE E. MACDONALD

The Piano Music of Charles-Valentin Alkan (1966)

The Invisible Art of Film Music: A Comprehensive History (1998)

The Invisible Art of Film Music: A Comprehensive History,
Second edition, revised and expanded (2013)

A Musical Legacy: The St. Cecilia Society from 1890 to 2015,
Based on the original text by Alice Lethbridge, with revisions,
corrections, and additional material by Laurence E. MacDonald (2015)

100 Greatest Film Scores, co-authored with Matt Lawson (2018)

Best Picture: A Critical Look at the Academy Award-Winning Films
1927-2022 (2024)

LAURENCE E. MACDONALD

OSCAR SNUBS

FROM CITY LIGHTS TO MAESTRO

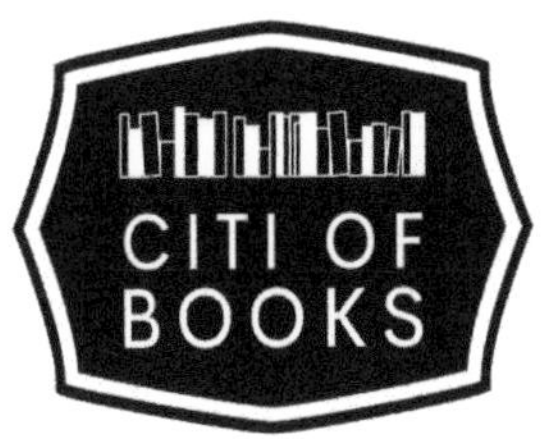

CITIOFBOOKS, INC.
3736 Eubank NE Suite A1
Albuquerque, NM 87111-3579
www.citiofbooks.com
Hotline: 1 (877) 389-2759
Fax: 1 (505) 930-7244

Ordering Information:
Quantity sales. Special discounts are available on quantity purchases by corporations, associations, and others. For details, contact the publisher at the address above.

Printed in the United States of America.

ISBN-13: Softcover 979-8-89391-812-0
eBook 979-8-89391-813-7

Library of Congress Control Number: 2025914675

TABLE OF CONTENTS

INTRODUCTION

In my last book, *Best Picture: A Critical Look at the Academy Award-Winning Films 1927- 2022,* I wrote a series of articles on the Oscar-winning films in the Best-Picture category. Along with profiles of the 95 films featured in the book I listed my personal choices for Best Picture, which differed from the Academy voters' choices about two-thirds of the time.

In this new book I have profiled 52 other films that are in my estimation highly significant examples of cinematic works that were denied any awards in the annual Oscar competition. Among the films discussed in the upcoming pages are those that were nominated in one or more categories, and some others that received no nominations at all. One thing these films have in common is that they were all snubbed by being completely deprived of awards.

It may be surprising for film enthusiasts to realize that many films that are now considered "classic" were totally ignored by the Academy. For instance, the two films by Charlie Chaplin that are discussed in this book, *City Lights* (1931) and *Modern Times* (1936), were totally snubbed by Academy voters, with no nominations awarded either of them. Others, such as *Double Indemnity* (1944) and *Taxi Driver* (1976), each received several nominations, including ones for Best Picture, but received no awards in their respective eligibility years.

I have conceived this book as a way of paying tribute to worthy films that did not get the Oscar recognition that they deserved when they were first released.

The format of each entry included in this volume matches that of my previous book. The films are again presented in chronological order, beginning, as the subtitle of this book suggests, with *City Lights* (1931), and continuing up through Bradley Cooper's brilliant film biography of Leonard Bernstein's life – *Maestro* (2023). Each film entry includes the screen credits, followed by the following aspects of each film: Background, Plot, Memorable Moments, Summation, and a final short section that reflects my view on what awards this film should have won.

It is my hope that through this series of verbal portraits, readers will come to better appreciate the lasting value of films that, like other works in the various visual media, may be overlooked when first introduced, but over time come to be regarded as historically significant contributions to the visual arts.

As I indicated in my previous book, everyone is entitled to their personal opinions. There are no rules regarding one's liking or disliking of anyone's creative efforts, but hopefully this series of presentations will help readers gain insight on the value of the films presented herein.

OSCAR SNUB #1: *CITY LIGHTS* (1931)

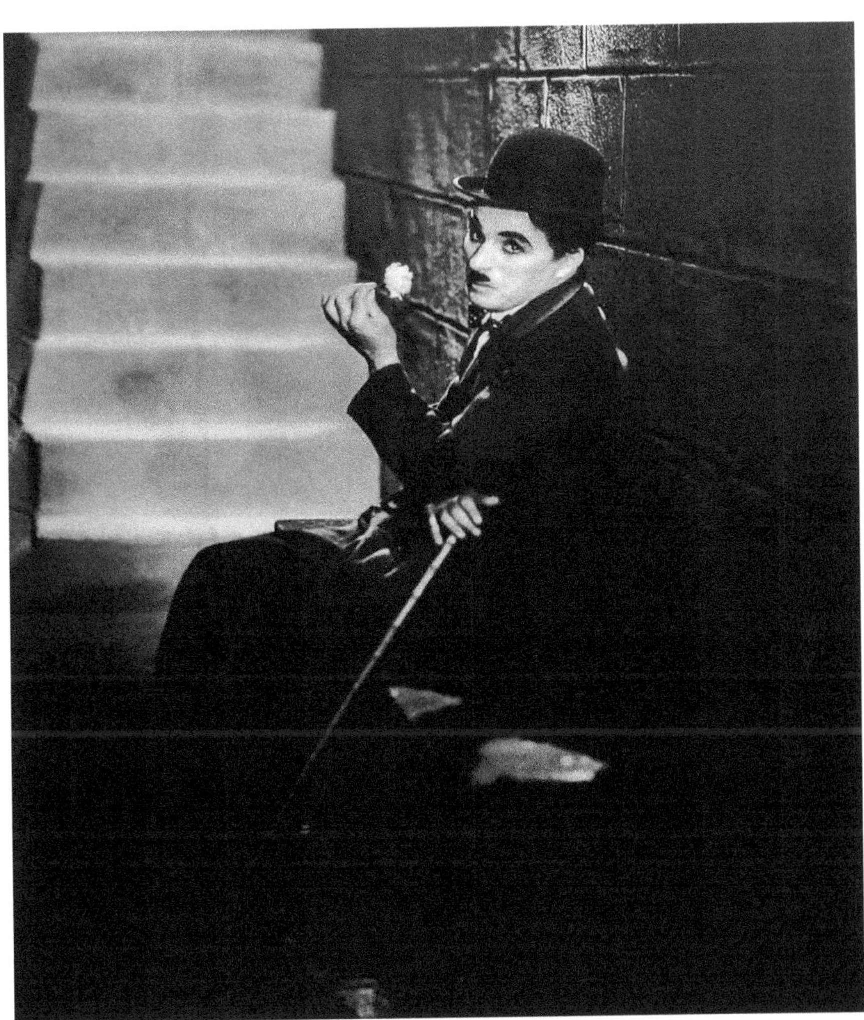

Studio: United Artists; **Director:** Charles Chaplin; **Producer:** Charles Chaplin; **Screenplay:** Charles Chaplin, Harry Carr, and Harry Crocker; **Cinematography:** R. H. Totheroh; **Art**

Direction: Henry Clive and Charles D. Hall; **Costume Design** N/A; **Editing:** Charles Chaplin and Willard Nico; **Sound:** Theodore Reed; **Music:** Charles Chaplin and Arthur Johnston; **Cast:** Charles Chaplin (Charlie, a Tramp); Virginia Cherrill (a Blind Girl); Harry Myers (An excentric Millionaire); Al Ernest Garcia (the Millionaire's Butler); Hank Mann (a Prizefighter); Florence Lee (the Blind Girl's Grandmother). **Running Time:** 86 minutes.

BACKGROUND: As a silent-film comedian, Charlie Chaplin was a jack-of-all-trades who from 1914 to 1921 wrote, produced, directed, and starred in a large number of short films that often featured his most-famous screen creation, a tramp character whose comical antics usually disrupted the lives of those around him. Over time Chaplin gave this prankish character a more benign personality, which is evident in his first feature-length film, *The Kid* (1921).

The success of this film led to such classics as *The Gold Rush* (1925) and *The Circus* (1927), but it was Chaplin's next picture, *City Lights* (1931), that featured the tramp as someone who could truly draw the viewer's sympathy as an itinerant vagabond who falls in love with a blind flower seller.

Because Chaplin started production on *City Lights* at the end of 1928, when the film industry was beginning to abandon silent filmmaking altogether, the film includes a recorded soundtrack with both music and sound effects, but there is no spoken dialogue, since Chaplin did not think he could reinvent the essentially wordless nature of his tramp character.

PLOT: *City Lights*, which is set in an unnamed city, begins when a large sword-bearing male statue is being unveiled in a city park, and the tramp is discovered sleeping in the statue's arms. The plot really begins in the following scene, when the tramp comes across a young woman selling flowers on a street corner. Somehow the seller mistakenly believes the tramp is actually a wealthy man who seeks not only to buy her wares but also to become her friend.

The tramp then encounters an inebriated millionaire who tries to kill himself (his heavy drinking has apparently caused his wife to move out). After a comical rescue from a nearby river, the tramp is invited to join his new friend for an evening of drinking and carousing. However, when the man awakens the next morning, he doesn't recognize the tramp and has him evicted.

The tramp continues to see the young woman, and when he finds out that there is a surgical way to restore the young woman's sight, he goes out of his way to earn the money that is needed for the procedure. At one point he signs up to fight in a boxing ring but is injured in the bout. Soon thereafter he receives a large sum from the millionaire, who rewards the tramp for his ongoing friendship by giving him the funds needed for the young lady's sight to be restored.

After spending time in jail for allegedly stealing the rich man's money, the tramp is on the street once more, and in the film's final scene, the tramp and the girl are reunited when she recognizes by touching his hand that he is the benefactor who has given her a new lease on life.

MEMORABLE MOMENTS: This film is filled with wonderful moments that are alternately comical and touching. The opening scene is very funny, with the tramp getting stuck on the sword of the statue's outstretched arm. The scene also includes a clever use of musical instruments to imitate the sounds of voices as the statue is unveiled, and again when the mayor makes remarks to the crowd that has gathered for the unveiling ceremony.

The scene by the river includes several hilarious moments as the drunk millionaire tries to drown himself by tying a rope to a large stone, but in his inebriated state he gets it wrapped around the tramp's neck instead. Soon both characters find themselves performing a weird sort of ballet as they first fall into the water and then try to pull each other out.

A later scene in a nightclub is also laced with humor as the tramp, who himself becomes tipsy, spins several people around, including a waiter carrying a huge food tray, and several dancers. When he and the millionaire are seated, he attempts to eat spaghetti but finds himself also ingesting long strings from a group of paper streamers used to celebrate the occasion.

The scenes where The tramp visits the humble apartment where the blind girl lives with her grandmother are quite touching, even though there are bits of humor, especially when the girl starts rolling up a ball of thread that actually comes from the tramp's shirt.

The boxing scene is very inventively staged, with a crazy balletic movement involving the tramp, his much larger opponent, and a referee, all of whom spin around as Charlie tries to avoid being hit by the other boxer.

SUMMATION: *City Lights* remains one of Chaplin's most masterful creations, wherein the moments of humor and sentiment are mixed in an ingenious way. As is the case with many of his later films, this movie was in production for almost four years, during which the sound revolution caused filmmakers to adapt their filmmaking techniques to embrace spoken dialogue. The silent nature of this film may have harmed the box-office chances for *City Lights*, which failed to get a single nomination in the 1930-31 Oscar eligibility year.

Despite the lack of awards for this film, it stands as one of the most memorable comedies in the history of film. In a poll conducted by a critics' group in the early 2000s, *City Lights* was voted the greatest comedy film of all time.

WHAT AWARDS SHOULD THIS FILM HAVE WON?: *City Lights* should have won for Best Picture and Chaplin should also have been recognized with an award for his acting. His work towers over Lionel Barrymore's hammy performance in *A Free Soul,* in which he won Best Actor for a trial scene in which he collapses and dies after making a soulful speech in defense of the accused, who happens to be his daughter's boyfriend, played by a youthful Clark Gable.

OSCAR SNUB #2: *LOVE ME TONIGHT* (1932)

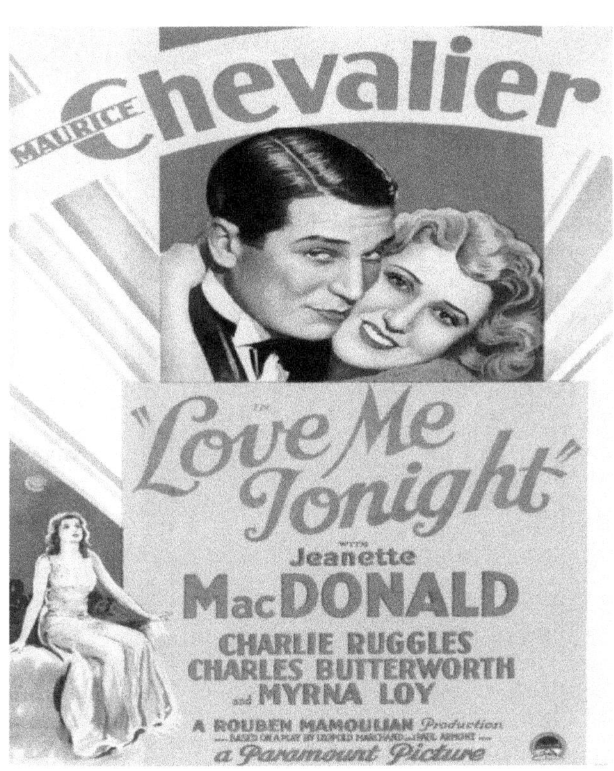

Director: Rouben Mamoulian; **Producer:** Rouben Mamoulian; **Studio:** Paramount; **Screenplay:** Samuel Hoffenstein, Waldemar Young, and George Marion, Jr.; **Cinematography:** Victor Milner; **Art Direction:** Hans Drier; **Costume Design:** Travis Banton and Edith Head; **Editing:** William Shea and Rouben Mamoulian; **Sound:** M. M. Paggi; **Songs:** Richard Rodgers and Lorenz Hart; **Music Direction:** John Leipold and Nat Finston; **Running Time:** 104 minutes; **Cast:** Maurice Chevalier (Maurice Courtelin); Jeanette MacDonald (Princess Jeanette); Charlie Ruggles (Count Gilbert de

Vareze); Charles Butterworth (Count de Savignac); Myrna Loy (Princess Valentine); C. Aubrey Smith (the Duke).

BACKGROUND: Between 1927 and 1932 American movie screens were filled with musical films. Hot on the heels of *The Broadway Melody*, the 1928-29 Best-Picture winner, came an abundance of film musicals, many of which have largely been forgotten. But two talented young actors, Maurice Chevalier and Jeanette MacDonald, charmed movie audiences in four films made between 1929 and 1934. Of these by far the most artistically produced and unforgettably entertaining is the 1932 Paramount film *Love Me Tonight.*

With its two stars singing original songs composed by the team of Richard Rodgers and Lorenz Hart, *Love Me Tonight* is based on a French play entitled *Tailor in the Chateau* by Leopold Marchand and Paul Armont.

It is worth noting that this film is the only one of the four Chevalier/MacDonald films to not be directed by Ernst Lubitsch. George Cukor was originally assigned the directing job on *Love Me Tonight*, but by the time filming began he had been replaced by theater director Rouben Mamoulian. It is largely due to Mamoulian's inspired and innovative direction that *Love Me Tonight* has become, despite its total lack of Oscar nominations, one of the most creatively produced of all film musicals.

PLOT: The film begins with a stunning visual and aural impression of Paris at the start of a typical day. After a number of beautifully photographed shots of the city are shown, the film then conveys a virtual symphony of sounds created by people beginning their work day by doing the most mundane things, but doing them in a rhythmically coordinated way. There are sounds of brooms brushing, nails being hammered, and carpets being beaten, along with such sounds as horns honking, whistles blowing, and chimneys belching smoke.

Following this cacophony of sounds, the scene provides a close-up of Maurice getting out of bed and closing a window to block out the raucous noises coming from outside. Shortly thereafter, Maurice opens his tailor shop and the plot begins when the financially-deprived Count

Gilbert de Vareze comes into Maurie's shop and not only takes out a number of newly tailored clothing items, but actually asks Maurice to loan him some money. When Maurice is soon after informed of the count's dishonest business dealings, he determines to go to the count's country estate to collect the money the count owes him.

While on route, Maurice begins singing "Isn't It Romantic," melodic bits of which are successively picked up by several others, including a cab driver, a small group of marching soldiers, a number of gypsies in a camp, and finally by Princess Jeanette, who despondently admits to being lonely and forlorn since the death of her much older husband.

Once Maurice arrives at the lavish estate, the count slyly introduces him to the family as his friend, a man of aristocratic title.

Maurice quickly becomes welcome amid the large household that includes Jeanette's elderly gentleman suitor, Count de Savignac, a bored young countess named Valentine, three busybody aunts who act as a kind of Greek chorus in the style of Shakespeare, and the family's patriarch, known only as the Duke.

Following the Princess's initial snubbing of Maurice, who is presented by the prankish count Gilbert as Baron Courtelin, Maurice manages to win her affection, but she soon finds out, as does the entire household, that he is nothing but a tailor.

After Maurice hastily leaves the estate to return to Paris by train, Jeanette comes to her senses and goes after him by riding on horseback at breakneck speed, and even boldly stopping the train in a determined effort to keep Maurice from getting away.

MEMORABLE MOMENTS: The film's entire first section is hugely enjoyable, from the noise-making symphony of sounds at the very beginning through the multiple vocal renditions of "Isn't It Romantic," which cleverly begins with Maurice singing in his shop, and ending with Jeanette standing at her bedroom window in the lavish country estate.

Another highlight is Maurice's singing of "Mimi," which he sings to Jeanette even though the song does not bear her name. Chevalier's voice is not one of operatic quality, but his rendering of the song's melodic line is undeniably charming.

When Maurice's true identity is made known, the three aunts quickly scamper about in comic fashion as the entire cast sings bits and pieces of "The Son-of-a Gun Is Nothing but a Tailor."

The last scene, although lacking a big final musical number, is highly dramatic as Jeanette gets off her horse and stands defiantly in front of the moving train, which stops just feet away from her as Maurice jumps off the vehicle for a final clinch with the woman he loves.

SUMMATION: *Love Me Tonight* benefits greatly from the Rodgers and Hart songs that are ingeniously woven into the plot, especially "Isn't It Romantic." While there are no big dance scenes anywhere in the film, the mixture of song and comedy results in a timeless classic that can be watched over and over without any loss of enjoyment by the viewer. Of all the films profiled in this book, *Love Me Tonight* is one of my all-time personal favorites.

WHAT AWARDS SHOULD THIS FILM HAVE WON?: Because *Love Me Tonight* was released just a few days into the Academy's 1932-33 eligibility season, there was a long period between its arrival in theaters and the time the Academy balloting for awards took place. That may explain why *Love Me Tonight* was completely snubbed by the Oscars. In any case, there were many other worthwhile films among the ten nominees for 1932-33, especially *42nd Street, A Farewell to Arms, Little Women, and The Private Life of Henry VIII.* The winner, *Cavalcade,* has dated badly and doesn't seem like an award-worthy film. In my estimation, *Love Me Tonight* is superior to all the official nominees and very worthy of a place in this book.

OSCAR SNUB #3 – *RUGGLES OF RED GAP* (1935)

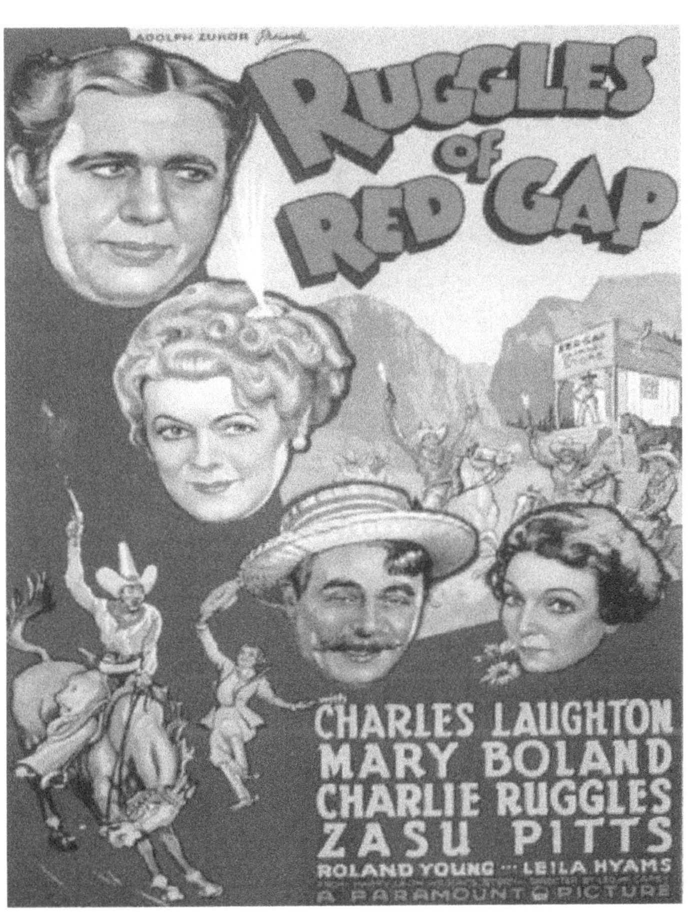

Director: Leo McCarey; **Producer:** Arthur Hornblow, Jr., **Screenplay:** Walter DeLeon, Harlan Thompson, and Humphrey Pearson, from the novel by Harry Leon Wilson; **Cinematography:** Alfred Gilks; **Art Direction:** Hans Drier and Robert Odell; **Costume Design:** Travis Banton; **Editing:** Edward Dmytryk;

Sound: no listing; **Music:** Ralph Rainger and Sam Coslow; **Cast:** Charles Laughton (Ruggles); Charlie Ruggles (Egbert Floud); Mary Boland (Effie Floud); ZaZu Pitts (Mrs. Judson); Roland Young (George Bassingwell, Earl of Burnstead); Leila Hyams (Nell Kenner); **Running Time:** 92 minutes.

BACKGROUND: Harry Leon Wilson's best-selling novel has been filmed several times, beginning with silent versions released in 1918 and 1923. A 1950 musical version called *Fancy Pants*, featuring Bob Hope and Lucille Ball, was a modest hit. But the most acclaimed film of Wilson's novel was released in 1935, with Charles Laughton as Marmaduke Ruggles, a gentleman's gentleman whose English master loses him in a poker game to a *nouveau riche* married couple, Egbert and Effie Floud, who are vacationing in Paris. When Ruggles accompanies the Flouds to their home in Red Gap, Washington, a rowdy town that has prospered due to the gold rush, most local residents mistakenly believe Ruggles is an English aristocrat.

The novel's story pokes fun at both members of high society and newly arrived would-be high society folks that seem to delight in badly pronouncing French expressions and wearing fancy formal clothing. The 1935 film is clearly intended as a starring vehicle for Laughton, who in that single year appeared in three films that were nominated for Best Picture (the others include *Les Misérables* and the Oscar-winning *Mutiny on the Bounty*).

PLOT: The film begins the morning after the poker game, when the Earl tells Ruggles that he must leave the Earl and begin working for the Floud family. Although taken aback by this news, Ruggles obligingly does as he is told and meets his new employers at their hotel in Paris. Although Effie treats Ruggles like a servant, Egbert sees his new butler as a friend and takes him along on an outing that is intended as a means by which Egbert should buy formal clothing to replace the ones of which his wife does not approve. In the course of several hours Egbert drags Ruggles on a series of adventures that include several stops in local bars where the two, along with another newly rich American, get thoroughly intoxicated.

Shortly thereafter, the Flouds take their new employee with them to Red Gap, where the local inhabitants immediately think Ruggles is a rich European with the title of colonel. Egbert is not inclined to deny Ruggles' new identity, and many misadventures stem from this mistaken idea, including Ruggles' reading of books in the Floud's library on American history which convey the concept that all men are created as equals.

While Effie and her houseguest, a stuffy Englishman with a fancy title, disapprove of Ruggles' newly gained American attitude, Egbert enjoys Ruggles' company, especially when hanging out in bars. In one special scene, when talk of Abraham Lincoln's freeing of the slaves is discussed, no one can remember the exact words Lincoln spoke at Gettysburg. When everyone starts asking around what Lincoln actually said, Ruggles starts reciting word-for-word the text of Lincoln's Gettysburg address.

After Effie's houseguest indignantly fires Ruggles and tells him to take a train out of Red Gap, Ruggles decides he finds his new freedom to his liking and starts planning to open a restaurant with the help of his newfound friend, Mrs. Judson, a widow who shares Ruggles' appreciation of fine cuisine.

In the final scene Ruggles opens his establishment, the Anglo-American Grille, and most of Red Gap's prominent citizens show up to admire their English friend's accomplishments.

MEMORABLE MOMENTS: The early scenes in Paris are highly amusing, as Egbert goes through a transformation, aided by Ruggles, who gets increasingly intoxicated as Egbert drags him along from one place to another. An especially humorous moment occurs when Egbert gets his bushy moustache trimmed and then turns on the barber by clipping one side of the latter's moustache.

The film's most memorable scene takes place in the bar, when Ruggles quietly starts reciting the words of Lincoln's famous address. The camerawork masterfully shows closeups of several faces of bar customers who seem mesmerized by Ruggle's quiet but sincere delivery of the speech. The result is a calm and quiet respite from the film's otherwise highly comical style.

In the final scene, as Ruggles and Mrs. Judson toil in the kitchen on the opening night of the Grille, they hear the gathered customers singing "For He's a Jolly Good Fellow," without realizing that it is Ruggles who is being toasted with the song. When he is pushed out of the kitchen to observe the singing, he becomes the happy recipient of everyone's affection.

SUMMATION: Director Leo McCarey became known for a series of sentimental but highly entertaining films. Prior to *Ruggles* he had directed the Marx Brothers in the 1933 film *Duck Soup,* and went on the win two directing Oscars, the first for the 1937 romantic hit *The Awful Truth,* and the second for 1944's number one box-office success, *Going My Way,* which swept the Oscars with seven Academy Awards. Despite these wins, *Ruggles of Red Gap* remains one of McCarey's most supreme achievements.

WHAT AWARDS SHOULD THIS FILM HAVE WON?: The only Oscar recognition *Ruggles Of Red Gap* received from the Motion Picture Academy came in the early months of 1936 when it was named as one of the twelve nominees for Best Picture of 1935. There was plenty of competition for the award, with some real classics among the nominees, especially *Captain Blood, David Copperfield, The Informer, Les Misérables,* and two musicals, *Top Hat* and *Naughty Marietta.* That year's Best-Picture winner, *Mutiny on the Bounty,* with Laughton as the infamous Captain Bligh, remains a classic film, but if there was a category similar to the comedy/musical one in place when determining the nominees for the Golden Globe Awards, *Ruggles of Red Gap* would very deservedly have won in that category. It remains a superlative film entertainment.

OSCAR SNUB #4 – *MODERN TIMES* (1936)

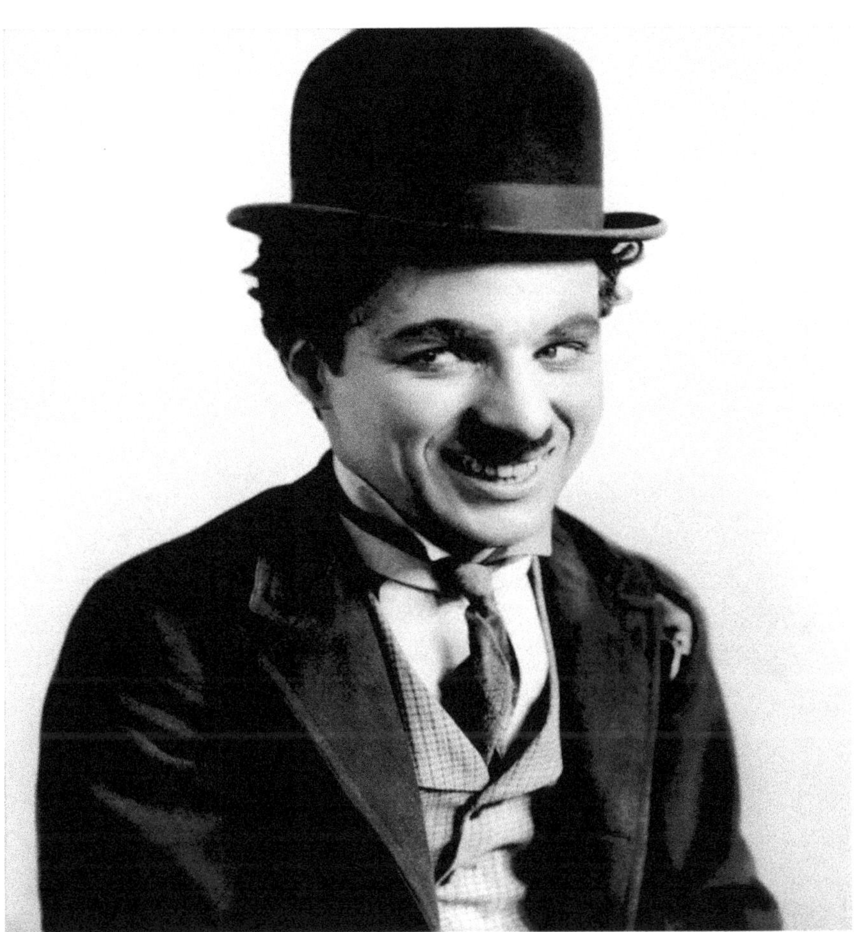

Director: Charles Chaplin; **Producer:** Charles Chaplin; **Screenplay:** Charles Chaplin; **Cinematography:** Rollie Totheroh and Ira Morgan; **Art Direction:** Charles D. Hall and J. Russell Spencer; **Editing: C**harles Chaplin and Willard Nico; **Sound:** Paul Neal and Frank Maher; **Musical Score:** Charles Chaplin, arranged by Edward Powell and David Raksin; music direction by Alfred Newman; **Cast:** Charles Chaplin (a tramp); Paulette Goddard (a gamin); Henry Bergman café proprietor); Chester Conklin (a mechanic); Stanley Sandford (Big Bill); Allen Garcia president of the steel company); **Running Time:** 83 minutes (in Chaplin Collection, mk2 DVD).

BACKGROUND: Following the 1931 release of *City Lights*, Chaplin took the next three years planning and filming his next film, *Modern Times.* As with the earlier film, he resisted the idea of making a talking picture, despite the fact that silent films had become a thing of the past by 1930. Instead, he devised a scenario that would once again feature his silent tramp character and surround him with a cast of actors that would likewise avoid spoken dialogue.

As with *City Lights,* there is a recorded soundtrack with sound effects and a synchronized musical score. The new film, however, includes voices heard on recording devices, along with a large screen mounted on a wall near the assembly line that shows the president of the steel company speaking to his employees at the beginning of the film.

Less sentimental than *City Lights, Modern Times* was designed as a satirical look at the world of manufacturing, with heartless business foremen forcing workers to maintain increasingly fast speeds while tinkering with mechanical parts that move along a conveyor belt.

Chaplin's film also reflects labor troubles by way of a flag-waving workers' protest that reflects the Great Depression that was in full swing at the time *Modern Times* was in production.

PLOT: the film begins with an assembly-line scene wherein the tramp has difficulty keeping up with the speed of the factory's conveyor built. During a lunch break the tramp is selected to help demonstrate an automatized feeding machine that would make meal breaks take up less time. It is obvious that the tramp is mentally challenged by his difficulties in surviving this one day, and he suffers a nervous breakdown that leads him to be arrested and placed in a hospital.

When he recovers his sanity, he is released from custody and soon gets caught up in a workers' protest and gets arrested again for carrying a provocative banner.

When he is released from jail, he meets a young woman (described as a gamin), who is struggling to feed her unemployed father and two younger sisters. At one point she steals a loaf of bread from a local bakery but the tramp takes the blame and winds up in prison.

The tramp and the girl meet again after he helps foil a prison break and is released from confinement. This time he gets a job as a night manager in a department store, and he hides her in a furniture display. Trouble again arrives when a break-in occurs and once again the tramp falls victim to circumstance.

When both the tramp and the girl get employed at a café, the tramp gets the chance to perform a song with strutting dance moves. They hastily depart the scene when a pair of vagrancy authorities come to arrest the girl as a child runaway whose father has now died.

In the touching last scene they find themselves outside the city and decide that no matter what may befall them, they will remain together.

MEMORABLE MOMENTS: The first segment of the film is filled with hilarious sight gags, including the scene in which the tramp is strapped into a feeding machine, which starts working erratically when a robotic arm tips a bowl of soup on him and then stuffs food into his mouth in rapid movements.

More hilarity occurs when he gets so dizzy from the fast-paced assembly-line work that he spins around and wanders outside the building where he dizzily uses his fastening tools on people on the street, especially a buxom woman who gets chased down the block until she hails a nearby policeman.

Another highlight occurs when the incarcerated tramp foils a prison break and gets a letter of commendation from the warden. This letter sets up a job in a department store where at one point he and the girl put on roller skates and spin around in a comical dance-like manner.

The café episode includes one of the film's most entertaining scenes when the tramp's voice is heard in a song that has Italian-style gibberish lyrics. Chaplin's dance moves add charm to this part of the film, which includes the only time in Chaplin's 1930s films when the viewer is allowed to hear his actual voice.

SUMMATION: While less unified in its plotline than the earlier *City Lights, Modern Times* is filled with comical moments which highlight Chaplin's extraordinary abilities as a silent comedian. His hyper movements as a worker on an assembly line, combined with the moment when he is at the mercy of the feeding machine, prove Chaplin's mastery at pantomime.

More than in *City Lights,* Chaplin used this film as a means of expressing concern for the troubles that afflicted America during the Great Depression. There is a defiant attitude in the misadventures that the tramp experiences in *Modern Times* that clearly lay the groundwork for his next film, the 1940 Oscar-nominated film *The Great Dictator,* in which Chaplin daringly plays the tramp as a persecuted Jewish barber while also portraying Adolph Hitler himself in scenes that still resonate today as examples of the Nazi leader's horrific cruelty.

The clever use of musical scoring and sound effects helps in making *Modern Times* a prime example of filmmaking art. Chaplin's original melodies are significant in defining the human side of the tramp character, while the love theme, which is used to confirm the affection between the girl and the tramp, has become well known through the later addition of lyrics that led to the familiar song "Smile."

WHAT AWARDS SHOULD THIS FILM HAVE WON?: Ten 1936 films competed for the Best-Picture award. Among the classics are *Mr. Deeds Goes to Town, San Francisco, Anthony Adverse, Dodsworth,* and *A Tale of Two Cities.* The lengthy and elaborate MGM film *The Great Ziegfeld* won the big prize, but *Modern Times* deserved to be recognized as that year's winner.

OSCAR SNUB #5 – *THE PRISONER OF ZENDA* (1937)

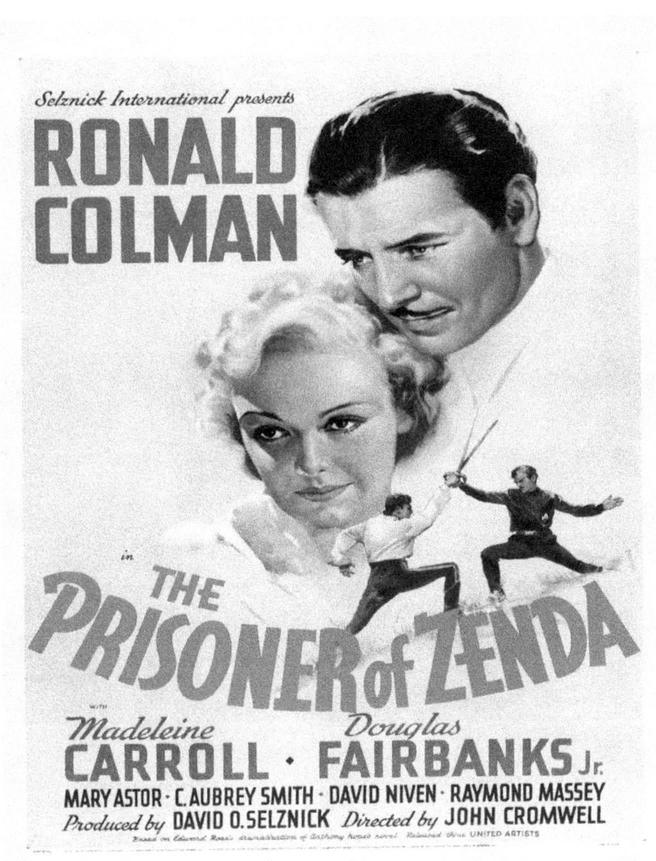

Director: John Cromwell; **Producer:** David O. Selznick; **Studio:** Selznick International/ U.A. **Screenplay:** John Balderston, from the novel by Anthony Hope; **Art Direction:** Lyle Wheeler: **Costume Design:** Ernst Dryden; **Editing:** James E. Newcom; **Sound:** Oscar Legerstrom; **Music:** Alfred Newman; **Special Effects:** Jack Cosgrove; **Cast:** Ronald Colman (Rudolf Rassendyll/

King Rudolf); Madeleine Carroll (Princess Flavia); Raymond Massey (Black Michael); Douglas Fairbanks, Jr. (Rupert of Henzau); C. Aubrey Smith (Colonel Zapt); David Niven (Lieutenant Fritz von Tarlenheim); **Running Time:** 100 minutes.

BACKGROUND: The idea of having the same actor playing multiple roles in the same film goes back to the beginning of the sound era when Lon Chaney relished the idea in such films as *The Unholy Three* (1930). Other actors have taken on the unique challenge of playing two look-alike characters in the same scene, including Bette Davis in two films, *A Stolen Life* (1946) and *Dead Ringer* (1964). Two films featuring teenage twins were made by the Walt Disney company, *The Parent Trap* (1961), with Hayley Mills as twins who swap roles, and the 1998 remake, with Lindsay Lohan enacting the same roles Mills had played in the earlier version.

The use of trick photography has allowed many actors to appear "together" in the same scene. That visual trickery is very evident in both the 1937 David O. Selznick production of *The Prisoner of Zenda* that stars Ronald Colman and the 1952 MGM version with Stewart Granger, which was conceived as a scene-for-scene duplicate of the earlier version. The addition of Technicolor photography in the latter version does little to erase the fact that in almost every aspect the earlier version of *Zenda* is superior to the remake. The black-and-white Selznick film is a classic example of a frequently exciting adventure film with a beautifully conceived romantic subplot at its core.

PLOT: In Anthony Hope's novel, an English traveler is vacationing in central Europe when he surprisingly meets his distant relative who is about to be crowned king of Ruritania. The night before the coronation the king is drugged, so that his half-brother, Black Michael, can usurp the throne. Thanks to a pair of men loyal to the rightful king, the coronation takes place as planned, but with cousin Rudolf standing in as the monarch. The ruse is only supposed to last one day, but when the monarch suddenly disappears, the pretense has to be extended.

To add complication to the plot, cousin Rudolf meets Princess Flavia, who has been betrothed to the king since they were children. When Rudolf meets her he is smitten, and Flavia finds him much more likeable than the king that she has not seen for several years. When the king is still not found in the days following the coronation, Rudolf agrees to continue the impersonation at a royal ball that has been planned to honor the royal couple's impending marriage. During the festivities both Rudolf and Flavia find themselves romantically attracted to each other.

In the midst of this intrigue, Rupert of Henzau, a handsome but dangerous colleague of Michael, learns of the impersonation and collaborates with Michael to kill both Rudolf and the rightful king, who has been sequestered at the castle of Zenda, a remote place used by the monarchs of Ruritania as a hunting lodge.

After Rudolf manages to sneak into the castle, he and Rupert face each other in a fateful fencing duel, while the king's loyal soldiers storm the castle and the king is rescued. In the final scene Rudolf and Flavia proclaim their mutual love, but they realize that they have no future together, since Flavia decides that she must honor her long-planned betrothal to the king.

MEMORABLE MOMENTS: The coronation scene is lavishly filmed, with a long row of trumpeters playing a brass fanfare at several points during the ceremony. A moment of anxiety occurs when Rudolf suddenly pauses in his recitation of the royal oath, but Rudolf quickly recovers his composure and resumes the recitation of the required words. During the oathtaking both Colonel Zapt and Fritz, who have helped to orchestrate the impersonation by coaching Rudolf in preparing the royal speech, breath huge sighs of relief.

The royal ball is one of the film's most lavish scenes, with the "king" and Flavia descending a lengthy staircase that leads to the ballroom floor. Once the dancing begins, with a Johann Straus waltz played by the royal orchestra, a fun moment occurs when Rudolf and Flavia cease their dancing. When the music suddenly stops, Rudolf learns from Flavia that when the monarch stops dancing the music has to stop.

To the consternation of the conductor, the waltz starts a total of four times. Each time the music commences the conductor gets increasingly agitated in his musical gestures in front of the orchestra.

The rescue sequence is visually exciting, especially during the duel between Rudolf and Rupert. The two make several jabs, during which there are impressive visual shots of their images appearing as dark shadows against the walls and pillars of the room.

The parting scene in which Flavia and Rupert express their mutual love is both well-acted and emotionally touching, with the help of the lovely background music of Alfred Newman helping to enhance this tender scene.

SUMMATION: Producer Selznick went out of his way to create a visually stunning film out of this classic story. With the help of Newman's great musical score, the scenes at the royal palace contain many moments of magnificent pageantry, while James Wong Howe's brilliant photography plays a huge role in helping this film achieve both excitement and glamour.

Both Colman and Carroll look properly majestic in their royal costumes, while Douglas Fairbanks, Jr. pretty much steals the show whenever he is onscreen, with the sinister smile that he flashes multiple times, especially when he spars with Colman in his royal impersonator role.

Of all the romantic adventure films of the 1930s, this version of *Prisoner of Zenda* remains a classic example of Hollywood filmmaking at its best.

WHAT AWARDS SHOULD THIS FILM HAVE WON?: The list of ten nominees for Best Picture of 1937 includes some first-rate films, including *The Good Earth, Lost Horizon, A Star Is Born, and Captains Courageous. The Life of Emile Zola* deservedly won as Best Picture, but *Prisoner of Zenda* should at least have won in the cinematography and music categories.

OSCAR SNUB #6 - *BRINGING UP BABY* (1938)

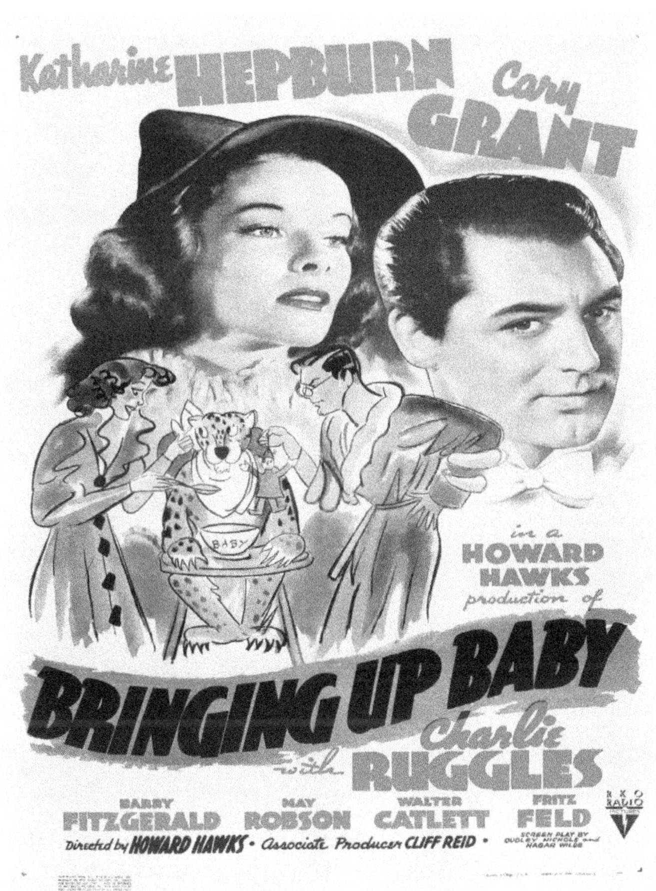

Director: Howard Hawks; **Producer:** Howard Hawks and Cliff Reid; **Studio:** RKO; **Screenplay:** Dudley Nichols and Hagar Wilde, from Wilde's short story; **Art Direction:** Van Nest Polglase and Perry Ferguson; **Costume Design:** Howard Greer; **Editing:** George Hively; **Sound:** John L. Cass; **Musical Score:** Roy Webb, with stock music by Max Steiner; **Special Effects:** Vernon L. Walker; **Cast:**

Katharine Hepburn (Susan Vance); Cary Grant (Dr. David Huxley); Charlie Ruggles (Major Applegate); Walter Catlett (Constable Slocum); May Robson (Elizabeth Random); Virginia Walker (Alice Swallow); **Running Time:** 102 minutes.

BACKGROUND: In the 1930s a type of light-hearted film known as "screwball comedy" began to gain popularity with moviegoers. In the middle of the Great Depression, audiences were delighted with films that included zany characters and crazy plot twists.

Howard Hawks's *Bringing Up Baby* is one of the most memorable examples of this genre, which lasted from the late 1930s well into the 1940s. Many major stars appeared in these films, including Cary Grant and Katharine Hepburn, who starred together in four films made between 1936 and 1940. *Bringing Up Baby* represents the second of these films, and even more than in the classic 1940 film *The Philadelphia Story,* Hawks's film proves that Grant and Hepburn could excel in truly hilarious screwball situations.

From the start *Bringing Up Baby* moves along with a crazy lack of traditional continuity, and thus the film clearly deserves to be categorized as "screwball."

PLOT: The film begins at the Stuyvesant Museum of Natural History where David Huxley, a skilled paleontologist, is assembling the skeleton of a prehistoric brontosaurus, with the help of his assistant, Alice Swallow, who is also his fiancée. David lacks only a single bone, an intercostal clavicle, to complete the construction project that has taken him four years. Good news comes when he learns that that this all-essential bone is being shipped to the museum.

Complications arise when David goes to a local golf course in hopes of meeting Mr. Peabody, a lawyer who represents a rich woman named Mrs. Random, who has agreed to donate a million dollars to the museum. Before David can engage Mr. Peabody, he is distracted by a young woman named Susan Vance, who uses David's ball for her next stroke. Despite his objections she hits the ball and thus starts a long series of unexpected complications, which escalate when Susan starts driving David's car and dents the vehicle in the process.

Later that evening, David again hopes to meet with Peabody at a golf club, but more complications arise when David runs into Susan and they both wind up with torn clothing and a hasty exit from the building.

The next day Susan calls David asking for his help with a pet leopard named Baby that her brother has shipped from Brazil. She claims she wants to take the animal to her aunt's home in Connecticut. After a wild ride into the country, they arrive at her aunt's lavish estate and lock the animal into a storage room by the garage.

Throughout this undertaking David carries the bone in a box that was delivered to him earlier that day. Anxious to get back to the museum and his fiancée, David is once again sidelined when the aunt's dog, George, finds the box and buries the bone somewhere in the yard.

In the meantime, David finds out that Susan's aunt is Mrs. Random, the potential donor to the museum. Before he can leave, he must find the bone and deal with two leopards, because another one, much more dangerous than Baby, has escaped from a nearby circus.

Complications escalate further when a local constable arrests both David and Susan when she tries to drive off in someone else's car. Several others, including Mrs. Random and Mr. Peabody, also get locked up in jail until the constable can figure out who is breaking the law.

After a frantic scene in which both leopards are on the loose, David is able to lock up the circus animal and get back to the museum, where Susan shows up with the missing bone and tries to hand it to David, who is on a scaffold above the precious skeleton. What happens next brings the film to a humorously conceived ending.

MEMORABLE MOMENTS: In the golf course scene, David keeps calling to his playing companions when he gets distracted by Susan's unexpected use of his ball and his car. Four times he hilariously yells, "I'll be with you in a minute, Mr. Peabody."

Later, when David and Susan are looking for Baby, who has gotten loose on the way to Mrs. Random's home, Susan instructs David to join her in singing "I Can't Give You Anything but Love," which is supposed to calm the animal down. This song is cleverly worked into several scenes in the film.

The film's most riotous moments occur in the extended sequence which takes place at the jail where the flustered constable tries to get the truth from the locked-up supposed wrong-doers. Everyone in the scene talks at a very rapid pace, with dialogue overlapping at times. At one point Susan tries to confuse the constable by calling herself "Swinging Door Susy," a gangster who has committed crimes with the help of David (whom she calls Jerry). When the circus leopard comes charging into the corridor, David saves the day by bravely maneuvering the wild animal into a jail cell adjacent to the one that everyone else, including the constable, has scampered into.

SUMMATION: Everyone in *Bringing Up Baby* contributes to the hilarity of the complicated situations that develop from the film's opening moments. Grant is especially good at conveying the annoyance that David faces from the moment he meets the scatter-brained Susan. His numerous pratfalls add nicely to Grant's portrayal of this mightily put-upon character.

Supporting performers add greatly to the fun, especially Walter Catlett as the flummoxed Constable Slocum, who keeps getting sidetracked during his investigation by the fast-talking repartee voiced by the other cast members.

Howard Hawks deserves special credit for instilling the rapid-paced dialogue that permeates the film. *Bringing up Baby* may not have anything serious to say, but as an exercise in slapstick comedy this is an exceptionally well-made film.

WHAT AWARDS SHOULD THIS FILM HAVE WON?: Cary Grant never won an acting Oscar, despite later nominations in 1941 and 1944. I would have given him one for *Bringing Up,Baby* because his comic timing is an impeccable example of superlative acting.

OSCAR SNUB #7 – *OF MICE AND MEN* (1939)

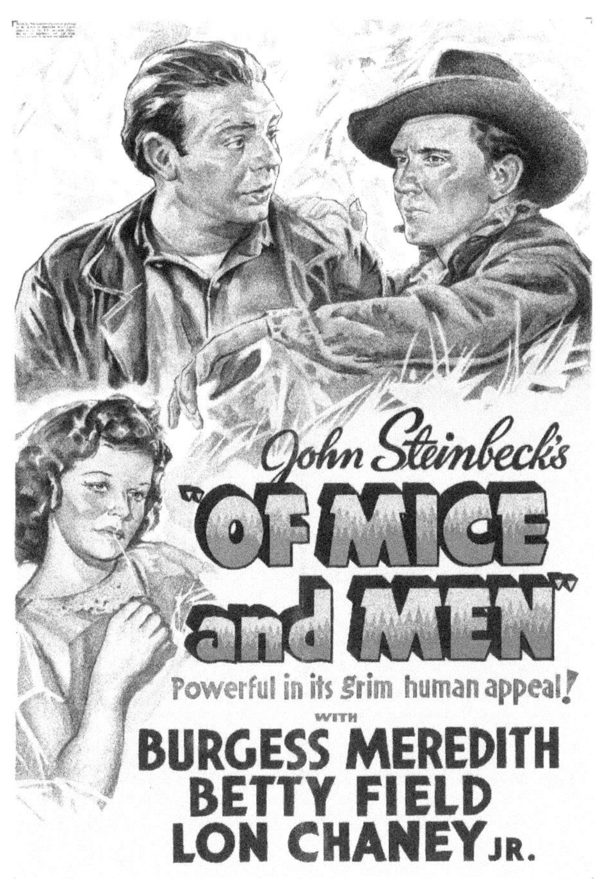

Director: Lewis Milestone; **Producer:** Lewis Milestone; **Studio:** Hal Roach, UA; **Screenplay:** Eugene Solow, from the play based on the novel by John Steinbeck; **Cinematography:** Norbert Brodine; **Art Direction:** Nicolai Remisoff and W. L. Stevens; **Costume Design:** Harry Black; **Editing:** Bert Jordan; **Sound:** William Randall; **Music:** Aaron Copland; **Cast:** Burgess Meredith (George

Milton); Lon Chaney, Jr. (Lennie Small); Charles Bickford (Slim); Betty Field (Mae Jackson); Roman Bohnen (Candy); Bob Steele (Curley Jackson); **Running time:** 107 minutes.

BACKGROUND: In the late 1930s author John Steinbeck wrote two novels that became immediate best-sellers – *Of Mice and Men* (1937) and *The Grapes of Wrath* (1939). Both became nominees for Best Picture when released as theatrical films, in 1939 and 1940 respectively. *Grapes of Wrath* may be the more critically acclaimed of the two, but *Of Mice and Men* has been fondly remembered (and memorably remade in 1992).

Steinbeck's story concerns two drifters in the central farming area of California during the Great Depression. George Milton, the smaller and smarter of the two, habitually travels with the much taller and huskier Lennie Small, who was hit in the head by a horse as a child and rendered mentally deficient. As Lennie's longtime caretaker, George always speaks for his companion, who has trouble remembering things.

PLOT: George and Lennie desire to have a little farm of their own, but first they need to find jobs so that they can raise the necessary funding. At the start of the film, they arrive at a barley farm after being pursued by several law enforcement officers. Lennie has habitually caused trouble, so George hopes that if Lennie does only what George tells him to do, they will succeed at their new workplace. Although things initially go well at the ranch, problems soon arise.

The first sign of trouble comes when they meet the boss's son, Curley. As one of the veteran farm hands explains, Curley, who is of small stature, hates big people like Lennie. Another complication is Curley's resentment concerning his lonely wife, Mae, who admittedly doesn't love him, and causes him to fly into a rage when anyone else comes near her.

George easily befriends some of the other workers, especially Slim and an elderly man named Candy, who has lost his left hand and spends most of his time tending an old dog that he keeps with him. When

Candy hears George talk about the little place that he and Lennie want to find, Candy begs them to let him join in the project.

Things go downhill when Curley attacks Lennie by punching him repeatedly, until George tells Lennie to hit back. When Lennie clenches Curley's upraised right hand, the sheer strength of Lennie's grip causes Curley to pass out.

Following this scene, things go from bad to worse when Mae, who is being evicted by her injured husband, visits some pups in the barn and causes Lennie to react when she gets excited and starts yelling. She winds up being suffocated when he puts his huge hand over her mouth.

After Lennie runs off to a river where George has told him to go if trouble arises, George uses a gun to shoot Lennie and thus prevent the enraged Curley from carrying out his own vengeance.

MEMORABLE MOMENTS: In an early scene, when George and Lennie are in a woods near a river, Lennie asks George to repeat a dream he has told many times, about having a ittle place all their own where they can raise their own crops, raise animals (especially the rabbits that Lennie often refers to) and live off the fat of the land. In this long unedited shot, they sit close together near a fire and heat beans for dinner as George gets Lennie to picture this ideal place. As they bed down for the night George tells Lennie to remember these bushes by the river, so that if trouble comes their way, Lennie knows where to go.

A later worthy moment takes place in the bunkhouse when Lennie listens as George once again paints a verbal picture of their little place. But this time their friend Candy, who has been listening from a distance, comes towards them and asks if he can join them in their search. Candy even counts out money to help pay for the place and writes out a detailed monetary proposal concerning the benefits of raising rabbits. At one point Lennie and Candy both look mesmerized when George agrees to put this plan into action.

The film's most dramatic scene occurs when Curley starts punching Lennie in the bunkhouse. Aaron Copland's highly dramatic chords emphasize each one of Curley's blows, until the closeup shot of fists raised in the air brings about a hugely energized and long-sustained dissonant chord that powerfully evokes the crushing of the bones in Curley's hand. When Curley falls to the floor, the music includes a really dramatic sound.

The last scene is hauntingly memorable, as George fires the shot and then stands in a trance-like state when a sheriff arrives to take the gun from his hands. When they move out of view the idyllic hoped-for home in the woods is also left behind.

SUMMATION: *Of Mice and Men* is without doubt one of the saddest films described in this book, and it is also one of the most unforgettable. Besides the terrific acting by the entire cast, especially Lon Chaney, Jr., in the best role of his career, the film excels in many other ways, including outstanding cinematography by Norbert Brodine. In many scenes the actors are seen in long unedited shots that have humans surrounded by such visual devices as bunkbed frames and woodwork that surrounds windows and doors.

Another superlative aspect of the film is the emotional score by Aaron Copland, whose cues are often highly dramatic, while others emphasize the story's sadness, especially when Candy awaits the shooting of his dog while lying in his bunk.

Lewis Milestone also deserves credit for bringing this tragic story to the screen.

WHAT AWARDS SHOULD THIS FILM HAVE WON?: Despite stiff competition from the other nominees, this film should have been awarded for its excellent screenplay plus Aaron Copland's superbly dramatic score.

OSCAR SNUB # 8 - *THE SHOP AROUND THE CORNER* (1940)

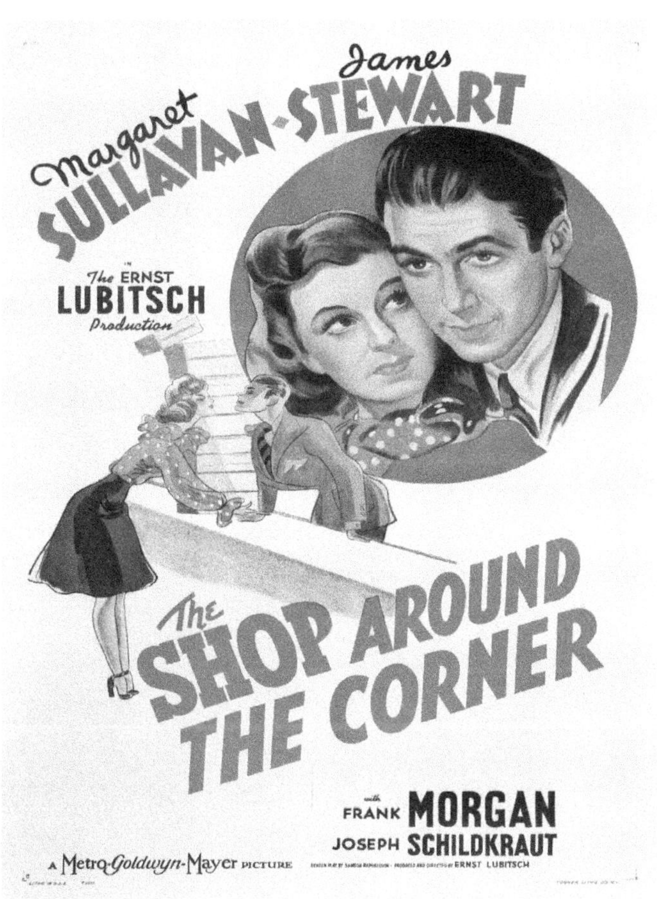

Director: Ernst Lubitsch; **Producer:** Ernst Lubitsch; **Studio:** MGM; **Screenplay:** Samson Raphaelson, from the play by Nikolaus Laszlo; **Cinematography:** William Daniels; **Art Direction:** Cedric Gibbons and Edwin B. Willis; **Costume Design:** N/A; **Editing:** Gene Ruggiero; **Sound:** Douglas Shearer; **Music:**

Werner Heymann; **Cast:** Margaret Sullavan (Klara Novak); James Stewart (Alfred Kralik); Frank Morgan (Hugo Matuschek); Joseph Schildkraut (Ferenz Vadas); Felix Bressart (Mr. Pirovich); William Tracy (Pepi Katona); **Running time:** 97 minutes.

BACKGROUND: Ernst Lubitsch became a very popular film actor, writer, and director in his native Germany during the second decade of the 20th century. After migrating to Hollywood he continued to make noteworthy films that concentrated on the basic theme of love among the rich. It was during the 1920s that Lubitsch's brand of romance, humor and sometimes rather risqué plotlines earned the soubriquet "the Lubitsch Touch" and led to back-to-back Oscar nominations for both producing and directing *The Patriot* (1928) and *The Love Parade* (1929), the latter of which was his first talking picture. He won acclaim again in 1939 for directing *Ninotchka,* which he made at MGM. The following year he shifted gears by making a love story about ordinary people, *The Shop Around the Corner,* based on a Hungarian play called *Parfumerie.*

While this film failed to receive any Oscar nominations, *Shop Around the Corner* has gained fame as one of the classic romantic comedies of the 1940s. It has also been the plot inspiration for two later films, including the Judy Garland musical *In the Good Old Summertime* (1949) and *You've Got Mail* (1998).

PLOT: Lubitsch's film, which is set in Budapest during the 1930s, takes place mostly in a notions shop run by a well-to-do businessman named Hugo Matuschek. Among the employees is Alfred Kralik, a hard-working clerk who has been with the company for nine years. On the same day that he hopes to convince the boss that he should be given a raise, Alfred meets Klara Novak, a pretty young woman who he thinks has come into the shop to buy something, when what she really wants is to meet Matuschek personally and ask for a job. When Alfred finds out what her true intentions are, he feels that she has misled him and he becomes a bit aggravated with her.

Over the next six months their dislike is observed by the other employees, who hear Klara speak disparagingly about him, while Alfred finds her petulant and annoying. As Christmas nears, each of them asks for the same evening off because they say they have made other arrangements. What they have been planning is the chance to meet the persons they have been corresponding with by letters. Kralik has a habit of sharing with his fellow employee Mr. Pirovich the contents of letters he has been receiving, while Klara often quotes to Alfred some of the things her pen pal has been writing to her.

On the evening of the fateful meetings that they have each arranged, it turns out that they have plans to meet at the same place. It is Alfred who first comes to the awareness that the woman he desires to have dinner with is none other than Klara herself. When he comes into the restaurant to speak with Klara, he doesn't let on that he knows how they are connected, and they remain unfriendly, especially Klara, who resents Alfred when he sits in the chair that she has reserved for her date.

Earlier on that same day Alfred loses his job when Matuschek expresses displeasure with him but writes him a letter of recommendation. That evening becomes additionally troublesome when word comes that Matuschek has tried to shoot himself when he learns that his wife has become romantically linked with one of Matuschek's other employees.

In the wake of these difficulties, Alfred not only gets rehired, but he becomes the business manager. When Matuschek returns and hands everyone bonus checks as Christmas presents, Alfred takes the opportunity to confront Klara about their real connection and they wind up falling into each other's arms.

MEMORABLE MOMENTS: In the opening scene, as the employees of Matuschek's shop wait on the sidewalk for the boss to arrive and unlock the door, Alfred reads a portion of the latest letter he has received from his mystery pen pal to Pirovich, Alfred's fellow employee is impressed when Alfred reads the inscription "Dear Friend" that appears in the letter. In the letter the woman also claims to be an avid reader and is currently reading Tolstoy's *Anna Karenina.*

The memorable restaurant scene begins when Alfred asks Pirovich to look through the window and see if his female pen pal is there. When Pirovich looks in and spots a woman with the book *Anna Karenina* he says, "You're not going to like her because she IS Miss Novak." This scene becomes additionally noteworthy when Klara says that that he is nothing like the man who has been writing letters to her. Alfred wants to prolong the conversation and find a way of telling Klara the identity of her "Dear Friend," but he gets up and leaves the premises after she says that he is definitely not the type of person she is waiting for.

The film's last scene is also memorable, as Alfred and Klara stay at the shop after the others have left. When Alfred starts quoting from the latest letter he has sent to post-office box number 237, Klara finally realizes that Alfred is her "Dear Friend."

SUMMATION: Upon a first viewing, much of *Shop Around the Corner* may seem a film of no special merit, but its appeal improves with repeated viewings. Not only do the extended conversational scenes featuring Alfred and Klara become much more beguiling, but the moving final scene is a real tug at the heartstrings as Klara finally makes the connection that Alfred is actually her beloved pen pal.

Many romantic films have conventional happy endings, but the final minutes of *Shop Around the Corner* should leave viewers misty-eyed and deeply moved. Few other films contain such a heightened level of emotional impact.

WHAT AWARDS SHOULD THIS FILM HAVE WON?: The ten nominees for 1940's Best Picture include many fine films, including *The Grapes of Wrath, The Great Dictator, The Letter, Kitty Foyle,* and the prize-winning *Rebecca. Shop Around the Corner* is a small gem of a film that at least should have been cited for its fine screenplay, direction, and production design.

OSCAR SNUB #9 – *SULLIVAN'S TRAVELS* (1941)

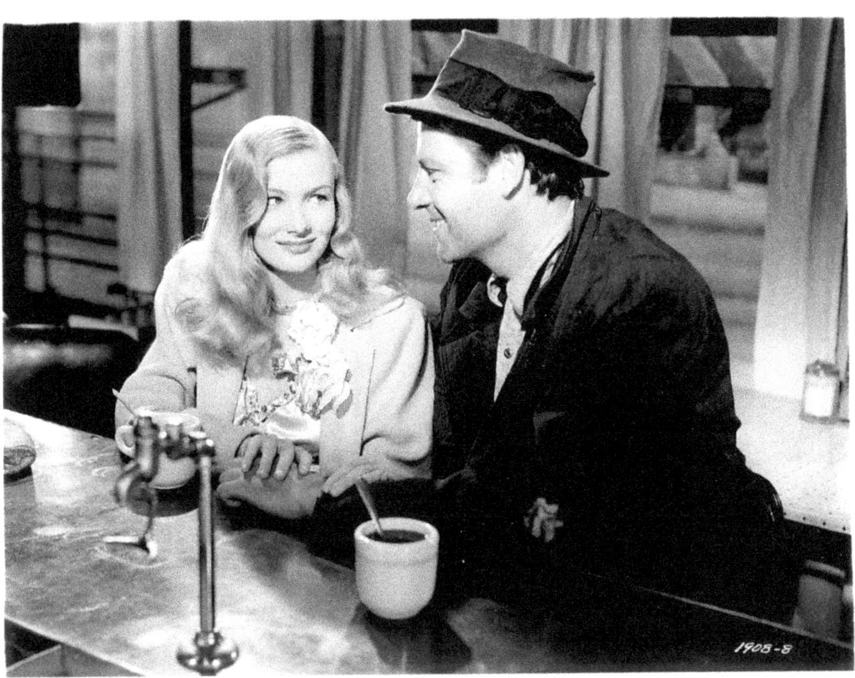

Sullivan's Travels (1941)
Directed by Preston Sturges
Shown: Veronica Lake, Joel McCrea

Director: Preston Sturges; **Producer:** Preston Sturges; **Studio:** Paramount; **Screenplay:** Preston Sturges; **Cinematography:** John Seitz; **Art Direction:** Hans Drier and Earl Hedrick; **Costume Design:** Edith Head; **Editing:** Stuart Gilmore; **Sound:** Harry Mills and Walter Oberst; **Music:** Leo Shuken and Charles Bradshaw; **Cast:** Joel McCrea (John L. Sullivan); Veronica Lake (the girl); Robert Warwick (Mr. Le Brand); William Demarest (Mr. Jones); Franklin Pangborn (Mr. Casalsis); Porter Hall (Mr. Hadrian); **Running Time:** 91 minutes.

BACKGROUND: Preston Sturges (1898-1959) was the rare type of filmmaker who could write, produce, and direct most of his films. He was born into a prominent family that was known for their creation and marketing of various cosmetics products. In addition to marketing many of the family products to local department stores in New York City, in 1920 Preston created a long-lasting lipstick called "Red-Red-Rouge." [1]

By the late 1920s Preston started writing theatrical plays, the second of which, *Strictly Dishonorable,*was filmed twice, the first time by Sturges himself.

His first film work was as a dialogue writer for such Paramount films as *The Big Pond* (1931). His first screenplay was for the 1933 film *The Power and the Glory* with Spencer Tracy. In 1940 he won an Oscar for the original screenplay of *The Great McGinty*, which was also his first film as director.

Sturges' next project was *Sullivan's Travels*, which over the years has gained recognition as a classic film about filmmaking and a director's vision of creating films that contain social relevance. Sturges' film tells the story of successful film-director John Sullivan's attempts to find out what it's like to survive without money and social standing. To the chagrin of his studio executives, Sully sets out on a number of adventures dressed as a hobo. What happens to him during these experimental outings provides the plot for Sturges' film.

PLOT: The first scene in the film is actually a film-within-a-film that is being shown privately to a group of studio heads who are expecting Sully's latest project to be a comedy like the ones that have made him one of Hollywood's best-known filmmakers. To their chagrin the footage that we see involves a nighttime scene set on top of a moving train where two men are fighting it out and ultimately falling into a river as the film ends. After much arguing Sully wins the debate by promoting the idea that he will dress like a bum for two weeks and go in search of what is really going on in America.

His first outing includes a frantic scene in which a group of studio employees aboard a bus try to keep up with Sully once he hitches a ride in a souped-up car driven by a 13-year-old. He tries again, but promises to keep in contact with his "handlers." Ironically both of his first outings lead him right back to his lavish home in Hollywood.

On his travels he meets a young woman who has unsuccessfully tried to get a job as a movie actress. At one point she convinces Sully to let her accompany him looking like a fellow hobo. On one of their adventures, they hop on a moving train to become better aware of the attitudes of homeless people.

When Sully leaves for his last outing, during which he plans to give out to all passersby a large series of five-dollar bills, misfortune overtakes him when he is knocked out and robbed of his money. When he wakes up he can't remember his name and is accused of killing John Sullivan, whose body is found on railroad tracks where the bum had been fatally run over by a moving train. Troubled with raging headaches, Sully is convicted of killing the robber, whose identity is thought to be that of Sully himself.

Sentenced to six years of hard labor, Sully suffers one painful situation after another. But on one occasion he is brought along with a group of other convicts to a small church where the prisoners join the congregation to see an old movie, which turns out to be an early silent cartoon featuring Mickey Mouse and his dog, Pluto. At first Sully is skeptical about the film but he soon joins in laughing along with everyone else when Pluto gets tangled up in pieces of sticky flypaper.

In a wild final sequence Sully is able to prove his innocence and returns to Hollywood a changed man. Now he can see that films that make people laugh are of great value after all.

MEMORABLE MOMENTS: When tramp-dressed Sully hitches a ride with the young boy, the bus that follows them is forced to travel at such a high speed that everyone aboard the bus is tossed about, with dishes and supplies flying everywhere.

When Sully and the girl get on a moving train, they annoy two fellow tramps when they try to engage them in conversation about their situation. The other two quickly depart the train car and seek to find another one.

While in prison, when the prisoners start watching the cartoon being shown at the church, the infectious laughter gives Sully a whole new perspective about the relevance of movies in people's lives.

SUMMATION: Although there is much slapstick in the film, the real significance of *Sullivan's Travels* is its insightful commentary about Americans during the Great Depression. Sully learns that films don't necessarily have to make people think when the best thing they can provide is laughter.

Some of the film strays far from its comic origins, especially when Sully is chained to other prisoners and forced to do strenuous manual labor. But the film provides an interesting perspective about the difference between real life and that which is portrayed on film. As such, *Sullivan's Travels* deserves to be recognized as a classic example of a comedy-based film that also represents socially conscious filmmaking.

WHAT AWARDS SHOULD THIS FILM HAVE WON?: 1941 is the year of Orson Welles's masterpiece *Citizen Kane,* which became one of the biggest snub in movie history when it was overlooked in the Oscar competition for Best Picture by *How Green Was My Valley.* Other nominated films include *The Little Foxes, The Maltese Falcon, Sergeant York,* and *Suspicion. Sullivan's Travels* should have been on that list. It should have been cited for its screenplay and for its star, Joel McCrea, who never received any nominations in his long career.

---

[1] Donald Spoto, *Madcap: The Life of Preston Sturges* (Boston: Little, Brown, and Co., 1990), p. 44.

OSCAR SNUB #10 – *THE MAGNIFICENT AMBERSONS* (1942)

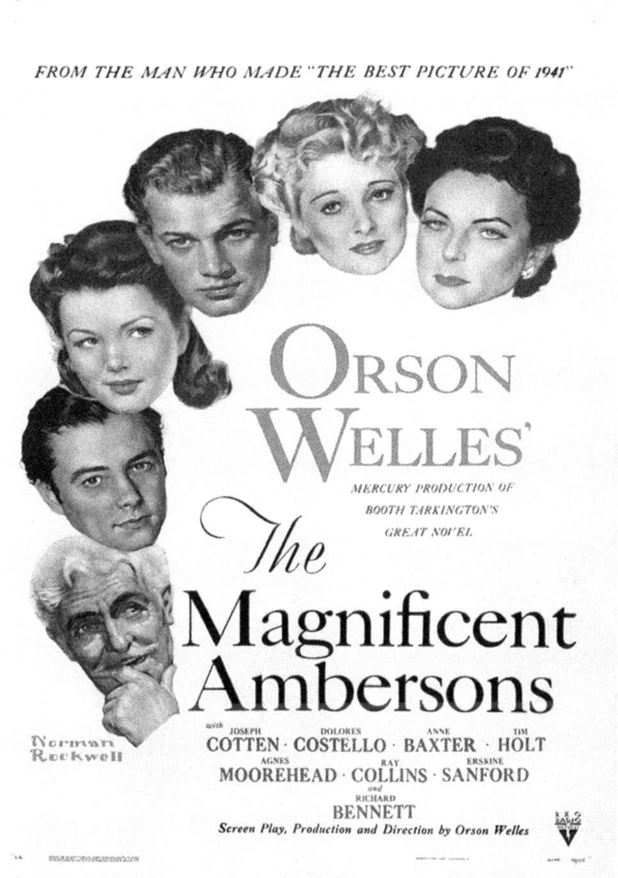

Director: Orson Welles; **Producer:** Orson Welles; **Studio:** RKO; **Screenplay:** Orson Welles; **Cinematography:** Stanley Cortez; **Art Direction:** Albert S. D'Agostino and Mark-Lee Kirk; **Costume Design:** Edward Stevenson and Earl Leas; **Editing:** Robert Wise; **Sound:** Bailey Fesler and James G. Stewart; **Music:** Bernard Herrmann and Roy Webb; **Special Effects:** Vernon L. Walker; **Cast:**

Joseph Cotten (Eugene Morgan); Dolores Costello (Isabel Minafer); Tim Holt (George Minafer); Agnes Moorehead (Fanny Minafer); Anne Baxter (Lucy Morgan); Ray Collins (Jack Amberson); Richard Bennett (Major Amberson); **Running Time:** 88 minutes.

BACKGROUND: When Orson Welles got his contract with RKO in 1940, he received carte blanche to make whatever movies he wanted, and with free rein to make them without studio interference. Thus came the controversial 1941 film *Citizen Kane*, which became a critical success but a commercial disappointment, largely because of the negative attitude many people in Hollywood had towards a film that was unflatteringly based on the life of newspaper publisher William Randolph Hearst, who was also a well-known film producer.

Despite *Kane*'s lack of box-office success, Welles went on to produce a film based on Booth Tarkington's novel *The Magnificent Ambersons,* which Welles had earlier adapted in 1938 for his radio series *Mercury Theatre on the Air.*

Production on the new film proceeded without the negativity surrounding *Citizen Kane,* but when preview audiences saw the finished film they were very unimpressed. Without Welles's involvement (due to his being assigned a project that took him to Mexico), the studio drastically altered the film by removing a great deal of the original footage and replacing it with several scenes that were not in the original version.

The result of RKO's tampering resulted in a much-shorter film than was originally planned, with new scenes directed by Robert Wise, the film's original editor, and with music by RKO employee Roy Webb. Bernard Herrmann, the original composer, refused to have anything to do with the alterations made to the original film, and asked that his name not be included in the vocal credits that Orson Welles, the film's narrator, verbally announced at the end of the film.

PLOT: Welles's film, which is set in an unnamed city (presumably Indianapolis because that is where the novel's author came from), tells the story of an old-money family, the Ambersons, and a struggling automobile pioneer named Eugene Morgan. At the start of the film young Eugene becomes infatuated with Isabel, the Amberson's only daughter. When Eugene comes to the Amberson residence he is turned away because he is considered a business failure and Isabel winds up marrying Wilbur Minafer, a wealthy man of whom her family approves.

After many years the paths of Isabel and Eugene cross once again, but now Isabel has a son named George, who is very spoiled and largely disdained by local residents who resent the boy's holier-than-thou attitude. When Isabel's husband dies, Eugene, who is now a prosperous auto pioneer, thinks he has another chance with her, but George, now a young adult with no desire for employment, resents Eugene and blocks any attempts by Eugene to woo George's mother.

Ironically, George becomes infatuated with Eugene's daughter, Lucy, but she is troubled by George's insistence that he will not pursue a career of any kind and instead plans to live off of the Ambersons' wealth. Even when Isabel is dying of consumption George prevent Eugene from seeing her.

Over time, changes occur in the city due to the growing popularity of the automobile and the construction of streets that provide access to an increasing number of outlying residential neighborhoods. The Amberson mansion becomes a decaying remnant of things past and the only survivors of the once-prominent family are financially destitute. After George is injured while working on a good-paying but dangerous job, Eugene steps in to help with George's medical expenses and there is a final reconciliation between the Amberson and Morgan families.

MEMORABLE MOMENTS: The opening sequence of *Ambersons* is a brilliantly filmed documentary-style look at changing fashions amid the prominent residents of the city, with Joseph Cotten seen wearing different styles of evening attire as they evolve. This leads to an introduction to the Ambersons and the huge mansion in which they reside. Orson Welles's spoken narration adds greatly to the impact of this sequence, in which the viewer sees short clips of young Eugene trying to serenade Isabel, and the spoiled young George being a torment to many of the Ambersons' neighbors.

Another memorable scene occurs at one of the Ambersons' deluxe balls, at which Eugene dances with Isabel, while George tries to court

Eugene's teenage daughter, Lucy. The impressive set design of the interior of the Amberson mansion adds greatly to the charm of this scene.

Other impressive moments occur on the grand staircase of the Amberson home when George has heated discussions with George's Aunt Fanny, who has lived at the mansion ever since her brother Wilbur married Isabel. The outstanding camerawork by Stanley Cortez adds greatly to the effectiveness of these scenes, especially when George relentlessly pursues his suspicions that his mother's affection for Eugene is causing a lot of idle gossip among townspeople.

SUMMATION: it is difficult to appraise the last section of the film, due to the rather obvious incorporation of replacement scenes that were inserted to help conclude the saga of George and his cruel determination to thwart Eugene's pursuit of George's mother. A feeling of hasty plot resolution often interferes with the sheer brilliance of the film's early segments.

Still, RKO's meddling does not totally ruin the effect that this film conveys. With Welles's expert narration and the brilliant staging of outdoor winter scenes featuring Eugene's stalled motorcar versus George's recklessly overturned sleigh, *Magnificent Ambersons* remains a visually stunning and dramatically compelling look at a time in America when changes in technology resulted in growing prosperity for some and economic ruin for others.

WHAT AWARDS SHOULD THIS FILM HAVE WON?: *Magnificent Ambersons* was among the ten nominees for Best Picture of 1942 and competed against *Kings Row, Random Harvest, The Pride of the Yankees, Yankee Doodle Dandy,* and that year's winner, *Mrs. Miniver.* Welles's film also earned for Agnes Moorehead an Oscar nomination in the Best Supporting Actress category, and two other nominations were earned for the film's brilliant cinematography and art direction. In a just world *Ambersons* would have won in all three of these categories.

OSCAR SNUB #11: *THE OX-BOW INCIDENT* (1943)

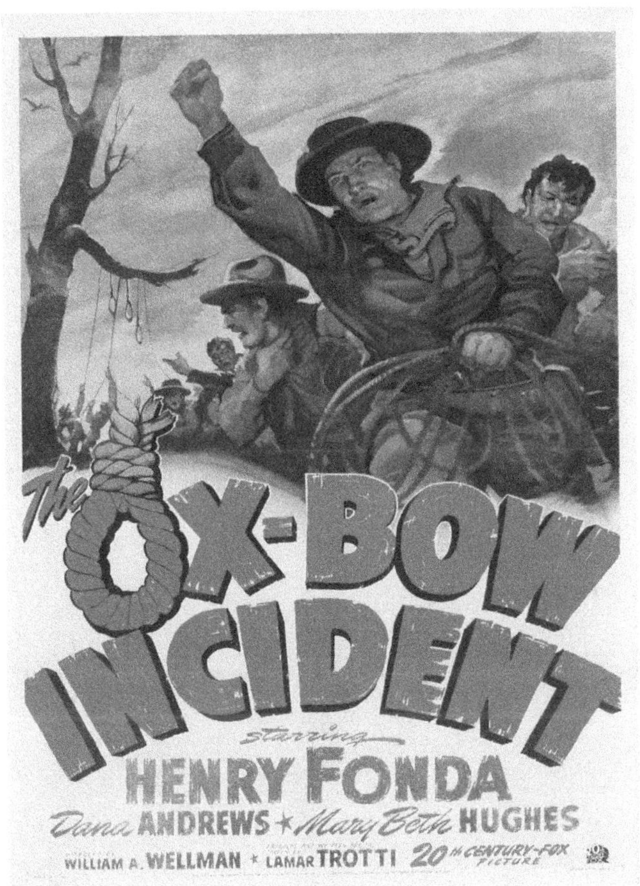

Director: William A. Wellman; **Producer:** Lamar Trotti; **Studio:** 20th Century-Fox; **Screenplay:** Lamar Trotti, based on the novel by Walter van Tilburg Clark; **Cinematography:** Arthur Miller; **Art Direction:** Richard Dix and Frank E. Hughes; **Costume Design:** Earl Luick; **Editing:** Allen McNeil; **Sound:** Alfred

Bruzlin and Roger Heman; **Music:** Cyril J. Mockridge; **Cast:** Henry Fonda (Gil Carter); Dana Andrews (Donald Martin); Mary Beth Hughes (Rose Mapen); Anthony Quinn (the Mexican); William Eythe (Gerald Tetley); Henry Morgan (Art Croft); Jane Darwell (Ma Grier); **Running Time:** 75 minutes.

BACKGROUND: Although Walter Van Tilberg Clark set most of his literary works in the state of Nevada, he was actually born in Maine. As a Western writer he created a classic novel, *The Ox-Bow Incident*, which gained critical and popular claim following its publication in 1940. Henry Fonda, after earning an Oscar nomination for *The Grapes of Wrath*, approached studio executives at 20th Century-Fox about starring in a movie based on Clark's novel. At first there was little interest in the project, but Fonda agreed to make several other pictures for Fox if they agreed to let him do it. The result was not a box-office success, but today *Ox-Bow Incident* is recognized as a true classic in the Western genre.

PLOT: The story, which takes place in Nevada during 1895, begins with two cowboys, Gil Carter and Art Croft, who have just come off the range and enter Canby's saloon in the town of Bridger's Wells. After Gil has too much to drink and gets involved in a fistfight, he and Art witness a dramatic situation that starts when a young man comes running into the saloon to report a cattle rustling and the killing of a cattle owner named Kinkaid, who is a close friend of the guy Gil has just fought with. When it is learned that the sheriff is out of town, the deputy sheriff decides to take the law into his own hands by forming a posse and going after the rustlers. Despite the objections by several people, who think the sheriff should take charge of the situation, several townsfolk get illegally deputized to find the supposed murderers. Gil and Art, although initially reluctant to join what is turning into an angry mob, are pressured to join them.

Once the posse finds three men who happen to have a herd of cattle with Kinkaid's brand on them, there is no stopping the lynching from taking place. Once the lynching happens, the posse is soon met by the sheriff, who informs them that Kincaid is alive, and that they've acted in total disregard for the law.

Back at the bar in the saloon, Gil reads to several posse members a letter written by Donald Martin, one of the lynching victims, that was addressed to his wife and their two kids. In the letter Martin deplores the fact that he was denied a proper court hearing regarding the accusations against him and his partners. After finishing his recitation, Gil leaves town with Art to offer comfort to Martin's family.

MEMORABLE MOMENTS: When the posse arrives at a place called Ox-Bow, the riders stop near an ominous tree that has a long horizontal branch that juts out from its trunk. It is in this foreboding place that they find three men sitting by a campfire. Without hesitation the three are taken into custody and a superficial examination leads the posse members to presume that these three are the killers.

Another notable moment comes when General Tetley, a former Confederate officer who has taken upon himself the role of leader of this disorderly bunch, decides to let the posse decide the fate of the captured men by having those opposed to the lynching come forward. In a quiet moment with no dialogue, only seven men, including Gil, Art, and the general's horrified son, Gerald, stand up for the prisoners.

Ater the lynching there is a continued silence as the members of the posse start the return trip to Bridger's Wells. As they move off, the shadows of the three dead men are reflected on the ground by the moonlight.

Back at the saloon after the lynching, one of the film's most powerful moments occurs when Art reads aloud Martin's letter. As Gil reads, his face is blocked from view by the wide brim of Art's hat. The words, intoned rather softly, tell all that needs to be said about the reckless abandon of justice that has befallen Martin and his two unfortunate companions.

One further noteworthy aspect of the film is the framing shots of Gil and Art, who at the start of the film ride towards the camera as they venture downhill into the town and the saloon. The last moment of the film includes a reverse shot of the two dismayed riders going up that same hill on horseback until they move out of view. In both shots a quiet rendering of "Red River Valley" is sounded on a solo accordion. Interestingly, that closing shot closely resembles the noteworthy ending of the 1952 Western film *High Noon*, wherein the buckboard carrying the now-resigned marshal and his bride goes uphill and out of sight, accompanied by the singing voice of Tex Ritter.

SUMMATION: In many ways *Ox-Bow Incident* resembles a Biblical parable, especially when the three prisoners are hanged in a manner not unlike the Crucifixion of Jesus and the two thieves on the hill known as Calvary. The raucous laughter of Ma Grier, the sole female member of the posse, seems reminiscent of those in the crowd attending Jesus's trial in front of Pontius Pilate who yell "Crucify him! Crucify him!"

The film's screenplay is faithful to Clark's novel, with one significant exception. In the book the contents of the letter are never revealed. Perhaps these words are not necessary to the film, but they allow the filmmakers to make a powerful plea that no one should ever take the law for granted and deny an accused person's right to a fair trial. This scene provides the film's most unforgettable moment and confirms the lasting legacy that *Ox-Bow Incident* has earned as an example of extraordinary filmmaking.

WHAT AWARDS SHOULD THIS FILM HAVE WON?: Although *Ox-Bow Incident* earned a Best-Picture nomination it lost to *Casablanca*. There were no other award citations for this film, which sadly should have been cited for its incisive screenplay and William Wellman's excellent direction.

OSCAR SNUB #12 – *DOUBLE INDEMNITY* (1944)

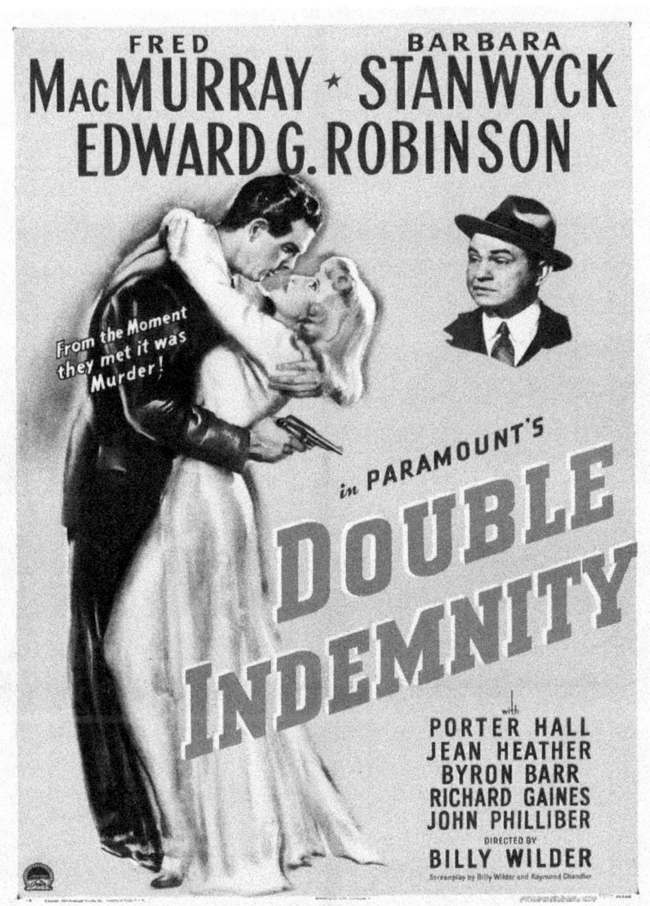

Director: Billy Wilder; **Producer:** Joseph Sistrom; **Studio:** Paramount; **Screenplay:** Billy Wilder and Raymond Chandler, based on the novel by James M. Cain; **Cinematography:** John Seitz; **Art Direction:** Hal Periera and Hans Drier; **Costume Design:** Edith Head; **Editing:** Doane Harrison; **Sound:** Stanley Cooley and

Walter Oberst; **Musical Score:** Miklós Rózsa; **Cast:** Fred MacMurray (Walter Neff); Barbara Stanwyck (Phyllis Dietrichson); Edward G. Robinson (Barton Keyes); Porter Hall (Mr. Jackson); Jean Heather (Lola Dietrichson); Tom Powers (Mr. Dietrichson); **Running time:** 107 minutes.

BACKGROUND: James M. Cain (1892-1977) was a successful writer who specialized in hard-boiled fiction based on true-life crimes. He is best remembered for three novels, *The Postman Always Rings Twice* (1934), *Double Indemnity* (1936), and *Mildred Pierce* (1941). All were successfully filmed in the 1940s, with *Double Indemnity* the first to reach the silver screen.

This film's story is based on a factual event from the 1920s, when a woman named Ruth Snyder enticed her lover Henry Gray to kill her husband. Both were convicted of the crime and executed at Sing Sing prison on January 13, 1928.[1] In 1943 filmmaker Billy Wilder secured the film rights to Cain's novel, and the film was released the following year, when it received seven Oscar nominations, including a bid for Best Picture.

Once he arrived in Hollywood in the 1930s, Wilder became a comedy screenwriter at Paramount. But after directing the 1942 farce *The More the Merrier,* he made the 1943 World War II drama *Five Graves to Cairo*, and followed that film with *Double Indemnity*, Wilder's only foray into *film noir*, which remains one of the most critically acclaimed examples of this genre.

PLOT: The film, which is set in Los Angeles during 1938, begins with a car racing at night through the city's downtown streets until arriving at a large insurance office building. The auto's sole occupant, whose left arm appears to dangle in a useless manner, is admitted to the premises by a night watchman and takes an elevator to an upper floor. Soon thereafter he sits at a desk in one of the offices with sweat on his face and starts talking into a Dictaphone.

What follows is the narration by insurance agent Walter Neff about his fateful relationship with Phyllis Dietrichson, who has engaged Walter in preparing a life-insurance policy for her husband with herself as the sole beneficiary. Through this narration Walter confesses to fellow employee Barton Keyes how he and Phyllis conspired to kill Mr. Dietrichson.

As Walter continues his confession, he explains how Phyllis claimed to be in in love with him and that they could take advantage of her husband's life-insurance policy by scheming to kill him and make it look like an accident. Complications arise when Lola, Dietrichson's daughter by his deceased first wife, tells Walter that Phyllis had been working as a nurse to Lola's mother, and that Phyllis had caused her mother's untimely death. This revelation causes Walter to have serious doubts about Phyllis's feelings for him and eventually Phyllis shoots him, but before she can take a second shot Walter gets the gun and fatally shoots her.

Before Walter can finish his confession Keyes arrives, and Walter is left with a full awareness that he will undoubtedly face a death sentence for killing both Phyllis and her husband.

MEMORABLE MOMENTS: The structure of Wilder's film in ingeniously devised in that the actual murderer is revealed in the opening scene, before any of the crime's details are known.

The first meeting between Walter and Phyllis, as detailed in the Dictaphone confession, includes one of the film's best scenes, in which Walter drives to the Dietrichson's home to get a signature on an auto insurance policy, but he becomes distracted by an ankle bracelet she's wearing. In the ensuing dialogue there is a fast-paced repartee in which Walter, who learns her name is Phyllis, suggests he would have to drive around to see if he likes it. When he asks how fast he is going, Phyllis hints that he is doing around ninety. He then refers to her as a police officer and asks if she should give him a speeding ticket. When he asks if he could cry on her shoulder, she suggests he cry on her husband's shoulder. At this point he says, "That tears it."

There are several scenes in which Keyes, the insurance company's claims manager, talks in a furiously fast manner about various claims, including the ones concerning Dietrichson's death. Especially noteworthy is the scene in which cinematographer Fred Seitz's shot emphasizes the difference in height between actors by having MacMurray parked against a desk at the left of the shot while the much-shorter Robinson steals the scene as Keyes walks about spouting theories. Adding to the effect of these scenes is the uninterrupted nature of the shots, which allows the actors to perform without many editor's cuts.

The closing scene, in which Keyes enters his office while Walter is still recording his confession, contains the memorable last moment when Keyes helps the mortally wounded Walter light a cigarette and Walter tells Keyes for the second time in the film, "I love you, too." These words are the last ones spoken in the film, which ends with the sure knowledge that Walter will pay the ultimate penalty for his crimes.

SUMMATION: This film's screenplay contains some of the best dialogue ever written for a film. The script provides clever ways in which the characters address each other. For instance, Walter never calls his partner-in-crime "Phyllis"; instead, he always calls her "Baby." Walter also calls the claim manager simply "Keyes," and Phyllis always refers to Mr. Dietrichson as "my husband." In fact, no first name is given to this crucial character, whose name appears in the cast list as simply "Mr. Dietrichson."

There is little doubt that, with its many exceptional moments, *Double Indemnity* is an unforgettable example of *film noir* and is one of the best films of the 1940s.

WHAT AWARDS SHOULD THIS FILM HAVE WON?: *Double Indemnity* is by far the best of the five Best-Picture nominees, which includes the pleasant but overly sentimental winner, *Going My Way.* Wilder's film should also have won for its direction, writing, and musical score.

---

[1] Alain Silver and James Ursini, *From the Moment They Met It Was Murder: Double Indemnity and the Birth of Film Noir* (Philadelphia: Running Press, 2024), pp. 10-13.

OSCAR SNUB #13 – *MEET ME IN ST. LOUIS* (1944)

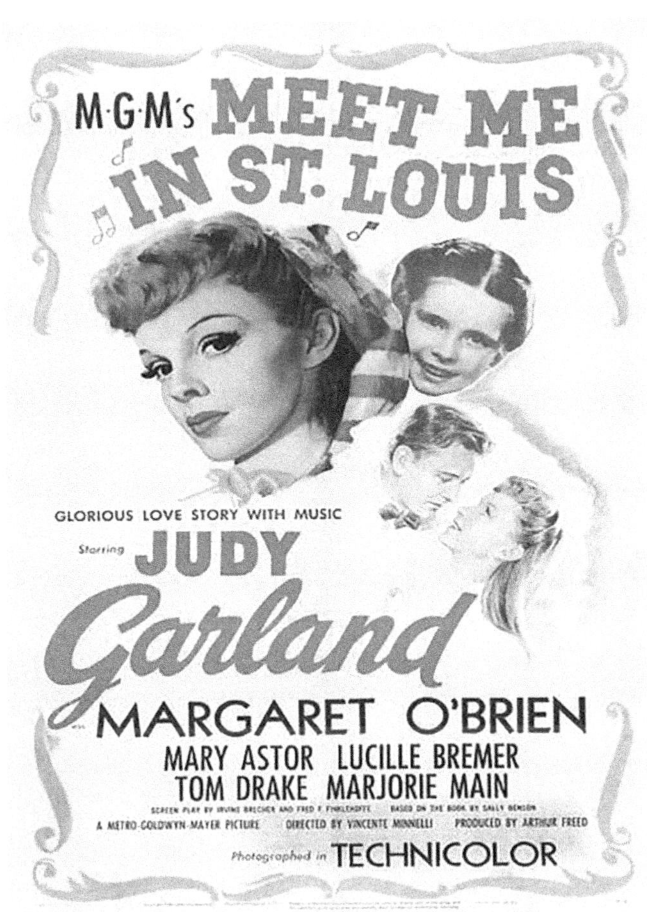

Director: Vincente Minnelli; **Producer:** Arthur Freed; **Studio:** MGM; **Screenplay:** Irving Becher and Fred F. Finklehoffe, based on stories by Sally Benson; **Cinematography:** George Folsey; **Art Direction:** Cedric Gibbons and Edwin B. Willis; **Costume Design:** Irene Sharaff; **Editing:** Albert Akst; **Sound:** Douglas Shearer;

Songs: Ralph Blane and Hugh Martin; **Musical Direction:** George Stoll; **Cast:** Judy Garland (Esther Smith); Margaret O'Brien (Tootie Smith); Lucille Bremer (Rose Smith); Leon Ames (Lorenzo Smith); Mary Astor (Anna Smith); Tom Drake (John Truett); **Running Time:** 113 minutes.

BACKGROUND: By the time Judy Garland starred in *Meet Me in St. Louis* she had been under contract at MGM for almost a decade. Because of her unique singing voice, which had matured at a very early age, she was assigned mostly musical films, including several in which she costarred with Mickey Rooney.

At age seventeen she reached stardom by being given the role of Dorothy in MGM's elaborate version of L. Frank Baum's *The Wizard of Oz* (1939), in which she sang several songs created for the film by Harold Arlen, especially "Over the Rainbow."

With the exception of *Oz,* Judy's early films were all made in black-and-white, and she continued to star in black-and-white films into the early 1940s, until producer Arthur Freed picked her for the role of Esther, one of the five Smith children who live in St. Louis right before the World's Fair of 1904. With *Meet Me in St. Louis* Judy began making a number of Technicolor musicals which were set in the historic past and paired her with such versatile performers as Gene Kelly and Fred Astaire.

PLOT: As with the Oscar-winning film of 1944, Paramount's *Going My Way,* there is not much of a plot in *Meet Me in St. Louis.* The film concentrates on several events involving a prominent banker and his family in St. Louis during the year that leads up to the opening of the St. Louis World's Fair in early 1904. During the summer that precedes the fair, Esther becomes Smitten with John Truett, a young man who has recently moved into the house next door to the Smith's sprawling Victorian-style home in a respectably up-scale St. Louis neighborhood.

Much of the film revolves around Esther's attempts to get romantic with her neighbor, while she also involves herself in the love life of her older sister, Rose. Esther additionally spends time with her youngest sibling, Tootie, whose juvenile adventures cause trouble, especially when Tootie learns that her father, Alonzo, plans to accept a promotion that would require relocating to New York City. It is Tootie's visible sadness about moving away from St. Louis that finally convinces their father to change his mind and allow the family to remain in St. Louis and attend the opening of the World's Fair.

MEMORABLE MOMENTS: The title song, which had been composed specifically for the World's Fair in 1904, provides an entertaining centerpiece for the first part of the film, which begins with an unseen chorus that sings the song during the opening credits. This is followed by the opening scene in which various cast members take turns singing portions of the song. Even Esther's grandfather gets a turn at singing it as the viewer is introduced to the Smith family during a hot summer day.

Especially enjoyable are three songs that were specifically composed for the film. The first is "The Boy Next Door," in which Esther speculates about falling in love with John Truett, who has recently moved into the neighboring home. The second is "The Trolley Song," in which Esther at first refrains from singing because John has not shown up to ride the trolley with her, but when he comes running down the street and hops on, she starts singing a portion of this lively tune.

The third of the film's original songs is a piece that has become a perennial holiday favorite called "Have Yourself a Merry Little Christmas." It appears towards the end of the film, when Esther tries to console little Tootie about leaving St. Louis. In Judy Garland's inimitable singing style, this somewhat melancholy version of the song is far different from the voluminous renditions by many later recording artists that have included the tune on albums of Christmas songs. In the film there is a portion of the lyrics that was changed for subsequent recordings. The more familiar phrase "Hang a shining star on the highest bow" was originally sung as "Until then we'll have to muddle through somehow." Garland's version stresses the need to find a way to celebrate Christmas even though it's going to be the last one the family will have in St. Louis.

SUMMATION: The four-part structure of the film allows the viewer to understand the trauma that a relocation to New York might cause. The opening "Summer" section is filled with joyful singing and several moments of light-hearted storytelling. By contrast the "Autumn" scenes become darker, especially when the two youngest Smith children, Tootie and Agnes, dressed in scary Halloween costumes, go out with a bunch of neighborhood children who plan to approach nearby homes and frighten the occupants by throwing handfuls of flour at them. The camera focuses on Tootie as she takes it upon herself to prove her bravery in one dramatic moment.

Although the last two sections of the film include less music, the film's rich Technicolor cinematography provides viewers with a vivid view of life at the turn of the 20th century. Garland shines as her character evolves from a carefree teenager to a young adult that finds love for the first time. *Meet Me in St. Louis* confirms Garland's abilities to dominate every scene in which she appears, even though Margaret O'Brien gives her some stiff competition, especially in the scene where they perform "Under the Bamboo Tree" together.

Although Vincente Minnelli's later films, especially *An American in Paris* and *Gigi*, may have brought him more Oscar recognition, *Meet Me in St. Louis* remains one of his best film accomplishments.

WHAT AWARDS SHOULD THIS FILM HAVE WON?: Leo McCarey's highly sentimental *Going My Way*, with Bing Crosby as a singing priest, swept the Oscars with seven awards, including one for Best Picture, but *Meet Me in St. Louis* should have won Oscars in these three categories: color cinematography, color art direction, plus an award for its lilting song score, which includes some timeless classics.

OSCAR SNUB #14 – *IT'S A WONDERFUL LIFE* (1946)

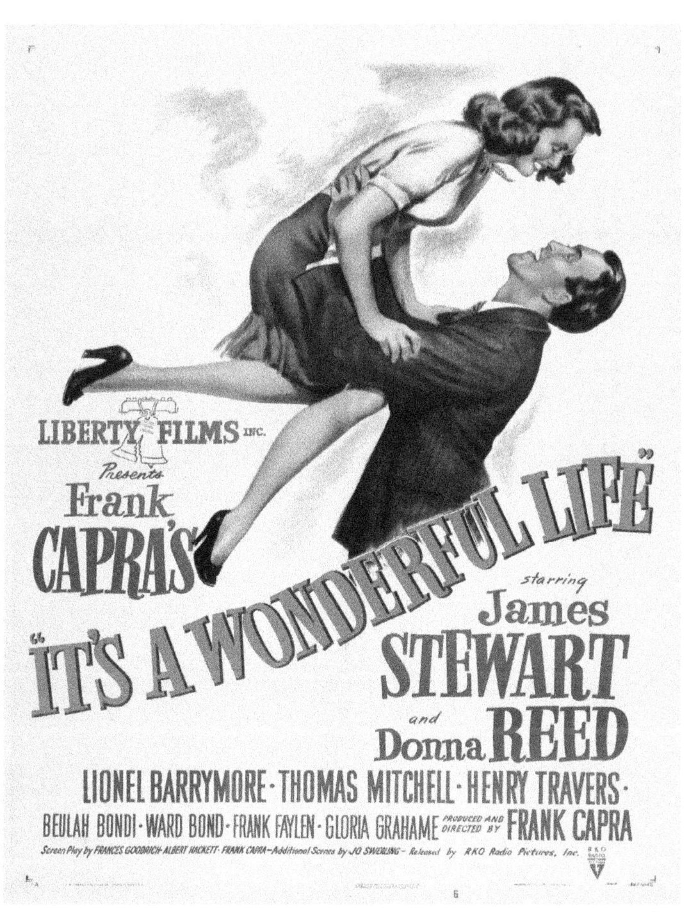

Director: Frank Capra; **Producer:** Frank Capra; **Screenplay:** Frances Goodrich, Albert Hackett, and Frank Capra, from story by Philip Van Doren Stern; **Cinematography:** Joseph Walker and Joseph Biroc; **Art Decoration/Set Decoration:** Jack Oakie, Emile Kuri; **Costume Design:** Edward Stevenson; **Editing:** William

Hornbeck; **Sound:** Clem Portman and Richard Van Hessen; **Musical Score:** Dimitri Tiomkin; **Cast:** James Stewart (George Bailey); Donna Reed (Mary Hatch); Lionel Barrymore (Henry Potter); Thomas Mitchell (Uncle Billy); Henry Travers Clarence); Beulah Bondi (Mrs. Bailey); Ward Bond (Bert); Gloria Grahame (Violet); H.B. Warner (Mr. (Gower); Todd Karns (Harry Bailey); **Running time:** 131 minutes.

BACKGROUND: At the conclusion of World War II both Frank Capra and James Stewart returned from active military duty to resume their film careers: Capra set up a new production company called Liberty Films, while Stewart made it known that he would like his next film to be directed by Capra. The result was *It's a Wonderful Life,* which Capra planned as yet another of his films that celebrated the triumph of an ordinary man over the dark forces at work in his life.

Stewart plays George Bailey, who inherits a small building and loan company upon the death of his father and struggles to keep it going in the face of competition from the town's wealthiest man, Henry Potter, who owns the town's only bank and a lot of Bedford Falls's real estate.

PLOT: on Christmas Eve, George's company is on the brink of failure and he is facing financial ruin. Up in the stars, angels' voices are heard discussing George's plight, and two senior angels, Franklin and Joseph, assign one named Clarence, who has yet to earn his wings, the task of becoming George's guardian angel in order to save his life.

For Clarence to learn about George, Joseph narrates George's life story, beginning with a winter day in 1919 when twelve-year-old George rescues his younger brother, Harry, from a break in the ice on a large pond. George is next seen working as a young assistant to the local druggist, Mr. Gower, who George observes accidentally combining a poisonous drug with a benign one. Gower at first roughly chastises George but later thanks him for his discovery. Clarence then sees George as a young adult taking over his deceased father's company and sacrificing his own savings so that his brother can go to college.

George is then seen marrying his childhood friend, Mary Hatch, and together they raise four children without ever getting financially secure, mostly due to a large home-building project sponsored by George's company. The last straw occurs when Billy, George's Uncle, misplaces $8,000 that is supposed to be deposited to keep the loan company solvent.

When George contemplates jumping off a bridge, Clarence suddenly appears and jumps into the water himself, correctly assuming that George will rescue him. When they both dry off, Clarence casts a spell in which George does not exist. In this way Clarence hopes to convince George that his life has had a positive impact on those around him.

MEMORABLE MOMENTS: One of the most humorous scenes occurs at a high-school dance when George is dancing with Mary. A jealous classmate of hers uses a key to unlock the latch on the moveable floor that covers the gym's swimming pool underneath it. As George and Mary kick up their heels in a Charleston number, they unwittingly move over the opening in the floor and fall into the pool. Soon lots other students and even some adults hilariously follow suit.

When George and Mary return to her home singing "Buffalo Gals" in a riotous off-key manner, he accidently steps on the tie of the bathrobe she has put on and it falls off, with Mary amusingly ducking into the hydrangea bushes in her parents' front yard.

A heightened dramatic moment occurs when George runs onto the bridge and winds up rescuing Clarence. When they get dry clothes on and Clarence hears George say that he shouldn't have been born, the spell begins with the snow suddenly stopping.

The following scene is the film's most downbeat, with George finding things around him greatly altered. He quickly perceives that something is wrong when Bert, the local cop, fails to recognize him, and both his mother and his wife don't remember him at all. The distraught George then runs back to the bridge and calls out three times, "I want to live again." He then prays, "Please God, let me live again." At this point the spell is lifted and the film begins to soar.

After George runs excitedly back home and becomes happily reunited with his family, a crowd of townsfolks shows up with donations that replace the missing bank money. Also noteworthy is the arrival of George's brother, Harry, who raises a glass to toast his brother by saying, "To my older brother, George, the richest man in town."

The film ends touchingly when George softly says "Attaboy, Clarence," after finding the book the angel has left behind in which are inscribed words of gratitude for finally getting his wings.

SUMMATION: As with Capra's previous films, *It's a Wonderful Life* contains lots of suffering felt by its principal character, but with a joyous final scene. Stewart's fine portrayal of George Bailey is easily on par with his playing of Jefferson Smith in Capra's 1939 classic *Mr. Smith Goes to Washington.* Both represent Stewart and Capra at a collective peak in their careers.

WHAT AWARDS SHOULD THIS FILM HAVE WON?: *Wonderful Life* received five Academy nominations but was snubbed by the critical recognition of William Wyler's *Best Years of Our Lives. Wonderful Life* should have won for Stewart's performance. Although the film was not a success in 1946 it has become a Christmas classic.

OSCAR SNUB #15 – *THE GHOST AND MRS. MUIR* (1947)

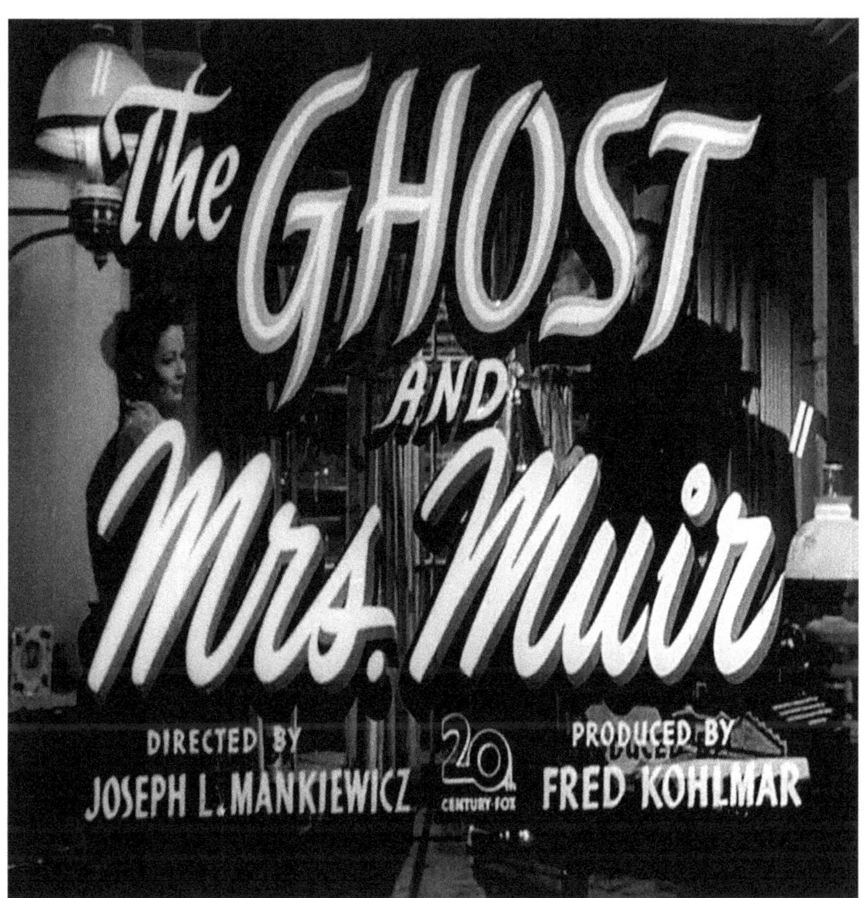

Director: Joseph L. Mankiewicz; **Producer:** Fred Kohlmar; **Studio:** 20th Century-Fox; **Screenplay:** Philip Dunne, based on the novel by R. A. Dick; **Cinematography:** George Folsey; **Art Direction:** Richard Day, George Davis, and Thomas Little; **Costume Design:** Eleanor Behm; **Editing:** Dorothy Spencer; **Sound:**

Bernard Freericks; **Musical Score:** Bernard Herrmann; **Cast:** Gene Tierney (Lucy Muir); Rex Harrison (Captain Daniel Gregg); George Sanders (Miles Fairly); Edna Best (Martha); Natalie Wood (Anna as a child); Vanessa Brown (Anna as an adult); **Running Time:** 104 minutes.

BACKGROUND: Movies with supernatural plot elements have been around for a long time. Especially popular have been ghost movies in which a spirit comes back from the dead to haunt the place where he had formerly lived. Movies like the 1982 film *Poltergeist* include plenty of frightening moments, along with the predictable possibility that there could be sequels that would give audiences even more numerous scary scenes. Some ghostly films have been far less nerve-wracking than *Poltergeist,* especially the many *Ghostbusters* films and Tim Burton's *Beetlejuice*, a comedic film with a hilarious performance by Michael Keaton as the titular ghost character. Yet another departure from the ghost-as-menace type of film is the 1990 *Ghost,* in which the spirit of Patrick Swayze's character tries to communicate with his grieving wife through a psychic woman memorably played by Whoopi Goldberg.

Perhaps the most charming ghost film ever made is Joseph L. Mankiewicz's *The Ghost and Mrs. Muir*, a distinct departure from the haunted-house movies mentioned above.

PLOT: In Mankiewicz's film, which is set in England around 1900, the titular ghost played by Rex Harrison is not scary, at least not to Lucy Muir, a widow with a cute five-year-old daughter, who wants to leave her in-laws and live near the sea. As the film begins, Lucy consults Mr. Coombe, a realtor in the town of Whitecliff-by-the-Sea, about renting Gull Cottage, a place that was formerly occupied by Captain Daniel Gregg, a sea captain who suddenly died there four years earlier. Despite Coombe's objections, Lucy defiantly rents the cottage, even after being confronted with the ghostly presence of its former owner.

Once Lucy moves in with her daughter, Anna, and her faithful maid, Martha, Lucy calls out to Captain Gregg to reveal himself. When he appears, she is not pleased with his negative attitude about anyone else occupying his home. After he tells her that his death was caused by a gas line that was left running one night without an open window, she makes a pact with him whereby he can stay in the house, on condition that he is confined to his former bedroom.

Over time Lucy develops feelings for the captain, who insists he should be called Daniel. When he becomes aware of her difficult financial situation, he dictates to her his memoir which, when published, becomes a highly popular book that provides Lucy with a tidy royalty income.

Lucy also becomes involved with Miles Fairly, a writer of children's books who helps her get Daniel's memoir published, but when she learns that Miles is already married she stops seeing him. By this time Daniel decides to stop appearing to Lucy and she remains alone in the cottage with only Martha and Anna.

The film suddenly advances many years to the point where the adult Anna gets married and moves away. After more years pass by, the aged Lucy and Martha still live in Gull Cottage, until the day when Martha puts a glass of warm milk on a table in Lucy's bedroom and leaves the room. When the glass falls from Lucy's hand, Daniel reappears, takes a revived and younger Lucy by the hands, and together they walk down the stairs and out the door into eternity.

MEMORABLE MOMENTS: *Ghost and Mrs. Muir* is filled with moments that will haunt the viewer, and not all of them include the actual haunting that is an essential part of the film. In the opening scene, when Lucy is debating with her in-laws (her late husband's mother and sister) her need to live on her own, the two women give her a hard time, but she prevails by simply saying that she is determined to leave London and find a house that is near open water. While the debate is occurring, the camera backs away to reveal Martha and little Anna, who are listening behind the kitchen door. When Lucy makes it clear that she is leaving and taking Martha and Anna with her, the little girl says to the maid, "Oh, Goodie," and they hug each other.

There are many special moments featuring Lucy and the spirit of Daniel. One of the best occurs when the memoir, which is to be called *Blood and Swash,* by Captain X, is finished. Lucy tells Daniel how happy she was during the writing of the book, and he responds by telling her how profoundly attractive she is. Her response is, "Daniel, I think we've got ourselves in a terrible mess."

The final scene is the most haunting part of the entire film. After the glass of milk is seen tipping over, Daniel's hands come into view as he reaches for Lucy, who now appears as a young woman, and he tells her she will never be tired again. This is the only moment in the film when they actually touch, as he takes her by the arm and they leave the room. With Bernard Herrmann's glorious emotion-filled music, this is one of the great movie endings of all time.

SUMMATION: This film was released just two years before the appearance of the back-to-back films for which Mankiewicz was awarded Oscars for both directing and writing. Although both *A Letter to Three Wives* (1949) and *All About Eve* (1950) have both become classics, *Ghost and Mrs. Muir* deserves a place of distinction among treasurable film romances.

Ghost and Mrs. Muir is blessed by two fine performances. Rex Harrison's speaking voice is often very gruff-sounding in his portrayal of a salty seafarer, but at times he achieves a mellow tone, especially when he indicates his growing affection for Lucy, who he prefers to call "Lucia." Gene Tierney shows great strength of character as a woman who survives the disappointment of being deceived by a married man and the fact that she has feelings for a man she cannot touch.

WHAT AWARDS SHOULD THIS FILM HAVE WON?: Mankiewicz's film is a masterpiece of romantic cinema and should have won awards for its beautiful cinematography and for Herrmann's memorably lyrical music.

OSCAR SNUB #16 – *STRANGERS ON A TRAIN* (1951)

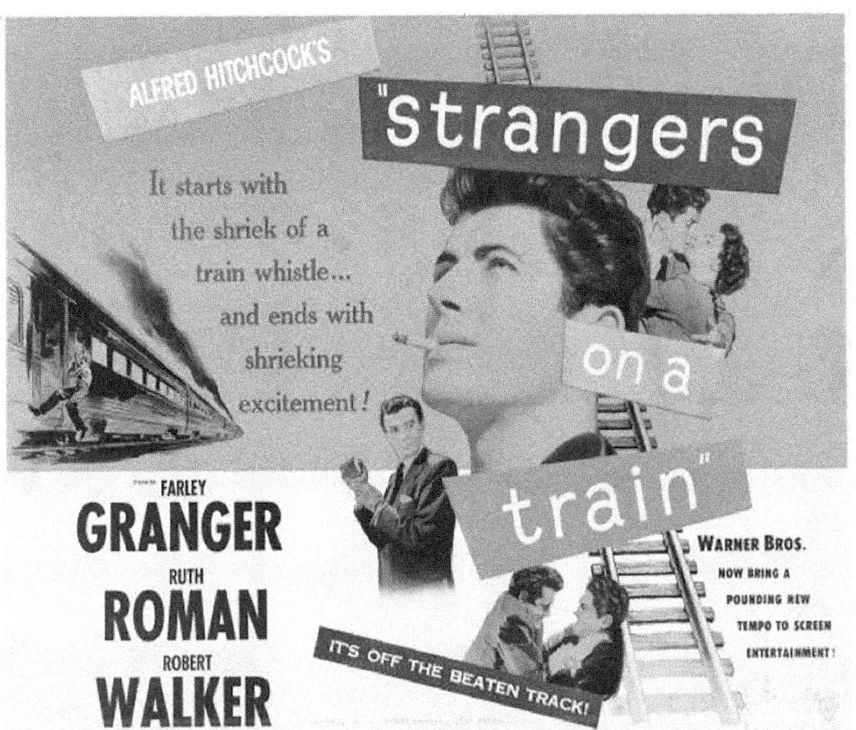

Director: Alfred Hitchcock; **Producer:** Alfred Hitchcock; **Studio:** Warner Bros. **Screenplay:** Raymond Chandler and Czenzi Ormonde, based on the novel by Patricia Highsmith; **Cinematography:** Robert Burks; **Art Direction:** Edward S. Hayworth and George James Hopkins; **Costume Design:** Leah Rhodes; **Editing:** William H. Ziegler; **Sound:** Dolph Thomas; **Music:** Dimitri Tiomkin; **Cast:** Farley Granger (Guy Haines); Robert Walker (Bruno Anthony); Ruth Roman (Anne Martin); Leo G. Carroll (Senator Morton); Patricia Hitchcock (Barbara Morton); Laura Elliott (Miriam Haines); Marion Lorne (Mrs. Anthony); **Running Time:** 101 Minutes.

BAACKGROUND: Since arriving in the United States in 1940 at the invitation of producer David O. Selznick to direct the film version of Daphne du Maurier's novel *Rebecca,* Alfred Hitchcock became one of the most prolific and successful directors in Hollywood history. From the 1940s to the early 1960s he cranked out films at the rate of one per year, and made some of the best films released during that period. Sadly, despite the high level of excellence in most of his films, Hitchcock never received a competitive Oscar for directing.

In the following pages of this book there are three examples of Hitchcock's best work. All of these films, which come within the period of 1951 to 1959, represent movies which in this author's estimation are classic examples of great filmmaking.

The first of these three is *Strangers on a Train,* one of several Hitchcock films in which an innocent man is unexpectedly drawn into a situation in which he is accused of murder and there is enough evidence against him that he could be convicted. Hitchcock's special way of handling such plot complications makes the story of this film very compelling.

PLOT: Guy Haines is a professional tennis player who, aboard a train on the way to his next tournament, meets Bruno Anthony, a man with whom Guy strikes up a casual conversation that leads to what appears to be a completely insane and unlikely situation. When Bruno learns that Guy is having difficulty getting his wife to agree to a divorce, he tells Guy that he hates his father and would like to get rid of him. This leads to Bruno's seemingly laughable proposal that they can resolve their respective situations by swapping murders. Guy thinks this idea is preposterous, but later learns that his wife has really been murdered.

When Bruno later approaches Guy about completing Bruno's fiendish plan, Guy is horrified and refuses to have anything more to do with this crazy man. As a result of Guy's refusal, Bruno goes out of his way to implicate Guy in the death of Guy's wife, and only some last-minute plot twists result in Guy being absolved of the crime.

MEMORABLE MOMENTS: The meeting of Guy and Bruno on the train in the film's opening sequence provides some noteworthy moments, despite the early casualness of their conversation. Guy's lighthearted reaction to Bruno's bizarre proposal adds a comic effect to the scene, but When Bruno holds onto Guy's cigarette lighter after Guy assists Bruno in lighting a cigarette, the attentive viewer should suspect that there may be dire consequences to this seemingly trivial act.

The murder scene in which Bruno follows Guy's wife, Miriam, and two young male companions to an amusement park begins unsettlingly as Bruno gets Miriam's attention when she looks back at him several times as they approach the Tunnel of Love attraction. After the two men proceed on and Miriam lags behind to possibly flirt with Bruno, he puts his hands on her neck and begins to strangle her. As his hands knock Miriam's glasses to the ground, the strangulation is ingeniously visible only through the reflection in one of her lenses.

Two other scenes where Miriam's glasses figure into the plot occur when Barbara, the sister of Guy's fiancée, is observed intently by Bruno as he looks at her and sees a resemblance to the victim because both women wear glasses. Especially absorbing is the second of these scenes, when Bruno is demonstrating a way to kill someone while seated on a couch with a woman at a party at the home of Senator Morton, Barbara's father. As Bruno puts his hands on the woman's neck, he looks up and is transfixed by Barbara's bespectacled appearance and almost chokes the woman to death.

The film's exciting last section begins with the scene where Guy is competing in a tennis match while Bruno is trying to retrieve the fateful cigarette lighter from a storm drain. As Guy repeatedly swings his racket, the camera keeps shifting between Guy and Bruno, whose hands reach deeper and deeper in stark close-ups as he tries to reach the lighter that can implicate Guy in the murder of his wife.

Surpassing the tension of this scene is the last sequence, when Guy and Bruno are struggling in a fight aboard a merry-go-round that is rapidly spinning out of control. This fast-edited scene, with intermixed close-ups of the two men fighting, mechanical horses bobbing, children screaming (plus one child laughing), is one of the most strikingly dramatic conclusions among all of Hitchcock's films.

SUMMATION: Hitchcock's films generally feature melodramatic situations that include action scenes that often lead to the deaths of significant plot characters. The level of violence in his films may account for the term "Master of Suspense" that was associated with Hitchcock throughout much of his career. Notwithstanding this recognition, Hitchcock had a team of production designers, cinematographers, editors, and composers who aided in making much of his work so memorable. Robert Burks received a richly deserved Oscar nomination for his work on *Strangers on a Train,* while Dimitri Tiomkin contributed a musical score which adds a great deal of dramatic tension. An added plus to the music is the use of carnival-like sounds for the merry-go-round, which plays a significant role in the film whenever Bruno sees Barbara's glasses, and especially when the climactic struggle on the carnival ride takes place in the film's concluding scene.

WHAT AWARDS SHOULD THIS FILM HAVE WON?: This film came at the beginning of a productive period in Hitchcock's career when he relished the opportunity to feature innocent persons who are drawn into extremely difficult situations. As the perpetrator of the plot in *Strangers,* Robert Walker gave the best performance in his career and should have been nominated for an acting award. Also award worthy were Burks's fine cinematography and Tiomkin's dramatic music.

OSCAR SNUB #17 – *THE DAY THE EARTH STOOD STILL* (1951)

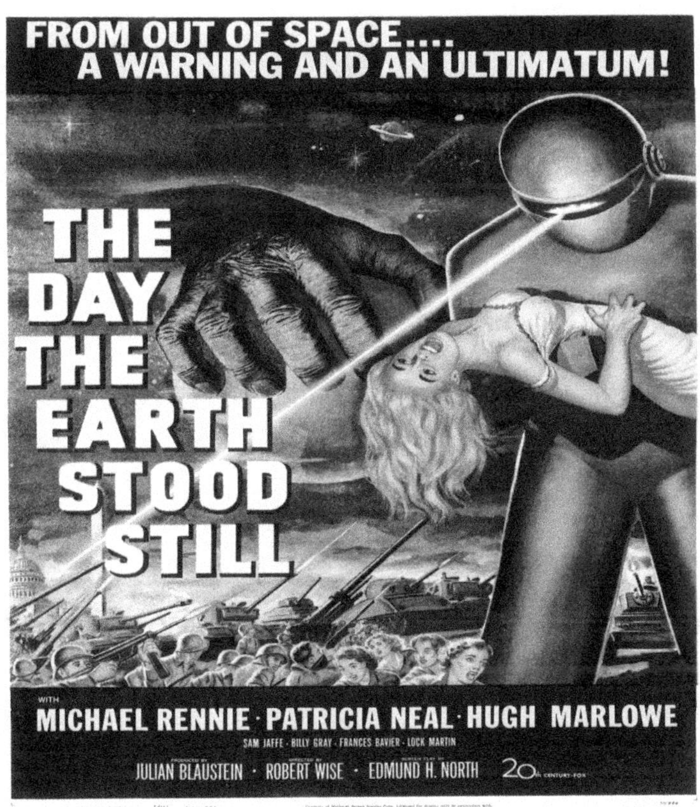

Director: Robert Wise; **Producer:** Julian Blaustein; **Studio:** 20th Century-Fox: **Screenplay:** Edmund H. North, based on story "Farewell to the Master" by Harry Bates; **Cinematography:** Leo Tover; **Art Direction:** Lyle Wheeler and Addison Hehr (Hehr also designed Gort); **Costume Design:** Perkins Bailey; **Editing:** William

Reynolds; **Sound:** Arthur Kirbach and Harry M. Leonard; **Musical Score:** Bernard Herrmann (including electronic theremin sounds); **Special Photographic Effects:** Fred Sersen; **Cast:** Michael Rennie (Klaatu/Mr. Carpenter); Patricia Neal (Helen Benson); Hugh Marlowe (Tom Stevens); Sam Jaffe (Prof. Barnhardt; Billy Gray (Bobby Benson); Lock Martin (Gort); Frances Bavier (Mrs. Barley); **Running Time:** 92 minutes.

BACKGROUND: Science fiction has been an important genre of filmmaking from the very beginning of the motion-picture medium. An early example is French director George Méliès' 1902 film *A Trip to the Moon,* which was later featured in the Prologue to the 1956 Oscar-winning film *Around the World in 80 Days.*

Sci/fi films got a real boost by the back-to-back releases in 1951 of two films, *The Thing (from Another World)* and *The Day the Earth Stood Still.* The success of these films, which both feature very tall and scary-looking extra-terrestrial beings, led to the large number of cinematic space fantasies that have flooded movie theaters ever since then.

The two aforementioned 1951 films both have one basic ingredient: the presence of flying saucers, although the saucer in *The Thing* is seen only as an immense circular object embedded in ice at the North Pole, while the one in *Day the Earth Stood Still* is immediately seen in the film's opening sequence when the saucer flies into the earth's atmosphere on route to the U.S.

The main difference between the two films is that in *The Thing,* once the human-like creature thaws out, it tries to kill everyone in its path, whereas the robot in *Day the Earth Stood Still,* while frightening to look at, is not inclined to harm anyone unless provoked by acts of violence.

PLOT: Following the opening credits, which show scenes of outer space accompanied by eerie music by Bernard Herrmann, a flying saucer comes into the earth's atmosphere and causes great alarm when it is spotted by radar. After it flies over several European cities it takes a course that leads to a landing on a field at the National Mall of Washington

D.C. After an arsenal of military soldiers, tanks, and local police arrives, the spacecraft opens and a huge robot appears, followed by a human-looking creature wearing a space suit. When a nervous soldier fires his gun, the spaceman is shot in the arm and then taken to Walter Reed Hospital.

When the alien quickly recovers and is interviewed, none of the attending medical and military personnel get much information from him. The alien then surreptitiously leaves the hospital and finds a place of temporary lodging at a nearby boarding house where he identifies himself as Mr. Carpenter.

He soon meets Helen Benson, a resident of the place, whose young son, Bobby, immediately becomes fascinated with the new tenant. When Carpenter leaves the house one evening while his mother is on a date with her boyfriend, Tom Stevens, Bobby follows Carpenter and is stunned to discover that he is the spaceman that everyone is looking for.

Soon thereafter, Stevens, who doesn't care about the reasons for the spaceman's visit, calls the authorities with the idea that he will become a celebrity for finding the missing spaceman.

Meanwhile, after scheduling a visit with Professor Barnhardt, a distinguished man of science, Carpenter arrives and identifies himself as Klaatu. After helping Barnhardt solve a difficult math problem, the professor believes this man really is from another planet, and learns that Klaatu has traveled with Gort, his robot protector, to deliver a warning to world leaders that if they decide to employ weapons of mass destruction, the result will be the earth's total annihilation.

Barnhardt is given the task of gathering together leaders from all over the globe to hear this dire warning, but first he asks for some kind of demonstration that will get everyone's attention.

Stevens's interference results in a fateful moment at the closely guarded spaceship when Klaatu is fatally shot by one of the soldiers. Although Klaatu temporarily recovers, he has instructed Helen to deliver a message to Gort that will stop the robot from doing any harm. Klaatu then appears at the spaceship to plea for intergalactic peace.

MEMORABLE MOMENTS: The very first scene includes fascinating shots of flight controllers studying radar screens, followed by glimpses of people in various foreign locales looking at the flying saucer as it approaches earth and finally lands on the National Mall.

When Carpenter takes Bobby on a walking tour of Washington they first visit the Lincoln Memorial, and then go to Professor Barnhardt's home, Bobby is amazed when Carpenter starts writing numbers on a chalkboard.

When Carpenter and Helen enter an office elevator at noon on a typical week day, The lights go out, the elevator stops, and Carpenter explains that the world's electricity has been neutralized. At this point Helen learns her companion's real identity. There are also shots from all over the world that help explain the film's title.

At the end of the film, after Klaatu is killed, Helen rushes to the spacecraft where Gort is ready to go into action. After she falls down, she remembers to say three words that Klaatu had earlier told her to speak to the robot if danger would arise: "Klaatu barada nikto." Gort carries Helen onto the spacecraft where she watches with wonder as Gort amazingly brings Klaatu back to life.

SUMMATION: *The Day the Earth Stood Still* is a well-produced film, with exemplary script and acting that help to separate it from the many other sci/fi films of the 1950s. When first released it had the distinction of being a rare film with extra-terrestrial visitors who are benign beings, even with Gort standing around.

Some later TV series portrayed aliens as friendly, specially *Mork and Mindy,* but the one later movie most inspired by Robert Wise's film is Steven Spielberg's Close Encounters of the *Third Kind.*

Earth Stood Still and Close Encounters both include stories about visitors from space who come to spread peace and not destruction.

WHAT AWARDS SHOULD THIS FILM HAVE WON?: *Day the Earth Stood Still* deserved awards for its excellent screenplay and for Bernard Herrmann's immensely inventive music.

OSCAR SNUB #18 - *SINGIN' IN THE RAIN* (1952)

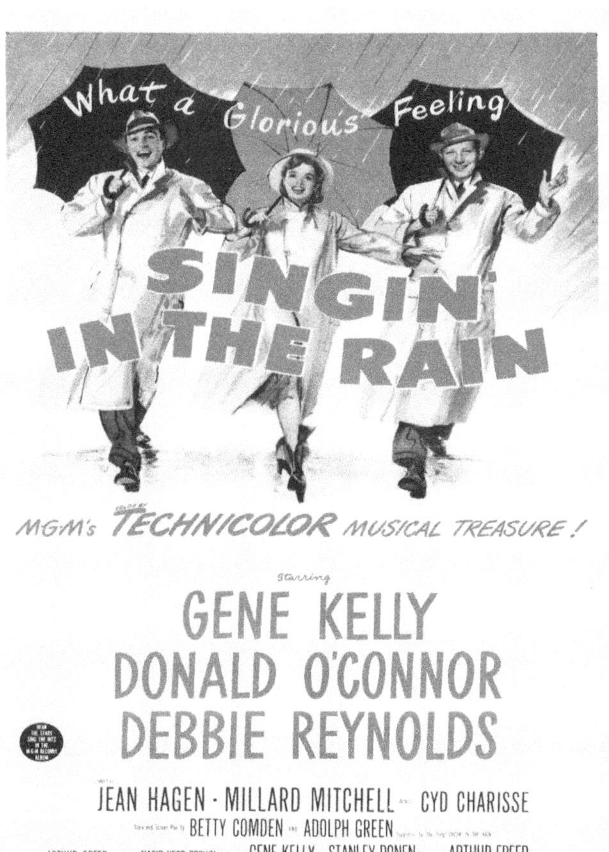

Director: Gene Kelly and Stanley Donen; **Producer:** Arthur Freed; **Studio:** MGM; **Screenplay:** Betty Comden and Adolph Green, based on their original story; **Cinematography:** Harold Rosson; **Art Direction:** Cedric Gibbons and Randall Duell; **Costume Design:** Walter Plunkett; **Editing:** Adrienne Fazan; **Sound:**

Douglas Shearer; **Musical Direction:** Lennie Hayton; **Choreography:** Gene Kelly and Stanley Donen; **Cast:** Gene Kelly (Don Lockwood); Donald O'Connor (Cosmo Brown); Debbie Reynolds (Kathy Selden); Jean Hagan (Lina Lamont); Millard Mitchell (R. F. Simpson); Kathleen Freeman (Phoebe Dinsmore, studio vocal coach); Cyd Charisse (dancer in "Broadway Ballet"); **Running Time:** 102 minutes.

BACKGROUND: In 1952 MGM made two films about the problems involved in making motion pictures. *The Bad and the Beautiful* is an inciteful film in which Kirk Douglas plays a Hollywood producer who desperately needs three of his former colleagues, a director, a writer, and a glamourous female star, to work with him again to salvage his failing career. By contrast, in *Singin' in the Rain* a movie studio faces difficulties caused by the transition from silent films to talking pictures at the end of the 1920s.

Both are fine films, but the second one is especially well-made, with Gene Kelly following his success in the 1951 Oscar-winning *American in Paris* by playing a Douglas Fairbanks-type actor who, with the leading lady that he despises, has to deal with the arrival of talkies.

PLOT: *Singin' in the Rain* is designed as a spoof of filmmaking from the very start. After arriving with Lina Lamont, his co-star, at a Hollywood theater for the premiere of their latest silent film, Don Lockwood is interviewed by a female radio host on the red carpet. As Don tells the story of his rise to fame the film includes a series of vignettes that differ greatly from those he is verbally relating.

The film then concentrates on the difficulties the cast and crew of Don and Lina's next silent picture face when they are ordered by studio head R.F. Simpson to convert the film into a talkie because of the surprise success of *The Jazz Singer.*

After Cosmo, Don's former vaudeville partner and current music director, proposes the idea of turning *The Dueling Cavalier* into a musical named *The Dancing Cavalier,* work begins anew. Problems arise due to the lack of experience with the use of new sound technology, and

Lina's terribly squeaky speaking voice is an even bigger problem. Cosmo again solves the problem by having Lina's voice dubbed. A starlet named Kathy Selden (Debbie Reynolds), who Don knows from having heard her sing at the Coconut Grove, is chosen and filming resumes.

When Lina finds that her voice is not being used, she has a fit and uses her contract to confine Kathy to doing only dubbing work, but at a screening, when Lina is asked to sing, Kathy is behind a curtain doing the vocal work until the curtain is slyly pulled open and the ruse is revealed. Don ends up with Kathy, who become his new costar.

MEMORABLE MOMENTS: The film swings into high gear in the first scene, when Don's narration of his early career is accompanied by highly entertaining short sketches in which Don and Cosmo cavort with violins as part of their stage act.

The humor continues when Cosmo performs a solo number called "Make 'em Laugh." Donald O'Connor's energetic body movements are a sight to see, with his thrashing about on a film set and somersaulting off walls.

There are two fine solo performances for Gene Kelly's character. In the first he serenades Kathy on a bare soundstage by singing "You Were Meant for Me," with the use of beautiful background lighting and the use of a ladder as a prop that they both stand on at one point. The other Kelly solo provides the film's most memorable scene, when Don kisses Kathy outside her home and then walks happily down a street during a downpour singing the film's title song. With an umbrella that he spins around while energetically dancing and splashing through puddles, this scene is a thorough delight.

Reynolds shines in a musical number called "Good Morning," in which she sings and dances energetically with her two male costars. The dancing involves synchronized stepping up and down a staircase and using a couch at one point. The result is one of the film's best scenes.

Two non-musical scenes also stand out. In the first one, Lina has trouble with a mic that has been placed in a bush being used as a decorative prop. After being told to project into the mic she says, "I can't make love to a bush."

In the other scene, during a sneak preview the film skips ahead at one point, and the film goes out of synchronization with the recorded sound. Hilariously, Lina's words are seen coming from the male actor in the scene, while his words are synced with hers.

SUMMATION: *Singin' in the Rain* has become a cinematic classic, with a fine combination of excellent musical performances and moments of raucous humor. Special acknowledgement goes to Jean Hagan, who normally had a low speaking voice as an actress but employed a high-pitched shrill sound as Lina. The Oscar nomination she earned for this film was richly deserved.

The only flaw in this film is the inclusion of the ballet scene known as the "Broadway Ballet." It was probably a suggestion by Kelly, who conceived the idea as an add-on to the *Dueling Cavalier* production in which Don, imagining himself just as he narrated at the beginning of the film, has a daydream about being a young performer working his way toward stardom on Broadway. This extended scene includes several interrelated dance numbers that lead to a fanciful scene in a casino where the young man starts dancing with a sexy lady (played by Cyd Charisse). This scene culminates in a lengthy section that takes place on a bare stage with Charisse wearing a white dress that has a very long train which blows about through the use of an enormous unseen fan. As visually impressive as this ballet is, the net result is extraneous to the film in which it occurs.

WHAT AWARDS SHOULD THIS FILM HAVE WON?: *Singin' in the Rain* should have won 1952's Best-Picture award. Jean Hagen's hilarious role was much more worthy of an award than the few moments that winner Gloria Graham had in *Bad and the Beautiful.*

Despite these snubs *Singin' in the Rain* is still one of the best musicals ever made.

OSCAR SNUB #19 - *A STAR IS BORN* (1954)

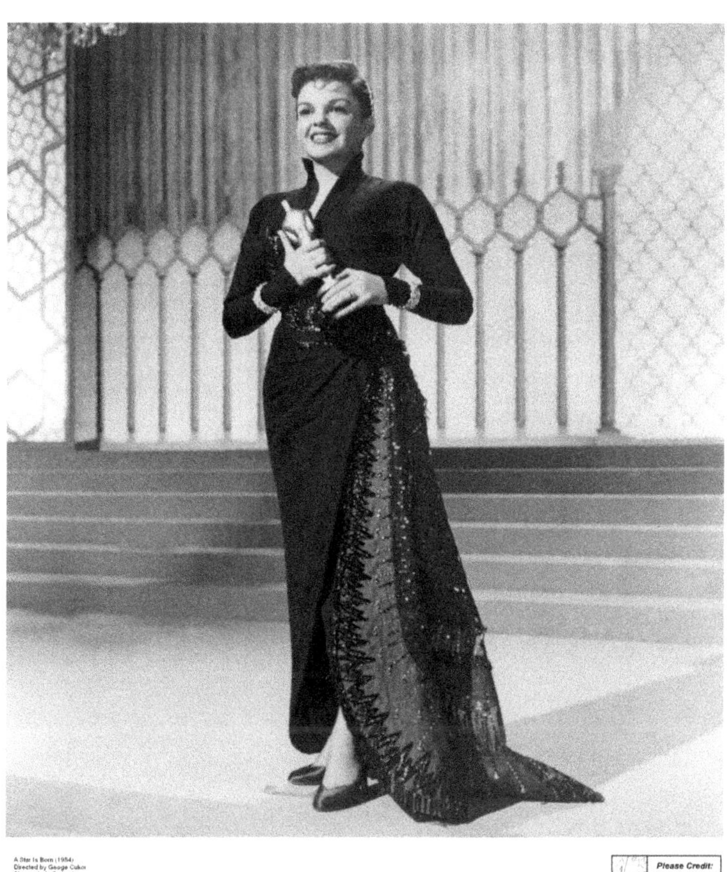

A Star Is Born (1954)
Directed by George Cukor
Shown: Judy Garland
Credit: © Warner Bros.

Rentals grant one-time EDITORIAL use only unless otherwise negotiated. Please inform us about usage or non-usage as soon as possible. Research fees may apply if no images are used

Please Credit:
PHOTOFEST
(212) 633-6330

Director: George Cukor; **Producer:** Sidney Luft; **Studio:** Warner Bros. **Screenplay:** Moss Hart, from screen story by William A. Wellman and Robert Carson; **Cinematography:** Sam Leavitt; **Art Direction:** Malcomb Bert; **Costume Design:** Jean Louis, Mary Ann Nyberg, and Irene Sharaff; **Editing:** Folmar Blangsted; **Sound:** Chaarles B. Lang and David Forrest; **Musical Direction:** Ray

Heindorf; **Original Song:** "The Man That Got Away," Harold Arlen and Ira Gershwin; **Cast:** Judy Garland (Esther Blodgett/Vicki Lester); James Mason (Norman Maine); Jack Carson (Matt Libby); Charles Bickford (Oliver Niles); Tom Noonan (Danny McGuire); Lucy Marlow (Lola Lavery); **Running Time:** 176 minutes (1983 Restoration).

BACKGROUND: Sometimes movies producers are not aware of the impact that their films may have over the years. That is certainly the case with David O. Selznick's 1932 film *What Price Hollywood?*. The scenario of this film, which was directed by Selznick's friend George Cukor from a story by Adela Rogers St. Johns, concerns a prominent director who discovers a waitress and makes her a movie star while he succumbs to alcohol abuse.

In 1937 William A. Wellman, director of *Wings,* the first Oscar-winning Best Picture, was hired by Selznick to make the first of four films entitled *A Star Is Born.* As coauthor, Wellman changed the director role to that of a popular film star who discovers a young woman who wants to pursue an acting career. As her star begins to soar his goes downhill, again due to the abuse of alcohol. This film earned seven Oscar nominations, including acting nods for Janet Gaynor and Fredric March and a citation for the film as Best Picture.

After Judy Garland was released from her MGM contract in 1950, she spent almost four years planning a comeback by starring in a musical version of *A Star Is Born.* With a screenplay by renowned playwright Moss Hart and direction by George Cukor (from the 1932 film), this musical version of the story became one of 1954's most highly anticipated films.

PLOT: The film begins with an all-star fund-raising event held at a theater in Hollywood. Among those in attendance is popular actor Norman Maine (James Mason), who drunkenly disrupts performers backstage. When he stumbles onstage, two male singers are performing as a trio with a young female singer named Esther Blodgett. As they perform, Norman gets in the way until Esther comes to the rescue by holding onto Norman to make it look like he is part of the act.

Despite Norman's drunken state he is impressed with Esther, and, after sobering up, he goes in search of her and finds her at a nightclub where she sings with a band in impromptu after-hours performances. With Norman observing from a distance, at the invitation of Danny McGuire, the group's pianist, Esther begins singing "The Man That Got Away." After she finishes, Norman urges her to come to the studio where he is under contract to make a screen test.

Thus begins Esther's climb up the ladder of success. She is renamed Vicki Lester, and with Norman's encouragement gets her first starring film role in a film that becomes a surprise hit.

This film's success leads to a film that earns her an Oscar nomination, but despite the fact that Vicki marries him, Norman's drinking causes him to be released from his studio contract.

At the Oscar ceremony, when Vicki comes onstage to be handed her award, Norman stumbles out and unashamedly tells the audience repeatedly that he needs a job.

Norman's downhill spiral is somewhat counterbalanced by Vicki's attempts to keep him sober, but Norman finally realizes that he is a detriment to his wife's career. He soon thereafter goes for a swim in the ocean and doesn't come back.

MEMORABLE MOMENTS: Early in the film, when Norman finds Esther at the nightclub, Judy Garland's singing of "The Man That Got Away" gets very emotional, especially when she stands up and spreads out her arms in muscular fashion to express the emotion in the song's lyrics. This is one of the most impressive musical performances in the film.

In a later scene, when Esther (now Vicki) is in the process of doing her first film role, she sits at the edge of a stage and sings "Born in a Trunk." This song forms bookends to a sequence in which Vicki's character relates the story of how she has come from Pocatello, Idaho to become a singing star. During this scene, Garland gives stylish renditions of such tuneful standards as "I'll Get By" and "Swanee."

In an emotion-filled later scene, Esther sits at her dressing-room table and tells Oliver Niles, the studio head, that Norman seems bent on destroying himself with alcohol. In one long take Garland reaches the pinnacle of her acting career with an outburst of tears that painfully reveals her suffering.

Toward the end of the film a dramatic moment occurs when Norman, who has just been released from jail through his wife's intervention, overhears Vicki talking to Niles about leaving Hollywood with Norman to keep him sober. As Norman listens his face becomes increasingly distraught, until he turns over in bed and starts sobbing uncontrollably. James Mason is heartbreaking in this wrenching scene.

SUMMATION: This film, which is the longest of the four *Star Is Born* movies, became the victim of studio interference when Jack Warner insisted, after the picture's less-than-successful premiere showings, that the film be shortened. The result, as the 1983 restoration clearly demonstrates, is a sometimes-frustrating viewing experience in which scenes include moments when the picture stops with freeze-frame shots (shown in a sepia-tinted color), with preserved audio tracks accompanying them.

Despite the editing problems, this *Star Is Born* remains the best of the four films. Garland's portrayal is the best work of her entire career and Mason is often heart-wrenching as Esther's troubled husband.

WHAT AWARDS SHOULD THIS FILM HAVE WON?: Although both actors were nominated, both were snubbed for their roles in this film. The Best-Actress award went to Grace Kelly, who impressed critics by avoiding makeup and wearing plain dresses as the wife of another alcoholic husband in *The Country Girl.* Meanwhile, Mason lost to Marlon Brando for the memorable role of Terry Malloy in *On the Waterfront.* Even without any Oscar wins, this version of *A Star Is Born* provides an unforgettable viewing experience.

OSCAR SNUB #20 – *THE NIGHT OF THE HUNTER* (1955)

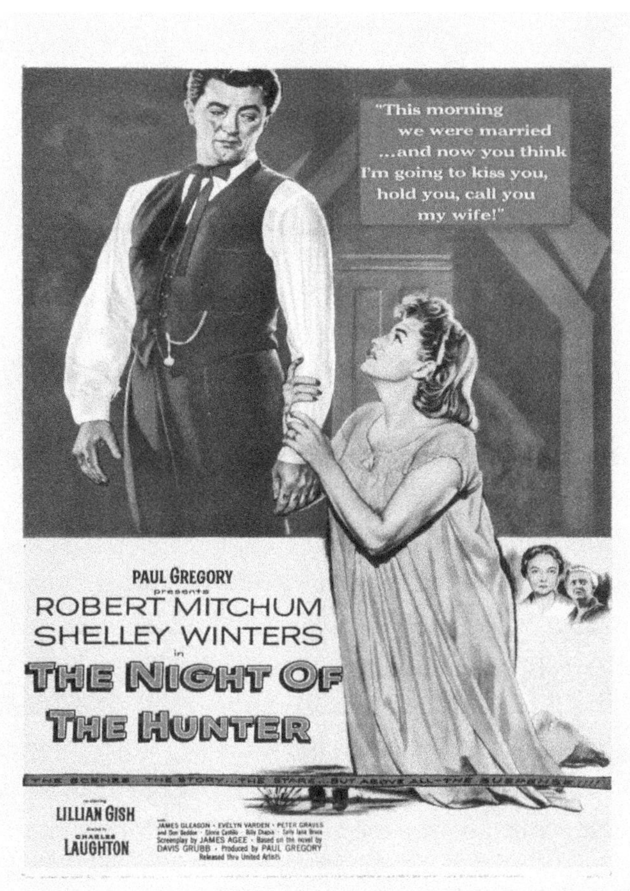

Director: Charles Laughton; **Producer:** Paul Gregory; **Screenplay:** James Agee, from the novel by Davis Grubb; **Cinematography:** Stanley Cortez; **Art Direction:** Holyard Brown and Alfred Spencer; **Costume Design:** Jerry Bos and Evelyn Corruth; **Editing:** Robert Golden; **Sound:** Stanford Houghton; **Musical Score:** Walter Schumann; **Cast:** Robert Mitchum (Harry

Powell); Shelley Winters (Willa Harper); Lillian Gish (Rachel Cooper); Peter Graves (Ben Harper); Billy Chapin (John Harper); Sally Jane Bruce (Pearl Harper); James Gleason (Uncle Birdie); **Running Time:** 93 minutes.

BACKGROUND: Many of the films that are profiled in this book have been highly regarded since the time of their original release. Others, however, did not receive much acclaim when they first appeared and have remained rather obscure films. *The Night of the Hunter* is a good example of the latter category; according to film historian Douglas Brode it was released without fanfare as part of a double bill that also included a low-budget Western.[1]

Despite its initial lack of popular recognition, this film has many outstanding qualities, including the direction by Charles Laughton, who never directed another film after the box-office failure of this production. This film also includes one of Robert Mitchum's most noteworthy acting roles as a self-styled preacher who is actually a despicable woman killer. There are additionally many other elements that make this film worthy of being included in this list of snubbed films.

PLOT: When an itinerant self-proclaimed preacher named Harry Powell occupies the same cell as convicted robber and murderer Ben Harper, the seeds are planted for Harry's search for the $10,000 that Harper had stolen. After Harper's execution, Harry is released and goes off to find Harper's two children, because Harper had mumbled in his sleep that his kids know where the money is hidden. An obstacle in Harry's quest is the fact that the children live with their mother.

Harry does find the children, and also Willa, their mother. After a quick courtship she agrees to marry him, completely unaware that Harry has a history of marrying widows and killing them. On their wedding night Harry convinces Willa that having sex is sinful, and not long thereafter he kills her, places her body in an old car, and sinks it into a nearby river.

---

[1] Douglas Brode, The Films of the Forties (Secaucus, N.J.: Citadel Press, 1976), p. 143.

When John and Pearl realize that their father is after the money, they know their lives are in danger. With Pearl carrying a doll into which the money has been stashed, John finds a small rowboat and they are pulled along by the current, with Harry pursuing them on horseback.

They are soon rescued by Rachel Cooper, a kindly older woman with a penchant for taking in homeless children. Harry comes calling but is chased away by Rachel, who threatens him with a rifle. Harry is finally identified as a killer, and after being trapped in a barn, he is taken into custody. While he is being escorted away, John hits Harry with the doll and the money flies out. Harry is last seen being moved from a jail as an angry mob tries to lynch him.

At the end of the film Rachel helps John and Pearl celebrate their first Christmas together, along with several other needy children.

MEMORABLE MOMENTS: After Willa's death an old man named Uncle Birdie discovers her body in the sunken car as he attempts to fish in the river. The shot of Willa's hair floating in the water is one of the most haunting images in the film.

Several times in the film Harry's voice is heard as he is moving along in pursuit of the money. Robert Mitchum's repeated singing of parts of the hymn "Leaning on the Everlasting Arms" adds an ironic effect as the hymn's soothing words provide a strange contrast to the menacing preacher's deadly intentions.

The sequence in which John and Pearl sleep in the boat as they are being pursued is one of the film's most memorable scenes, with lovely night shots of stars in the sky seeming like a protective blanket over the children as they float down the river. This scene is accompanied by composer Walter Schumann's lovely music that includes a lilting lullaby, "Hush, Little One, Hush," sung first by Pearl and later by an adult female voice. in a soothing manner.

SUMMATION: Despite the somber nature of the film's story, *Night of the Hunter* is masterfully designed, with the camerawork by Stanley Cortez adding greatly to the film's dramatic impact. The night shots in the middle section are particularly noteworthy, especially when accompanied by the film's memorable music.

The most noteworthy performance in the film is that of Robert Mitchum, whose maniacal behavior is on view from the very start. In the opening scene his prayer to the Lord gives ample indication of his murderous bent.

In later scenes Mitchum's singing voice in bits of the "Everlasting Arms" hymn provides a weird sort of warning that bad things are going to happen, even though Harry's presence in the town is at first seen to be comforting. It is ironic that the same people who initially think that this seemingly benign preacher should marry the hapless widow and provide proper care for her children form the lynch mob of angry townsfolk who cry out in fury for Harry's execution at the end of the film.

Night of the Hunter's mixture of tender and frightening moments is uniquely presented, with masterful direction by Charles Laughton. His many stellar achievements as an actor may have firmly prepared him for his accomplishments behind the camera. In any case, the direction of this film is just one of its many worthy facets that were sadly overlooked when the films of 1955 were been appraised by members of the Motion Picture Academy. In terms of the film's many excellent qualities, *Night of the Hunter* deserved accolades that it was regrettably denied.

WHAT AWARDS SHOULD THIS FILM HAVE WON?: The snubbing of this film by Academy voters can be considered one of the most shameful moments in the history of the Academy Awards. Mitchum should have been nominated for his chilling performance, and Lillian Gish deserved an Oscar for her supporting role.

Few other films of the 1955 film year, even *Marty* and *East of Eden*, reach the dramatic and artistic heights achieved by *Night of the Hunter.*

OSCAR SNUB #21 - *THE SEARCHERS* (1956)

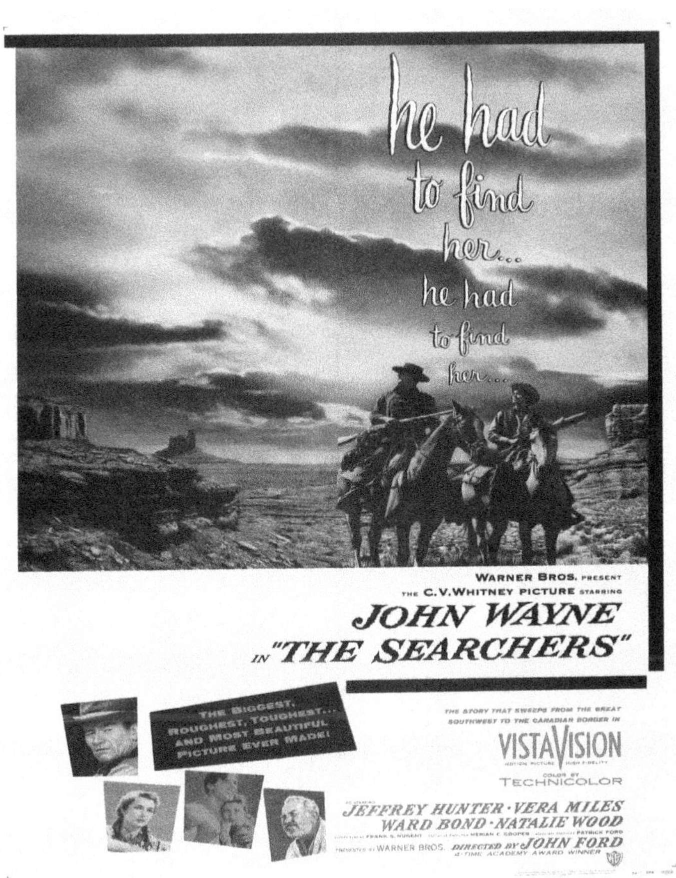

Director: John Ford; **Producer:** Merian C. Cooper; **Studio:** Warner Bros.; **Screenplay:** Frank S. Nugent, based on the novel by Alan LeMay; **Cinematography:** Winton C. Hoch; **Art Direction:** James Basevi and Frank Hotaling; **Costume Design:** Charles Arrico; **Editing:** Jack Murray; **Sound:** Hugh McDowell and Howard Wilson; **Musical Score:** Max Steiner; **Cast:** John Wayne

(Ethan Edwards); Jeffrey Hunter (Martin Pawley); Vera Miles (Laurie Jorgensen); Ward Bond (Rev. Capt. Samuel Clayton); Natalie Wood (Debbie Edwards, age 15); Harry Carey, Jr. (Brad Jorgensen); Henry Brandon (Scar); Walter Coy (Aaron Edwards); Dorothy Jordan (Martha Edwards); Ken Curtis (Charlie McCorry); **Running Time:** 119 Minutes.

BACKGROUND: John Ford (1894-1993) has the distinction of being the only film director to win four Oscars for his work. Having been born into an Irish-immigrant family in Maine, it is no surprise that two of his Oscars were earned for helming films set in Ireland: *The Informer* (1935) and *The Quiet Man* (1952). His other Oscars came in 1940 (for *The Grapes of Wrath*), set in America during the Great Depression) and in 1941 for *How Green Was My Valley* (set in Wales at the end of the 19th century). Surprisingly, none of Ford's Oscar winners is a Western.

Ford began his film career by making Westerns, and in the ten-year period beginning in 1920 he made thirty of them starring Harry Carey, who had a long career as a character actor.

Ford's fame as a Western-film director got a solid footing with the 1939 film *Stagecoach,* which helped make John Wayne one of the most popular actors of the 1940s through the 1960s. Ford directed Wayne in many of Hollywood's most revered Westerns, including the so-called Cavalry Trilogy that includes *Fort Apache* (1948), *She Wore a Yellow Ribbon* (1949) and *Rio Grande* (1950). In the 1950s Wayne's choice of films took a different direction, but in 1956 Ford lured him to star in a Western called *The Searchers,* based on a popular novel about a lengthy search for a nine-year-old female child in Texas whose family has been wiped out by a band of murderous Comanches. The role of Ethan Edwards, the man who leads the search, inspired Wayne to give one of his best performances on film.

PLOT: *The Searchers,* which is set in Texas, begins in 1868, when Ethan Edwards, a former Confederate soldier, rides up to the porch of a ranch and is greeted by Martha, Ethan's sister- in-law, and is then welcomed by his brother, Aaron, and their three children. After Ethan is invited to stay, he offers no explanation for his whereabouts since the war ended.

When word comes that a tribe of Comanches has been harassing homesteaders, Ethan goes along with a band of local ranchers in search of them. While they are away, the ranch is burned down and all of Ethan's family are presumed dead except for the youngest child, nine-year-old Debbie.

Thus is set in motion a search that lasts over five years. Ethan takes along Martin Pauley, a half-breed who has been raised by the Edwards family, and Brad Jorgensen, who has been engaged to the Edwards's older daughter. During the search Ethan finds details of her death but no sign of Debbie. Ethan concludes that Debbie has been captured and made to live as an Indian.

Brad gets killed by Comanches but the search continues, with Martin insisting on going along, if only to stop Ethan from killing Debbie, since Ethan has been known to be an Indian killer.

Eventually the searchers are aided by Reverend Samuel Clayton, who also serves as an Army captain, and a small troop of other army recruits.

When Debbie is found, she at first resists being taken into custody by Ethan, but later, during a raid on the Indian camp, Martin kills Scar, the tribe leader who had led the raid on the Edwards's ranch, and Ethan captures his niece, who at first thinks he is going to kill her, but Ethan has a change of heart and brings her back home.

MEMORABLE MOMENTS: There is a lot of comical repartee between Ethan and those around him, especially Captain Clayton, who joins the searchers for much of the attempted rescue. In an early scene Clayton questions Ethan about quitting the search. Ethan's reply is "That'll be the day," an expression that returns three more times in the film.

That phrase returns when Brad angrily says he will fight Ethan if he isn't allowed to continue searching. Ethan rejects the idea of Brad beating him up by again saying, "That'll be the day."

A much more serious retort comes when Ethan finds clothing that had been that of Debbie's big sister. When Brad demands more details about what happened to his fiancée, Ethan yells at him and shouts, "Do you want me to draw you a picture?"

Over the years that Ethan searches for his niece, Brad's sister Laurie waits patiently for news about the search team. In one memorable sequence Laurie reads aloud a letter from Martin that includes a humorous report of an Indian woman who accidentally gets traded to Martin in exchange for some merchandise. The sight of the woman following Martin around puts some extra levity into the film.

When Laurie gives up waiting for Martin, she plans to marry a guitar-playing rancher named Charlie McCorry. When Ethan and Martin return the night of the wedding, a fistfight with Charlie occurs, with Martin winning only after several humorous punches and knockdowns.

SUMMATION: Frank Nugent's insightful script and John Ford's inspired direction result in a film of high distinction. John Wayne is surrounded by an excellent supporting cast, several members of which graced many other John Ford films, including Ward Bond, John Qualen, and Harry Carey, Jr. (son of the western star).

Other worthy elements of the film are the excellent cinematography of Winton C. Hoch and the often-lyrical music of Max Steiner. Additionally, the film's framing device of a door opening and closing is an ingenious element. When Ethan leaves Debbie with the Jorgensons and walks out a door just as he had entered one at the start of the film, the story has come full circle, and the closing door suggests that Ethan's future will be just as uncertain as his past.

WHAT AWARDS SHOULD THIS FILM HAVE WON?: Although John Wayne finally won an Oscar in 1969 for playing Rooster Cogburn in *True Grit,* he should have won for *The Searchers.* He totally dominates the film and keeps the viewer engrossed throughout.

TRIVIA NOTE: 1950s rock singer Buddy Holly was so impressed with Wayne's cynical words that shortly after *The Searchers* was released Holly wrote the song "That'll Be the Day."

OSCAR SNUB #22 – 12 *ANGRY MEN* (1957)

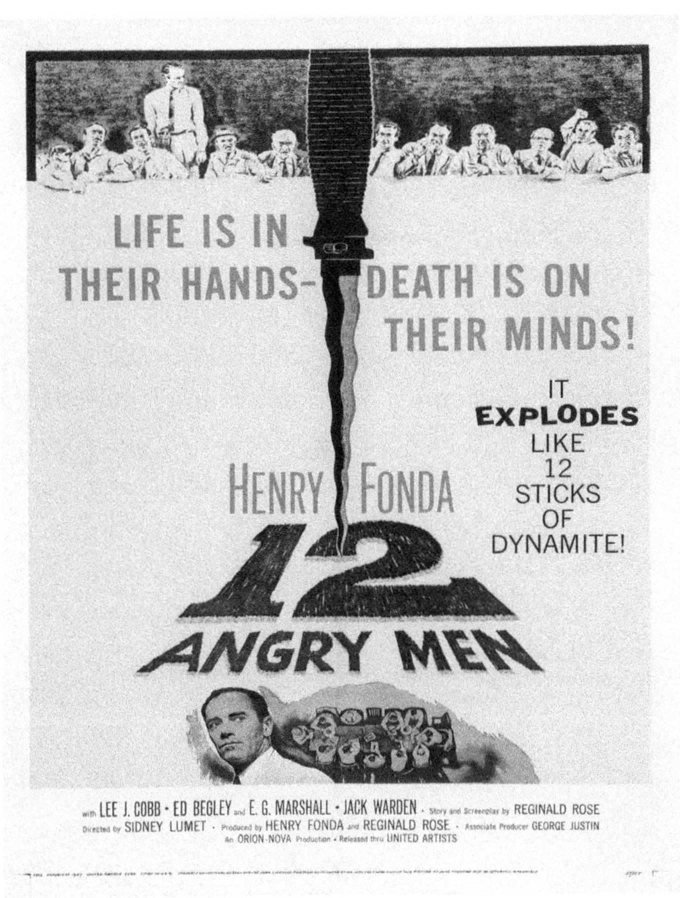

Director: Sidney Lumet; **Producer:** Henry Fonda and Reginald Rose; **Studio:** United Artists; **Screenplay:** Reginald Rose, from his teleplay; **Cinematography:** Boris Kaufman; **Art Direction:** Robert Markle; **Costume Design:** not listed; **Editing:** Carl Lerner; **Sound:** James A. Gleason; **Musical Score:** Kenyon Hopkins;

Cast: Martin Balsam (Juror 1); John Fiedler (Juror 2), Lee J. Cobb (Juror 3); E. G. Marshall (Juror 4); Jack Klugman (Juror 5); Edward Binns (Juror 6); Jack Warden (Juror 7); Henry Fonda (Juror 8); Joseph Sweeney (Juror 9); Ed Begley (Juror 10); George Voskovec (Juror 11); Robert Webber (Juror 12); **Running Time:** 95 minutes.

BACKGROUND: By the mid-1950s, the number of moviegoers paying to watch movies on a big movie screen had diminished greatly. During this same time there was a significant surge in contemporary dramas conceived by major writers for the small TV screens. Especially notable are the scripts by Paddy Chayefsky and Rod Serling. Especially ironic is the fact that *Marty*, Chayefsky's 1954 TV drama, came to the theater screen a year later and won several Oscars, including ones for Best Picture and Chayefsky's screenplay adaptation.

Also significant are the teleplays by Rod Serling that were adapted as Hollywood Films – *Patterns* in 1956 and the 1957 TV drama *Requiem for a Heavyweight*, which belatedly came to the screen in 1962.

Yet another talented screenwriter is Reginald Rose, whose one-hour live TV drama about a hung jury came to the screen in 1957 thanks to its producer-star, Henry Fonda, who relished the idea of playing a jury member who disputes the hasty judgment of the other eleven jurors.

There have been numerous films focused on jury trials, both fictional and factual ones, but Lumet's film, his first in a long and distinguished directing career, is unique because almost the entire film takes place in the sequestered jury room.

PLOT: The film begins in a courtroom where the judge, who seems rather bored with the proceedings, gives rather matter-of-factly a set of instructions to the jury concerning a murder case involving an eighteen-year-old defendant. The twelve jurors are then escorted into an adjacent room where they are instructed by the foreman, Juror 1, to cast their votes in writing. When the votes are tallied, eleven jurors have voted "guilty," but there is a lone hold-out from Juror 8, who feels that he doesn't want to cast a vote before some discussion takes place.

Thus begins a series of discussions that are reluctantly agreed to by most of the other jurors, who openly state their feeling that the accused is guilty. Juror 8 has no reasons at first for his holding off on a guilty verdict, but as the discussion ensues, several issues are soon addressed that lead Juror 9, the oldest man in the room, to express his doubts by voting "not guilty" on the next vote.

During the next hour several issues are brought up that result in more jurors changing their minds, until there is only one man, Juror 10, who refuses to agree with the others. The final discussion leads Juror 10 to confront his own prejudices against young people, stemming from his own difficulties as the parent of a rebellious teenager. His change of mind (and heart) leads to a vote to acquit the accused boy.

MEMORABLE MOMENTS: The film begins with a memorable shot, captured by the film's photographer, Boris Kaufman, of a courthouse building, with a roaming camera moving through a hallway until the door to a courtroom appears. Inside the room a judge is seen giving instructions, and then the face of the accused boy is seen in closeup. His face continues to appear as the jurors are escorted out of the room. This use of a slow dissolve shot effectively captures the conflict between the accused and the twelve men who will decide his fate.

Screenwriter Reginald Rose's script cleverly allows all twelve of the jurors to have moments when their individual personalities come forth during the many conversations that take place as the proceedings continue. There are too many moments for which there is space to acknowledge all the highlights of these scenes, but a few that stand out include a moment when Juror 8 tries to demonstrate the difficulties the accused would have had in inflicting the wounds that killed his father, who was much taller than his teenage son. A tense moment comes when Juror 3, the most volatile of the twelve men, takes the murder weapon and seems ready to stab Juror 8. Only the interference of some of the others in the room prevents his possible injury.

Later in the film, when Juror 10 is the only one left that clings to a guilty verdict, his verbal outburst shocks the other jurors (as well as viewers). Lee J, Cobb's acting in this scene provides the film's most emotional moment, when his character breaks down and starts to cry.

As Juror 8, Henry Fonda has no big dramatic speeches, but his character's determination to speak against those who want to get out of the room in a hurry provides a powerful statement regarding the responsibility that those assigned the task of deciding guilt or innocence have in carrying out their assigned task.

SUMMATION: By the end of *12 Angry Men* the viewer should come away with a better grasp of the legal system and the difficulties involved in the process of protecting innocent victims from their accusers.

Looking back at the films released in 1957, one can find a list of very worthy films, including the Oscar-winning picture *The Bridge on the River Kwai, Paths of Glory* [see next entry], plus the beautifully filmed *Peyton Place* and *Sayonara.* That list also includes *12 Angry Men,* which was no box-office hit when first released, but has gradually gained respect and become one of the most highly esteemed films of the 1950s.

To honor the twelve cast members whose performances are so uniformly excellent, all their names are listed in the credits found at the start of this entry.

12 Angry Men should be seen by all movie fans, especially those who want to discover "little" films that didn't win awards when first released.

WHAT AWARDS SHOULD THIS FILM HAVE WON?: Reginald Rose should have been awarded for his perceptive screenplay. Also, if there had been a way to give out collective Oscars, all twelve actors in *12 Angry Men* should have been awarded for Best Actor.

OSCAR SNUB #23 – *PATHS OF GLORY* (1957)

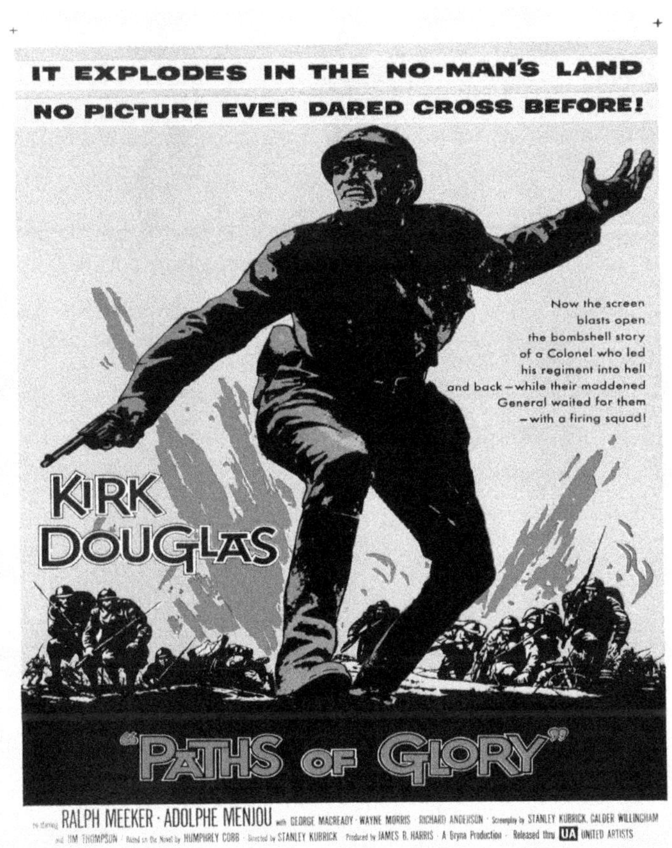

Director: Stanley Kubrick; **Producer:** James B. Harris; **Studio:** United Artists; **Screenplay:** Stanley Kubrick, Calder Willingham, and Jim Thompson; **Cinematography:** George Krause; **Art Direction:** Ludwig Reiber; **Costume Design:** Ilse Dubois; **Editing:** Eva Kroll; **Sound:** Martin Muller; **Musical Score:** Gerald

Fried; **Production Company:** Bryna Productions; **Cast:** Kirk Douglas (Colonel Dax); Ralph Meeker (Corporal Philippe Paris); Adolphe Menjou (General George Broulard); George Macready (Brigadier General Mireau); Wayne Morris (Lieutenant Roget); Joseph Turkel (Private Pierre Arnaud); Timothy Carey (Private Ferol); Susanne Christian (German singer in café); **Running Time:** 88 minutes.

BACKGROUND: Many new directors came onto the scene during the 1950s. Among them are tose that had worked in television, including Delbert Mann, Martin Ritt, Sidney Lumet, and John Frankenheimer. Another newcomer was Stanley Kubrick, although he started out as a magazine photographer and gravitated into filmmaking in 1950 with short documentaries. Three years later he made his first feature film, *Flesh and Desire*, which was not very successful, but in 1956 he made *The Killers,* which gained him high praise and brought him to the attention of Kirk Douglas, who was launching his own production company, Bryna productions. In 1957 Douglas hired Kubrick to direct a film based on Humphrey Cobb's 1935 novel, *Paths of Glory.*

There have been many antiwar films in motion picture history, including two that won Academy Awards as Best Picture. The first of these, *All Quiet on the Western Front,* has been filmed several times, but the earliest version, released in 1930, just a year after the great success of Erich Maria Remarque's novel, is the best one of them. The other Oscar winner is *The Bridge on the River Kwai,* which ironically was released in 1957, the same year that *Paths of Glory* came to the screen.

These films are set during different wars, with *River Kwai* depicting allied soldiers in a Japanese prison camp during World War II, while *Paths of Glory* and all the versions of *All Quiet on the Western Front* are set during World War I.

PLOT: *Paths of Glory*, which is set in France during 1915, tells the harrowing story of a highly dangerous mission to attack a place called the Anthill planned by General Broulard. Broulard's assistant, Brigadier General Mireau, believes the mission is too risky, but Mireau lures him on by promising him a promotion if he succeeds. When the mission fails, Mireau tries to save face by selecting alarge number of soldiers to face a court-martial for cowardice. After much debate, the number is reduced to three soldiers, one from each regiment.

After the selection of the soldiers takes place, Colonel Dax, a soldier in one of the regiments, becomes the defense attorney for the accused men. Dax is aware of the hypocrisy involved, but he volunteers to take on the task, largely because of his background as a trial lawyer.

The trial is held, but Dax is given little opportunity to defend the honor of the accused men. After the conviction Dax chooses Lieutenant Roget, a man whose cowardice has been no secret, as the leader of the firing squad. Roget reluctantly carries out the thankless task.

Following the execution Dax visits the two generals as they are enjoying breakfast together. Dax boldly accuses General Mireau of ordering one of the soldiers to fire on his own men. General Broulard relieves the other general of his command and offers the post to Dax, who defies the idea that he has plotted against Mireau in order to win the promotion for himself and angrily storms out of the room.

MEMORABLE MOMENTS: The first section, which includes the charge on the Anthill, is filled with impressive camera shots of men moving through the trenches, and then of the various soldiers making a bold attempt to get out of the trenches and move towards the intended destination. Closeups of frightened faces vividly indicate the hopelessness of their mission.

Another noteworthy moment occurs when General Mireau meets with the soldiers to discuss the selection of men to be punished for cowardice, Dax proclaims, "Why don't you shoot the entire regiment?" He then angrily states, "Shoot Me!" After more discussion, the proposed number drops from one hundred down to three.

When a priest arrives in a holding cell to hear the convicted men's confessions, Corporal Paris at first appears reluctant because of his non-religious background. When Paris begins talking to the priest, he hands him a letter that he wants delivered to his wife. Right before the execution Paris falls to his knees and tearfully shouts, "I don't want to die." He then bravely gets up and leads the procession of the three condemned men.

After the execution, Dax walks down the street and starts hearing shouting sounds coming from a nearby café. When he pauses to listen, the scene shifts to the interior of the building, in which lots of commotion is caused by the appearance of a young German female prisoner who is being teased by the café owner into performing. When she begins singing an old German folk song, she can barely be heard over the shouting and whistling of the gathered soldiers from Dax's regiment. But soon the noise dies down as the men start joining in the singing. Those who don't know the words just make sounds like "la-la-la," as the men appear transfixed. Some of them even wipe tears from their eyes as they realize this young woman is not really their enemy. This scene is the most emotionally moving moment in the entire film and should leave viewers haunted by the simple tunefulness of this song, the melody of which continues into the music that accompanies the closing cast credits.

Special note: the singer, billed as Susanne Christian, is Susanne Kubrick, the director's wife.

SUMMATION: *Paths of Glory* is a classic example of great filmmaking. Despite some awkward dialogue that stems from the use of American actors to portray Frenchmen, this film contains a powerful message about condemning soldiers without proper cause. In this sense *Paths of Glory* is far more memorable than *River Kwai,* in which captured British soldiers are forced into constructing a railway bridge in the jungles of Burma.

WHAT AWARDS SHOULD THIS FILM HAVE WON?: Regrettably, *Paths of Glory* didn't earn a single Oscar nomination. At least it should have been recognized for its impressive screenplay and photography. Kubrick also deserved an award for his excellent direction.

OSCAR SNUB #24 – *AUNTIE MAME* (1958)

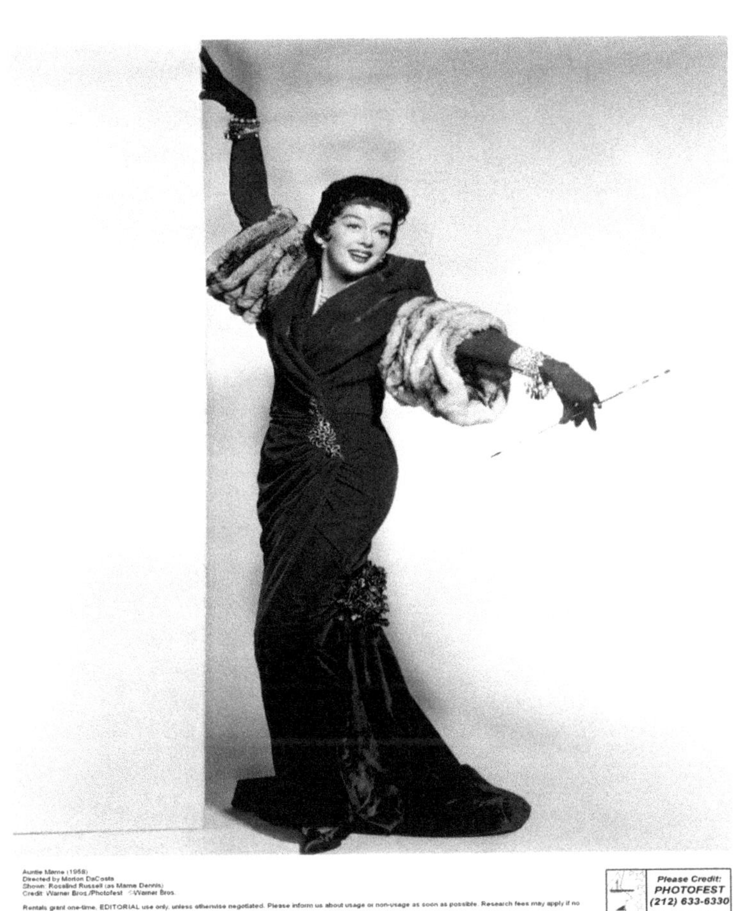

Director: Morton DaCosta; **Producer:** Morton DaCosta; **Studio:** Warner Bros. **Screenplay:** Betty Comden and Adolf Green, from the stage play by Jerome Lawrence and Robert E. Lee; **Cinematography:** Harry Stradling, Sr.; **Art Direction:** Malcolm Bert and George James Hopkins; **Costume Design:** Orry-Kelly; **Editing:** William Ziegler; **Sound:** M.A. Merrick; **Musical Score:**

Bronislau Kaper; **Cast:** Rosalind Russell (Mame Dennis); Forrest Tucker (Beauregard Jackson Pickett Burnside); Coral Browne (Vera Charles); Roger Smith (adult Patrick); Jan Handzlik (young Patrick); Peggy Cass (Agnes Gooch); Patric Knowles (Lindsey Woolsey); Fred Clark (Dwight Babcock); Robin Hughes (Brian O'Bannion); Pippa Scott (Pegeen Ryan); **Running Time:**143 minutes.

BACKGROUND: In 1955 a novel named *Auntie Mame* reached the New York Times best-seller list and remained on the charts for 112 weeks. It's author, Patrick Dennis, was in reality Edward Everett Tanner III, who claimed he wrote a fictionalized story about his aunt.

The popularity of the book led to a sequel called *Around the World with Auntie Mame*, which became a best seller in 1958. The books inspired a Broadway play written by Jerome Lawrence and Robert E. Lee. The play, which opened in October of 1956, became a huge success and ran for almost two years. It was also a personal triumph for Rosalind Russell, who played the role until January of 1958, when she left the show to star in the film adaptation.

The film was produced and directed by Morton DaCosta, who also directed the stage version, with several of the stage actors recreating their roles, including Russell, Peggy Cass, and Jan Handzlik, who played Patrick as a boy.

PLOT: *Auntie Mame* begins with a voice reading aloud the last will and testament of a wealthy businessman named Edwin Dennis, who has reluctantly agreed to give custody of his only child, Patrick, to his sister, Mame. Edwin's death is then revealed through a newspaper headline. Ironically, his fatal heart attack happens only a single day after the will is signed.

Little Patrick is brought to his aunt's apartment at No. 3 Beekman Place in Manhattan, and thus begins his unconventional upbringing, which is complicated by Dwight Babcock, an employee of the Knickerbocker Bank as well the will's executor, who is determined that Patrick will be raised in a very proper way.

When the stock market crashes the next year, Mame finds employment with little success until a wealthy southerner, Beauregard Burnside, meets her as a saleslady at Macy's when he tries to buy rollers skates for his nieces and nephews. Soon, Mame and Patrick arrive at Peckerwood, the Southern plantation owned by Beau's dictatorial mother. After a foxhunt planned in Mame's honor, Beau proposes marriage, and they soon go on a long honeymoon.

Some years later, after Patrick enters college, Beau dies while he and Mame are climbing in the Swiss Alps. After another year, Mame's longtime friend, publisher Lindsey Woolsey, proposes that she write her memoirs, and he hires Brian O'Bannion, an Irish poet, to assist her.

Complications arise when a frumpy but skillful stenographer, Agnes Gooch, becomes Mame's secretary and develops a crush on Brian. Further problems emerge when Patrick introduces Mame to his fiancée, Gloria Upson, whose parents live in a restricted area in Connecticut.

After some clever maneuvering by his aunt, Patrick marries a decorator named Pegeen Ryan and Mame eventually works her magic on their young son, Michael, who is unsurprisingly allowed by his parents to travel to India with his aunt.

MEMORABLE MOMENTS: *Mame* is filled with hilarious moments, beginning with the wild party she is hosting as Patrick arrives with a matronly woman who soon becomes the household maid. Among the crazy highlights of this event is a piano player who lies backward against the piano bench and plays with his hands reaching over his head.

Before meeting Mr. Babcock, Mame has her own ideas about Patrick's education, but her plan backfires when Babcock learns that Patrick is attending a school in Greenwich Village where students don't wear clothes in the classroom. Patrick's description of a school project is a hoot.

After losing her fortune in the Wall Street crash, Mame's friend Vera Charles finds her a very small role in a Broadway play. Unfortunately, Mame disrupts the last scene by wearing a bracelet that jingles so loudly that it distracts Vera, and then the bracelet gets caught on Vera's dress.

Mame's next job is that of a switchboard operator at the law firm of Widdicome, Gutterman, Applewhite, Bibberman, and Black. Russell's fast-paced attempts to pronounce the lawyers' names when she answers calls leads to a moment of sheer hilarity.

Mame's job at Macy's ends abruptly after her boss, Mr. Loomis, finds out that she can only do COD transactions. When Loomis looks at a big pile of tissue paper in Mame's hands he angrily says, "Miss Dennis, this sales book is a SHAMBLES!"

One of the film's most memorable highlights occurs during the foxhunt. As Mame manages to ride sidesaddle on a wild horse inappropriately called Meditation, a local sheriff tries to stop her from getting hurt. A loud crash occurs when Mame's horse hits the sheriff's car and Mame winds up in an icehouse, with the fox tucked into her riding jacket.

More hilarity occurs while Mame is working on her memoir and is being chased through her apartment by Brian, her writing associate, who suddenly seems a lot healthier than when he first arrived walking with a cane. Later that day, Mame arranges for Agnes to go with Brian to a fancy reception. When she drags Agnes up a staircase to make her more presentable, Mame utters the film's classic line: "Life is a banquet, and most poor suckers are starving to death."

SUMMATION: *Auntie Mame* was warmly received by both audiences and critics and received six Oscar nominations, including one for Best Picture. The film's success led to the 1966 stage adaptation with music by Jerry Herman, but despite the catchy title song and "We Need a Little Christmas," *Mame* is not as memorable as the original film. The 1974 film based on the stage musical is a badly conceived misfire, with a totally miscast Lucille Ball in the title role.

WHAT AWARDS SHOULD THIS FILM HAVE WON?: Rosalind Russell remains the most memorable of the many actresses who have portrayed Mame. Both Russell and Cass were Oscar-nominated, but neither won an acting award. Russell should have won for this role of a lifetime.

OSCAR SNUB #25 – *VERTIGO* (1958)

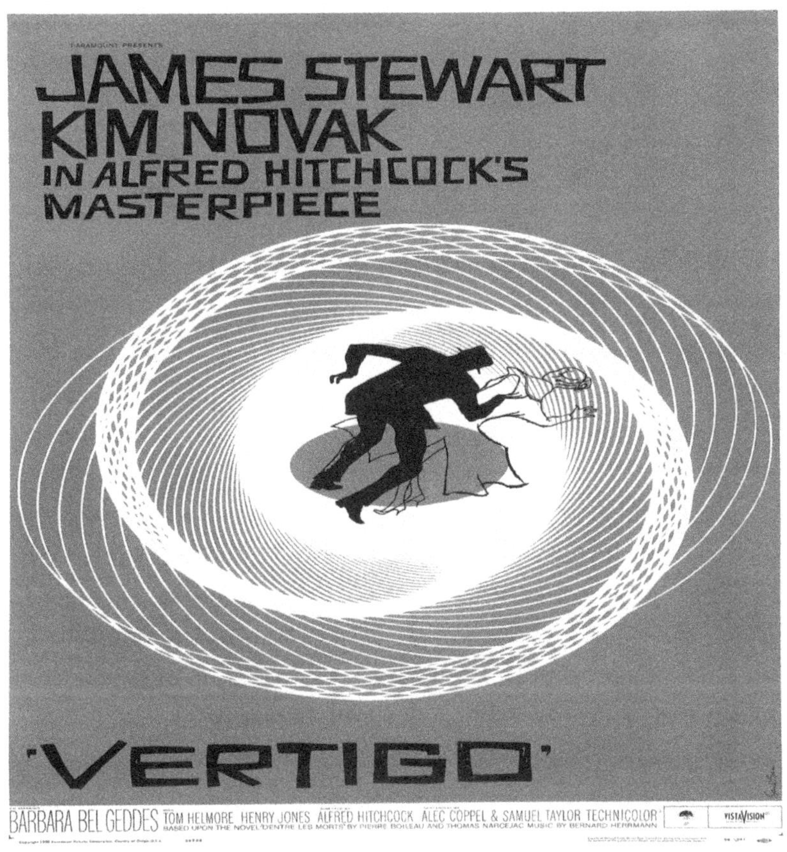

Director: Alfred Hitchcock; **Producer:** Alfred Hitchcock; **Studio:** Paramount; **Screenplay:** Alec Coppel and Samuel Taylor, from the novel *D'Entre les Morts* by Pierre Boileau and Thomas Narcejac; **Cinematography:** Robert Burks; **Art Direction:** Hal Pereira and Henry Bumstead; **Costume Design:** Edith Head; **Editing:** George Tomasini; **Sound:** Harold Lewis and Winston Leverett; **Musical**

Score: Bernard Herrmann; **Titles Design:** Saul Bass; **Cast:** James Stewart (John "Scottie" Ferguson); Kim Novak (Madeleine Elster/Judy Barton); Barbara Bel Geddes (Midge); Tom Helmore (Gavin Elster); Henry Jones (the coroner); Raymond Bailey (the doctor); **Running Time:** 120 minutes.

BACKGROUND: Since coming to the United States in 1940, Alfred Hitchcock steadily built a reputation as "the master of suspense." A common theme in his films is an ordinary man who has been accused of a crime and has no way to prove his innocence. This plot device is especially on view in such films as *Saboteur* (1942), *Spellbound* (1945), and the 1951 film *Strangers on a Train* [see article #16 elsewhere in this book].

Hitchcock often used actors such as Cary Grant, Henry Fonda, and James Stewart to portray basically decent characters who get involved in extremely difficult and dangerous situations. In the case of Stewart, Hitchcock used his likeable persona in three 1950s films. In 1954's *Rear Window* he plays a recuperating photographer who eavesdrops on neighbors from his apartment window, while in the 1956 remake of Hitchcock's 1934 film *The Man Who Knew Too Much,* Stewart plays a doctor who innocently learns of an impending assassination attempt.

In *Vertigo* Stewart plays Scottie Ferguson, a detective who gets drawn into a surveillance situation that becomes complicated when he falls for the woman he has been hired to follow (Kim Novak in a dual role).

As with several other Hitchcock films, *Vertigo* relies on the teamwork of such talented artisans as cinematographer Robert Burks, editor George Tomasini, and especially composer Bernard Herrmann, to create an aura of mystery throughout the film.

PLOT: The film begins with a nighttime chase in San Francisco involving a fugitive being pursued by a uniformed officer and Scottie. When Scottie missteps and clings to a gutter on the edge of a tall building, the cop holds out his hand to him but slips and falls to his death.

This accident causes Scottie to develop a fear of heights that plays a crucial role in the plot. Scottie quits the police force but agrees to help an old college friend, Gavin Elster, a wealthy businessman, by trailing Elster's wife, Madeleine, whose erratic behavior has led Elster to fear that she might try to harm herself.

In successive scenes, Scottie drives around the city by following her to several destinations, including a flower shop where she purchases a small bouquet that she carries to a mission where she stops to pay respects at the grave of a woman named Carlotta Valdes. Then she enters an art gallery where she sits for hours looking at a portrait of Valdes.

Madeleine later goes to a park adjacent to the Golden Gate Bridge where she tosses flower pedals into the bay and then jumps in. After Scottie rescues her, he brings her to his home and looks after her. It becomes evident in this scene that Scottie is developing feelings for Madeleine.

Scottie's affection is further enhanced when he accompanies her into a forest of redwoods and they kiss. His job of keeping an eye on her becomes an obsession that leads to the tragic event of her climbing up the steps at a mission tower and then falling to her death.

Scottie faces a police investigation and is exonerated of blame, but the outcome leaves him in a mentally disturbed state.

After his recovery, Scottie becomes obsessed with a woman named Judy Barton, who very much resembles Madeleine, and he convinces her to change her hair color and wear the same clothes that Madeleine had worn. Although Judy goes along with this idea, Scottie's romantic illusion only brings further tragedy into his life.

MEMORABLE MOMENTS: The opening chase scene in the predawn hours provides a stunningly dramatic prelude for *Vertigo.* The scene is particularly enhanced by the camerawork that depicts the dizziness that Scottie feels when he looks down from the gutter to which he is clinging. Herrmann's swirling musical sounds also help in depicting Scottie's fear of heights.

When Scottie is invited by Elster to Ernie's Restaurant to see what Madeleine looks like, Scottie is immediately intrigued by her, especially with the green gown she is wearing. Herrmann again adds to this scene, but this time the music has a romantically alluring sound that suggests Scottie's immediate infatuation with her.

There are several intriguing scenes where Scottie drives through San Francisco's hilly streets following Madeleine in her green car. In one of these scenes Scottie watches from a distance as Madeleine goes into a flower shop to purchase a small bouquet. In this scene she is wearing a grey suit with her hair pinned back. Again Scottie is fascinated with her looks and Herrmann assists greatly in musically depicting Scottie's growing affection for her.

One particularly memorable musical theme is a Spanish-flavored habanera theme that is used to reflect Madeleine's peculiar interest in Carlotta Valdez. In one scene Scottie observes Madeleine at an art museum staring at a painting of Carlotta and wearing a very fancy necklace. The repeated Habanera rhythm adds greatly to this scene.

Exciting music accompanies the moment when Madeleine jumps into San Francisco Bay, and Herrmann again adds suspense to the scene at the mission as Madeleine climbs the steps to the tower where she is seen falling to her death.

The most romantic scene in the film occurs when Judy is urged to wear a grey suit just like the one Madeleine had worn, with her blonde-tinted hairdo making her look exactly like the woman Scottie had loved. Herrmann's lush music works wonders, especially when Scottie kisses her.

SUMMATION: Despite the many suspense scenes, *Vertigo* is one of Hitchcock's most romantic pictures. Critics were divided about the film upon its initial release, and audiences stayed away, but *Vertigo* has gained enormous acclaim over the years and it currently ranks in some critics' polls as one of the best films of all time.

WHAT AWARDS SHOULD THIS FILM HAVE WON?: *Vertigo* received nominations for Art Direction and Sound but otherwise was totally overlooked by the Oscars. It deserved awards for Hitchcock's meticulous direction and especially for Bernard Herrmann's now-classic score.

OSCAR SNUB #26 – NORTH BY NORTHWEST (1959)

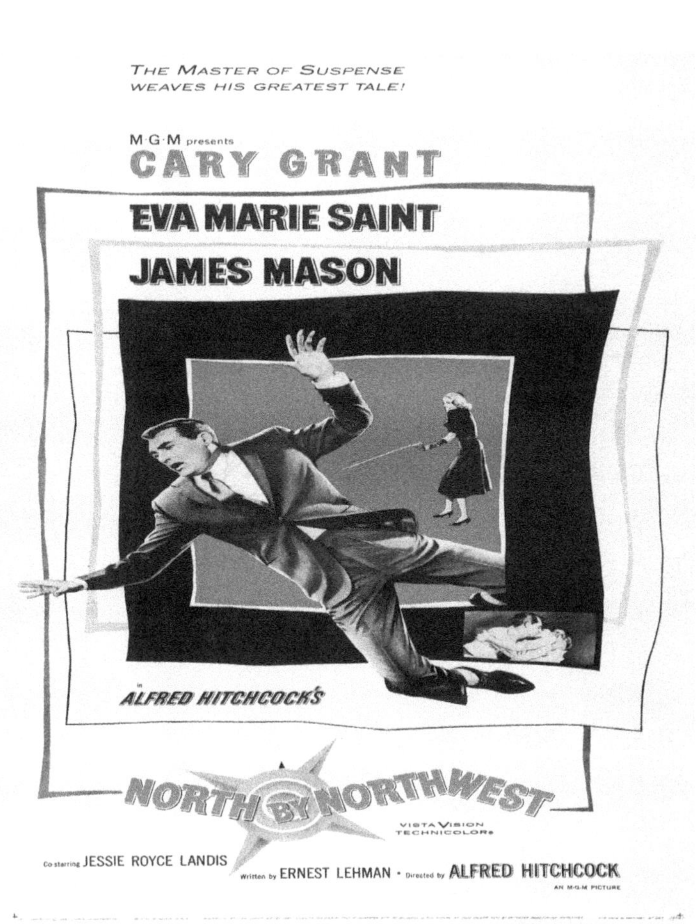

Director: Alfred Hitchcock; **Producer:** Alfred Hitchcock; **Studio:** MGM; **Original Screenplay:** Ernest Lehman; **Cinematography:** Robert Burks; **Art Direction:** William A. Horning, Robert Boyle, and Merrill Pye; **Costume Design:** Harry Kress; **Editing:** George Tomasini; **Sound:** Franklin Milton; **Original**

Score: Bernard Herrmann; **Cast:** Cary Grant (Roger Thornhill); Eva Marie Saint (Eve Kendall); James Mason (Phillip Vandamm); Jesse Royce Landis (Clara Thornhill); Leo G. Carroll (the Professor); Philip Ober (Lester Townsend); Martin Landau (Leonard); **Running Time:** 136 minutes.

BACKGROUND: Soon after finishing *Vertigo,* Alfred Hitchcock engaged Cary Grant to portray one of Hitchcock's favorite types of characters. Grant took the role of a New York advertising executive who innocently enters a restaurant for a business lunch and finds himself being abducted by two thugs who think he is someone else. As with several earlier Hitchcock films, here is a man who only has to be in the right place at the wrong time to set off a series of mistaken identities and wild chases.

Also figuring in the plot is a device that appears in several Hitchcock films, namely the use of familiar landmarks. While the 1942 film *Saboteur* winds up atop the Statue of Liberty, the climactic scenes of both the 1934 and 1956 versions of *The Man Who Knew Too Much* take place at the Royal Albert Hall in London. Screenwriter Ernest Lehman chose Mount Rushmore for the last episode of *North by Northwest,* after Cary Grant's character has been chased all the way from New York to Rapid City, South Dakota. In all these places, Hitchcock uses the locales to enhance the dramatic tension that made him worthy of the epithet "master of suspense."

PLOT: On a typical weekday in downtown Manhattan, advertising executive Roger Thornhill hurries out of his office building with his secretary in tow. They get into a cab, he dictates instructions, and they ride toward his destination for a business lunch. Up to this point all is as it should be, but moments later Roger is mistaken for a man named George Kaplan and two thugs physically abduct him, force him into another cab, and ride towards the home of a diplomat named Lester Townsend. After being dragged into the building, Roger meets Philip Vandamm, who thinks Roger is Kaplan. After being forced to drink a bottle of bourbon, Roger is placed behind the wheel of a stolen car and left to ride to his doom. Somehow Roger survives a wild ride, gets arrested, and is bailed out by his mother, who seems irritated at having her social schedule interrupted.

Things get worse as Roger seeks Townsend, who is scheduled to make a speech at the United Nations assembly hall. Roger finds Townsend, but the latter winds up with a knife in his back and Roger is seen holding the knife. Roger eludes capture, rushes off to Grand Central Station, and sneaks onto a train bound for Chicago, where he thinks he will find the real Kaplan.

Once aboard the train he avoids detection through the helpful services of Eve Kendall, who hides him in her compartment. After becoming infatuated with her he learns that she is the companion of Vandaam.

Once again Roger finds himself in danger when he follows Eve's instructions by going to a deserted place south of Chicago, where is almost killed by a pilot flying a cropduster. Once he finally gets to Chicago, he meets Vandaam and Eve at an art auction, where he again escapes with the help of the Professor, a leader of a secret government spy team that has been tracking Roger's moves in an attempt to stop Vandaam from carrying out a deadly plan that would seriously compromise American foreign relations.

Roger later learns that George Kaplan is actually just a fictitious ploy and that Eve is part of the Professor's team. After he follows her to Rapid City he manages to get her away from Vandamm, but in doing so has to climb with her down the monuments on Mount Rushmore.

MEMORABLE MOMENTS: Ernest Lehman's witty script provides lots of good moments for Cary Grant, who plays Roger Thornhill in a very playful manner, especially when he quips lines such as the one he says to Eve when he meets up with her in a Chicago hotel: "How did a girl like you get to be a girl like you?" Also included in that scene is the moment when Eve thinks Roger is taking a cold shower and hears him whistling "Singin' in the Rain."

One of the film's real highlights comes when Roger realizes that the airplane buzzing through the air is meant to run him down. The exciting climax to this scene comes when Roger ducks under a stopped fuel truck and narrowly escapes death when the plane plows into the side of the truck, with an explosive ball of flame rising out of the wreckage.

A humorous moment occurs after the Professor rescues Roger from the art auction and they fly to Rapid City. When Roger looks through a magnifying observation viewer at the monuments he says to the Professor, "I don't like the way Teddy Roosevelt is looking at me."

Shortly thereafter, when Roger survives being shot by Eve at a tourist center, he learns that she is part of the Professor's team. When she is driven away to join Vandaam on a plane Roger says, "I don't like the game you play, Professor," and Roger gets this response, "War is hell, Mr. Thornhill, even when it's a cold one."

The final climb down the faces on Mount Rushmore provides several exciting moments, especially when Roger saves Eve by holding onto her hand to pull her up as she dangles over the side of one of the granite sculptures.

SUMMATION: *North by Northwest* is greatly enhanced by the expert work of the creative team from *Vertigo*, including Robert Burks's cinematography, George Tomasini's editing, and Bernard Herrmann's thrilling music. Together with Ernest Lehman's clever script, these efforts make this one of Hitchcock's most supremely entertaining films.

WHAT AWARDS SHOULD THIS FILM SHOULD HAVE WON?: The 1959 film year was almost totally dominated by MGM's colossal epic *Ben-Hur*, which won a then-record eleven Oscars, but *North by Northwest* should have earned Grant a nomination for his seemingly effortless acting, and Lehman should have won an Oscar for his ingeniously devised original script.

OSCAR SNUB #27 – *ANATOMY OF A MURDER* (1959)

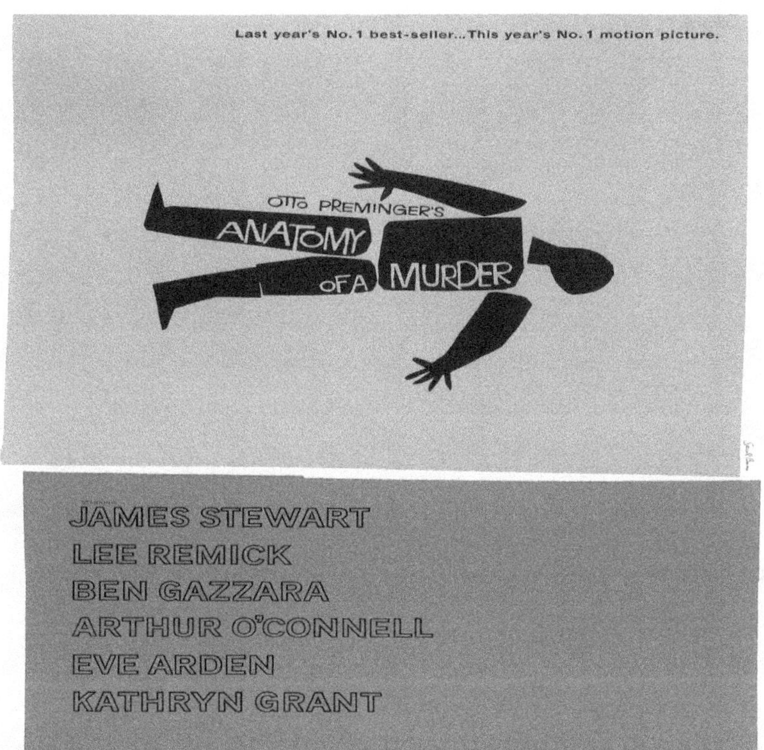

Director: Otto Preminger; **Producer:** Otto Preminger; **Studio:** Columbia; **Screenplay:** Wendell Mayes, based on the novel by Robert Traver; **Cinematography:** Sam Leavitt; **Art Direction:** Boris Leven; **Costume Design:** Hope Bryce; **Editing:** Louis R. Loeffler; **Sound:** Jack Solomon; **Musical Score:** Duke Ellington and Billy Strayhorn; **Cast:** James Stewart (Paul Biegler); Lee Remick (Laura Banion); Ben Gazzara (Lt. Frederick Banion); Arthur O'Connell (Parnell McCarthy); Eve Arden (Maida Rutledge), George C. Scott (Claude Dancer); Kathryn Grant (Mary Pilant); Joseph Welch (Judge Weaver); Murray Hamilton (Al Paquette); Brooks West (DA Mitch Lodwick); **Running Time:** 161 minutes.

BACKGROUND: Many popular novels have been utilized as the source material for motion pictures. In some case the results have been less than spectacular, but in the case of *Anatomy of a Murder,* the film adaptation of the 1958 runaway best-seller became one of 1959's biggest critical hits.

By the time the book reached the best-seller list, where it remained for over a year, filmmaker Otto Preminger had bought the rights to film this dramatically sensational fictionalization of an actual murder that had taken place during 1952 in a small town in Michigan's Upper Peninsula and the subsequent trial of an army lieutenant who is accused of killing a man in a bar owned by a man that the accused claims has raped his wife.

The origin of this decidedly adult subject is worth noting, since the factual details of the case are very similar to those in the film, wherein a local attorney defends the accused man in a trial that had originally taken place in the Marquette County Courthouse.

Little known at the time the film was made is the fact that the man who led the defense was also the writer of the novel who wrote using the pseudonym of Rober Traver. The author's real name is John Voelker, a prominent Michigan attorney who grew up in the U.P. and became the district attorney for Marquette County in 1934. He held many legal positions during his long career and at the time the film was in production in 1959 Voelker was serving as a justice on the Michigan Supreme Court. The book and subsequent film clearly derive from Voelker's legal experience in the courtroom.

PLOT: The film begins with Paul Biegler, a small-town Upper-Michigan lawyer, who is approached by Parnell McCarthy, Paul's former mentor, about defending Lt. Manion, who is accused of murdering Barney Quill, a bar owner in the nearby town of Thunder Bay. After interviewing both Manion and his wife, Laura, Paul agrees to become Manion's attorney.

In the course of his investigation, Paul learns that Manion is insanely jealous of anyone who comes near Laura, and Laura appears to Paul as a rather promiscuous woman who may have actually encouraged the attentions of the man that her husband killed.

With Parnell's help and that of Maida, Paul's secretary, the case doesn't appear to be an easy one to resolve in their favor, especially when Mitch Lodwick, the local DA, brings in a big-time attorney from Lansing, Claude Dancer, to help the prosecution's case. The only defense that Paul can find is to have his client proven temporarily insane by way of a little-known defense called "irresistible impulse."

MEMORABLE MOMENTS: Despite the seriousness of its plot, *Anatomy of a Murder* contains a lot of witty dialogue, much of which relates to the courtroom scenes. Most of the wit is expressed by Judge Weaver, a replacement for an unavailable local judge, who has a lot to handle when Paul and his adversaries, Lodwick and Dancer, start locking horns. When they all first appear in court, Weaver gets disgruntled when Paul admits that his client has been taken to Detroit for a competency exam. Weaver reacts by saying, "If it's customary for a man charged with first-degree murder to wander about at will, I don't suppose it behooves an outsider to point out that the law makes no provision for such quaint liberalism."

Many memorable moments occur during the trial. In one scene a bartender friend of the deceased Barney Quill gives testimony and makes a comical remark that causes the judge to say, "Just stick with the answers. Let the attorneys provide the wisecracks."

A clever trial moment occurs when Paul whispers some instructions to Maida, and when she objects he tells her she's fired. She whispers back that he can't fire her until she gets paid.

A visually striking moment comes when Dancer tells Laura during her testimony to remove her ugly hat and horn-rimmed glasses. The camera moves in closely to reveal her hidden beauty. Dancer then tries to get Laura to admit that Manion has physically hurt her. There is a moment of silence before she quietly admits that Manion has slapped her.

In the last scene, when Paul and Parnell try to collect their fee by driving to the trailer park where the Manions have been staying, they see a vacant space and then have a note handed them by the park owner in which Banion expresses his irresistible impulse to move on.

SUMMATION: *Anatomy of a Murder* is dramatically gripping throughout its extreme length, but there are some lighter scenes. One of these takes place in a nightclub where Paul is sitting at a piano to the right of the musical group's leader, Pie-Eye, played by Duke Ellington, the musician who along with his long-time collaborator Billy Strayhorn composed the film's jazz-inflected score. The film is also greatly enhanced by its location shooting in Michigan's Upper Peninsula, including places where the actual crime and subsequent trial had taken place.

WHAT AWARDS SHOULD THIS FILM HAVE WON?: With seven Oscar nominations, *Anatomy of a Murder* was one of 1959's most acclaimed films. Besides a nod as Best Picture, it received three acting nominations, including the last bid in James Stewart's long career and the first for George C. Scott. Arthur O'Connell also received a supporting nod. But this was the year of *Ben-Hur*, with Charlton Heston and Hugh Griffith dominating in the male acting categories.

Ironically, the film's best performance was given by Joseph Welch, an actual lawyer who famously defended the U.S. Army in a lawsuit brought by Senator Joseph McCarthy in 1954. As Judge Weaver, Welch steals all his scenes. Otto Preminger also got snubbed as director. In his long career he never received an Oscar and *Anatomy* was perhaps his very best film.

OSCAR SNUB #28 – *INHERIT THE WIND* (1960)

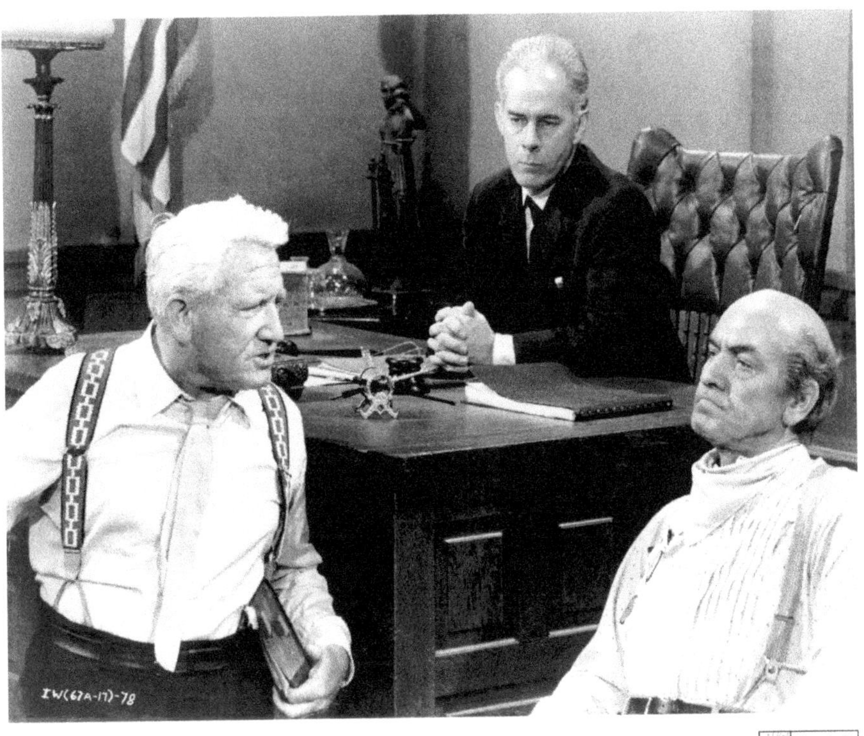

Director: Stanley Kubrick; **Producer:** Stanley Kubrick; **Studio:** United Artists; **Screenplay:** Nedrick Young and Harold Jacob Smith, from the play by Jerome Lawrence and Robert E. Lee; **Cinematography:** Ernest Laszlo; **Production Design:** Rudolph Sternad; **Costume Design:** Joe King; **Editing:** Frederick Knudtson; **Sound:** Walter Elliott; **Musical Score:** Ernest Gold; **Cast:** Spencer Tracy (Henry Drummond); Fredric March (Matthew Harrison Brady); Gene Kelly (E. K. Hornbeck); Dick York (Bertram Cates); Donna Anderson (Rachel Brown); Harry Morgan (Judge Mel Coffey); Florence Eldridge

(Sarah Brady); Elliott Reid (Prosecutor Tom Davenport); **Running Time:** 128 minutes.

BACKGROUND: In April of 1925 the state legislature in Tennessee passed a law that outlawed the teaching of evolution in state-run schools. Two months later John Scopes, a local teacher, was arrested for allegedly violating that law. In the ensuing trial two very prominent men came to the town of Dayton to participate in the legal proceedings: Clarence Darrow, who had gained fame in his defense of convicted killers Leopold and Loeb, and William Jennings Brian, a three- time nominee for President and a well-known expert on the Bible.

In 1955 Jerome Lawrence and Robert E. Lee wrote a fictional stage version of the trial that was named *Inherit the Wind* and played on Broadway for over two years. In 1960, Stanley Kramer both directed and produced a film version of the play that won accolades from critics but no awards during that year's Oscar competition.

In both the stage and screen versions of *Inherit the Wind* the names of the participants in the story have been fictionalized, and thus Clarence Darrow is renamed Henry Drummond, while William Jennings Brian becomes Matthew Harrison Brady. The teacher is also renamed Bertram Cates, and even the setting has been altered, and thus Dayton, Tennessee is called Hillsboro. Despite these changes, much of what took place in the actual trial is incorporated into the film's legal proceedings.

PLOT: The film begins with a discussion by Hillsboro's mayor and staff concerning the trouble that the newly passed evolution ban may cause. Moments later authorities come into a local school classroom to arrest Bert Cates when he discusses Darwin's theories during science class.

The film then shows a public demonstration in which a largely female group of citizens parades down Hillsboro's main street singing "Give Me That Old-Time Religion" while carrying hand-held signs that proclaim "Down with Darwin," among other anti-evolutionary epithets.

During the trial Drummond and Brady lock horns over the contents of the Bible, especially the book of Genesis, which Brady argues must be taken as absolute truth.

When the prosecution refuses to take testimony from science scholars that Drummond has brought to the trial, Drummond asks Brady to take the stand. In the ensuing questioning, Drummond succeeds in making Brady's non-questioning acceptance of Genesis stories as printed in the Bible seem questionable as to their historic accuracy.

Cates is convicted, but his sentence is extremely light, and Brady embarrasses himself by making a lengthy speech that he was hoping to make before the proceedings were concluded. By the time Brady begins, everyone in the courtroom is in a big hurry to leave. His subsequent collapse in the middle of the speech and death a few moments later bring the film to a close.

MEMORABLE MOMENTS: When Brady first arrives in Hillsboro for the trial, he is approached by Hornbeck, a cynical reporter, who Brady feels is an intruder bent on twisting the facts in the trial's proceedings for the benefit of newspaper readers. Hornbeck tells Brady that his job is to "comfort the afflicted and afflict the comfortable."

Much of the film concerns the on-going sparring match between Drummond and Brady. When the judge outright refuses to let Drummond's witnesses testify for the defense about the contents of the Bible, Drummond calls Brady to the stand. When Drummond refers to Genesis stories by raising an issue about Cain's wife and where she came from, Brady skirts the question concerning her origin. Brady's response is, "It frightens me to think of the state of the world if everyone had your driving curiosity."

At one point Drummond responds to Brady's citing of miraculous events recorded in the Bible by stating, "An idea is a greater monument than a cathedral, and the advancement of man's knowledge is a greater miracle than all the stakes turned to snakes or the parting of the waters."

The film's last scene is quietly memorable when Drummond is packing up his things after the end of the trial and the cynical Hornbeck observed him putting a Bible among his belongings. When Hornbeck chides Drummond for being a believer, Drummond returns the scorn by telling him there is nothing wrong with reading the Bible. The reporter then departs and Drummond, clutching his Bible, leaves in silence.

SUMMATION: *Inherit the Wind* is a well-made film about the value in freedom of thought. As playwriters, Lawrence and Lee gave the world a valuable lesson in their stage play, and Stanley Kramer's film version has successfully transferred the play's ideas to the silver screen.

The film's trial scenes are filled with dramatic moments that maintain viewer interest throughout the film's two-hour-plus running time. A capable supporting cast helps in several small roles, especially Florence Eldridge as Brady's wife. Curiously, Eldridge was Fredric March's wife, and they appeared in several films together.

The film has its flaws, especially in the often hammy acting by Fredric March as Brady, but Spencer Tracy is a revelation as Drummond. He completely dominates every scene in which he appears.

WHAT AWARDS SHOULD THIS FILM HAVE WON?: In the last twelve years of his life, Tracy was nominated five times, for his starring roles in *Bad Day at Black Rock* (1955), *The Old Man and the Sea* (1958), *Inherit the Wind* (1960), *Judgment at Nuremberg* (1961), and Tracy's last film, *Guess Who's Coming to Dinner* (1967). Although Tracy won back-to-back Oscars in the late 1930s – for *Captains Courageous* in 1937 and *Boys Town* in 1938, he reached the peak of his career with the above-named films, especially with his role in *Inherit the Wind.*

The award for Best Actor in 1960 went to Burt Lancaster for his flashy role in *Elmer Gantry*, but Tracy should have won that year, or for *Guess Who's Coming to Dinner*, in which he so commands the screen in the film's final minutes that you wonder how he could have been snubbed once again.

OSCAR SNUB #29 – *A RAISIN IN THE SUN* (1961)

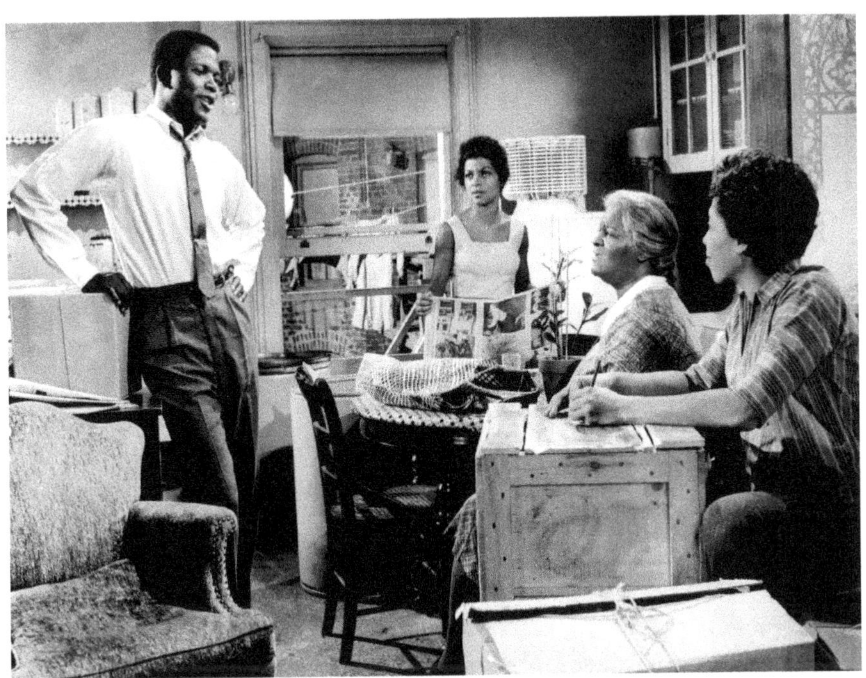

Director: Daniel Petrie; **Producer:** David Susskind and Philip Rose; **Studio:** Columbia; **Screenplay:** Lorraine Hansberry, from her stage play; **Cinematography:** Charles Lawton, Jr.; **Art Direction:** Carl Anderson and Louis Drage; **Costume Design:** no listing; **Editing:** Willian A. Lyon and Paul Weatherwax; **Sound:** Charles J. Rice; **Musical Score:** Laurence Rosenthal; **Cast:** Sidney Poitier (Walter Lee Younger); Claudia McNeil (Lena Younger); Ruby Dee (Ruth Younger); Diana Sands (Beneatha Younger); Stephen Perry (Travis Younger); Ivan Dixon (Joseph Asagai); John Fielder (Mark

Lindner); Louis Gossett (George Murchison); **Running Time:** 128 minutes.

BACKGROUND: In 1959, Lorraine Hansberry became the first black woman to win the New York Drama Critics Circle award when she was cited for her play *A Raisin in the Sun.* She was also the youngest female recipient of this prestigious award.

Hansberry's work, which was written in 1957, is based on her own experiences as a Chicago native growing up in an inner-city neighborhood filled with crowded tenements specifically designed for low-income families that were almost always Black. Hansberry's fictional family is headed by Lena Younger, who lives with her college-age daughter, her adult son, his wife, and their young son. The story of the play focuses on the money that Lena's now-deceased husband has left her in his will, which includes enough funds for her to help them in relocating to a better neighborhood.

PLOT: In the film, which Hansberry adapted, Lena deplores the fact that her family is crammed into such a confined space. She has long desired to move them into a real home, and when she receives a $10,000 payment from her husband's life-insurance policy, the opportunity arrives.

At first she meets resistance from her son, Walter Lee, who works as a chauffeur for a well-to-do white businessman. But when she learns that Ruth, Walter's wife, is expecting another child and is considering whether to terminate the pregnancy, Lena's mind is firmly made up.

Lena also has to deal with her daughter, Beneatha, who has a rebellious spirit, wants to become a doctor, and has stopped believing in God.

Lena's plan to buy a suburban home is complicated by Mr. Lindner, who represents the members of an improvement association in the neighborhood they plan to move into. When he attempts to pay the Youngers to stay out of their new domain, he is met with contempt.

Another problem arises when Lena learns that Walter has used most of the money to buy into a liquor business with two friends, one of whom suddenly disappears with all the money.

Despite all these setbacks, Lena and her family still manage to move into their new home.

MEMORABLE MOMENTS: In an early scene, when Lena tells her daughter-in-law about her late husband she tells how he worked his whole life as a laborer in order to make a better life for his family. At one point she says, "Seem like God didn't give the black man nothin' but dreams, but he did give us children the chance to make them dreams seem worthwhile."

Later that day, when Lena's daughter returns home after her college classes, Beneatha makes comments about how God does not provide for us, and that we have to make do on our own. When she says that there is no God, Lena becomes so offended that she slaps her daughter in the face and boldly tells her to repeat these words: "In this house there is still God. Claudia McNeil's performance in this scene, as with all the other scenes of the film in which she appears, is truly remarkable.

The film's most dramatic moment comes when Walter Lee's friend Bobo comes in a distressed state to reveal that Willie, their other investment partner, has absconded with all of the money they had raised. At one point Walter Lee goes down on his knees repeatedly yelling "WILLIE!," while Lena stands over him with clenched fists and appears to be ready to pound him into the floor as she cries out that Walter has squandered the remainder of the insurance money.

The last scene provides the film's most touching moment, when the family hurriedly carries out the last boxes to load into the moving van. When Lena suddenly remembers the potted plant that she has been nurturing throughout the film, she carefully picks it up and follows Walter out the door to take the first steps in beginning a better life.

SUMMATION: 1961 was a year of several big-budget films, including the historical epics *El Cid* and *King of Kings,* plus the elaborately filmed

Oscar-winning film version of *West Side Story*. It was also the year of the award-winning *Judgment at Nuremberg*, with great acting by Spencer Tracy as the trial judge and Oscar-winning Maximilian Schell as the defense attorney.

But along with these films, 1961 was also the year of the film version of Lorraine Hansberry's *A Raisin in the Sun*. Despite its low budget and its confinement almost throughout to the limited space of the Youngers' cramped apartment, this film remains a classic example of a wonderfully written story about ordinary people who just happen to be Black, and the obstacles they face in trying to improve the quality of their lives. With the original author's brilliant script as its source, *Raisin in the Sun* is one of the most memorable films of the 1960s.

WHAT AWARDS SHOULD THIS FILM HAVE WON?: Claudia McNeil's performance in this film is one of the finest ever given by an actress. At the very least she should have been awarded an Oscar nomination in the Best-Actress category. The 1961 winner was Sophia Loren, who plays a distraught mother of a teenage daughter who gets raped by soldiers during a time of war. She was the first actress to win for a foreign-language film and excelled in her role, which she played without the glamourous makeup and costumes that she displayed in that year's *El Cid*. Still, Claudia McNeil was regrettably snubbed by members of the academy.

Also overlooked was Sidney Poitier, whose performance in this film easily compares with his Oscar-nominated role in *The Defiant Ones* and his Oscar-winning performance in the 1963 film *Lilies in the Field*. *Raisin in the Sun* should also have been nominated for Best Picture and should also have been listed in the Adapted Screenplay category. In retrospect, *Raisin in the Sun* remains a classic example of exemplary filmmaking.

OSCAR SNUB #30 – *THE MANCHURIAN CANDIDATE* (1962)

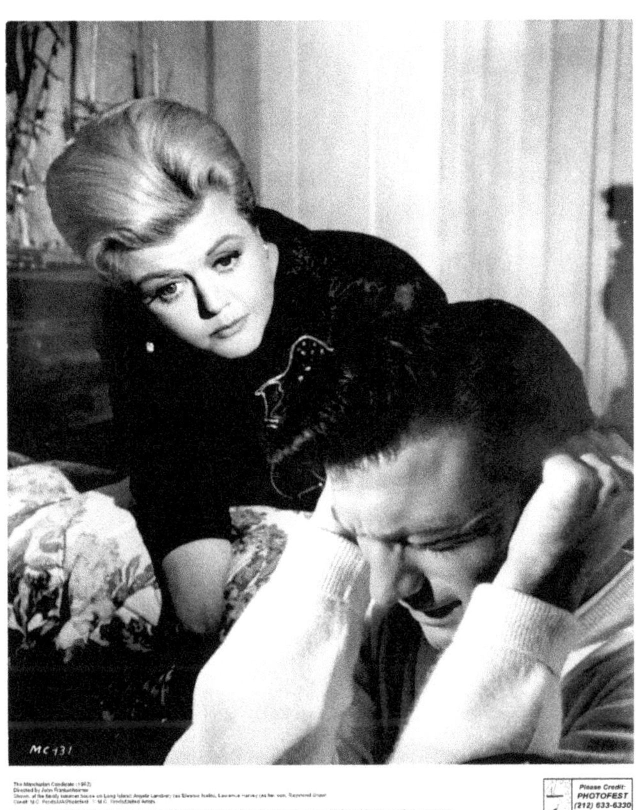

Director: John Frankenheimer; **Producer:** George Axelrod and John Frankenheimer; **Studio:** United Artists; **Screenplay:** George Axelrod, from the novel by Richard Condon; **Cinematographer:** Lionel Lindon; **Production Design:** Richard Sylbert; **Costume Design:** Mark Mabry; **Editing:** Ferris Webster; **Sound:** Joe Edmondson; **Musical Score:** David Amram; **Cast:** Frank Sinatra (Maj. Ben Marco); Laurence Harvey (Sgt. Raymond Shaw); Janet Leigh (Rose Chaney); Angela Lansbury (Eleanor Shaw Iselin);

James Gregory (Sen. John Iselin); Leslie Parrish (Jocelyn Jordan); John McGiver (Sen. Thomas Jordan); Henry Silva (Chunjin); **Running Time:** 126 minutes.

BACKGROUND): Richard Condon (1915-1996) was the author of over twenty novels written between 1958 and 1994. As exemplified in *The Manchurian Candidate,* which was published in 1959, Condon's stories specialize in political satire that he combined with elements of a suspense thriller. At its core, *Candidate* utilizes the furor that occurred back in 1954 when Wisconsin Senator Joseph McCarthy accused the U.S. Army of being infiltrated with communist sympathizers as the starting point for a drama in which a Senator and his wife threaten to start congressional hearings that would root out communist members.

In this fictional story, the senator's stepson is being used by foreign communist leaders through a Pavlovian process of mind control as a possible assassin. Members of the Army form a secret investigation to determine how this mind-control works and to find the assassin before he targets someone in the U.S. government.

PLOT: The film begins in 1952, during the war in Korea, when a small platoon of U.S. soldiers is captured and secretly taken to Manchuria, where a team of Chinese and Russian agents uses hypnosis on the captured soldiers.

Back in the U.S. two years later, Major Ben Marco (Frank Sinatra), who had headed up the small platoon, has recurring nightmares in which he envisions his troop being lectured to by a group of women that ostensibly belong to a garden club. Soon the female lecturer turns into an Asian man, and Raymond Shaw, one of the captives, is ordered to strangle one of the other soldiers. Upon awakening, Ben is so distraught that he reports these dreams to his commanding officers.

Soon Ben's nervous condition causes him to be put on leave, and he joins a group of military investigators to determine the root cause of his condition, especially when he becomes aware of two other soldiers in his outfit that have been having the same dreams.

Ben goes to New York, where he finds Raymond Shaw, another member of the outfit, who has amazingly been awarded a congressional medal for bravery while in combat. Ben soon discovers that Raymond has become the secret agents' target as a means of carrying out their nefarious plans, but he realizes the danger too late to stop Raymond from causing more deaths.

MEMORABLE MOMENTS: Early in the film, when Ben is on a New York-bound train, he meets Rosie when he nervously tries to light a cigarette and she helps him out. She gives him her phone number, which he uses after discovering one of the Asians in his dream arriving at Raymond's apartment. After a wild fight the police take Ben into custody, and then he and Rosie are seen in a cab after she comes to bail him out. In this scene, in one continuous take, Rosie explains that she has broken off her relationship with her former fiancé and that she is attracted to Ben. Janet Leigh does all the talking in this scene, which is one of the best moments in her film career.

When Ben later finds Raymond alone in his apartment and they have had too much to drink, Raymond relates his hatred for his mother and describes himself as unlovable. But he says he was lovable one summer when he met Jocie, the daughter of Senator Jordan, who lived across the lake from Raymond's mother and her new husband. In the flashback that comes next, Raymond describes how he and Jocie had fallen in love, only to have his mother cruelly force him to break off the relationship. His tearful description of these events is heartrending, and Laurence Harvey gives a very touching performance, possibly his best acting ever.

The last section of the film is extremely exciting, when Raymond, whom Ben has tried to deprogram from the Solitaire-triggering hypnosis, finds out from his mother that he is supposed to assassinate a presidential candidate during his acceptance speech at the Madison Square Garden. When Ben learns of this plot, he races through the arena to find Raymond, but his delay in reaching his former platoon member has tragic results. Through this scene there are 150-separate bits of film that have been edited together to add a terrific amount of tension.

SUMMATION: *Candidate* includes excellent performances, especially Angela Lansbury as a mother-from-hell, and from Harvey, whose multi-faceted role includes moments of great acting. This is a film that is as shattering to watch now as it was in 1962.

WHAT AWARDS SHOULD THIS FILM HAVE WON?: Lansbury was deservedly awarded a Supporting-Actress nomination but lost to Patty Duke, who played Helen Keller as a child in *The Miracle Worker.* Duke had the role of a lifetime, but it is sad when one person's much-deserved victory leads to another great performance getting snubbed.

Sadly, Laurence Harvey was not nominated, even though his performance was easily on the same level as that of Gregory Peck's Oscar-winning portrayal of Atticus Finch in *To Kill a Mockingbird.*

Manchurian Candidate's only other nomination was for Ferris Webster's brilliant editing, but he was also snubbed by the Academy, which awarded Anne Coates for her work on 1962's big winner, *Lawrence of Arabia,* which took home seven Oscars, including one as Best Picture.

PERSONAL NOTE: I fondly remember seeing *Manchurian Candidate* for the first time when CBS televised it with commercial breaks on a Thursday evening in 1965. I was tending my two toddlers that evening because their mother was called away to help take care of her ailing father. When the film started playing, all went well until I realized that the kids had not had their baths. During a commercial break, which came at the film's most exciting moment, I hurriedly carried my children upstairs, put them into the tub, sudsed them up, wrapped them dripping wet in towels, and rushed with them back down to watch the rest of the film, which remains one of my all-time favorites.

OSCAR SNUB #31 – *THE GREAT ESCAPE* (1963)

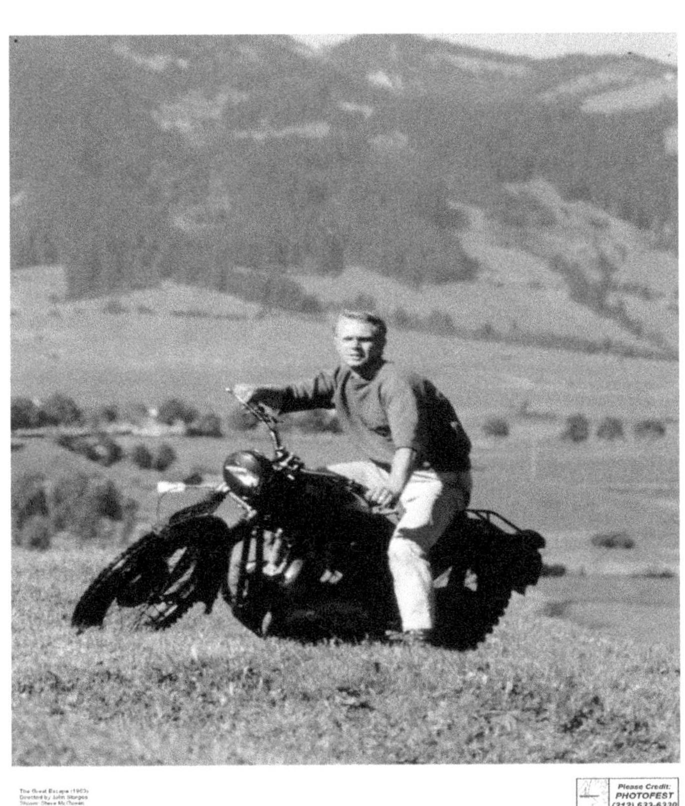

Director: John Sturges; **Producer:** John Sturges; **Studio:** United Artists; **Screenplay:** James Clavell and W. R. Burnett, from the book by Paul Brickhill; **Cinematography:** Daniel L. Fapp; **Art Direction/Set Decoration:** Fernando Carrere, Kurt Ripberger; **Costume Design:** Bert Henrikson; **Editing:** Ferris Webster; **Sound:** Wayne Fury; **Musical Score:** Elmer Bernstein; **Cast:** Steve McQueen (Hilts, the Cooler King); James Garner (Hendley, the Scrounger); Richard Attenborough (Bartlett, the Big X); James Donald (Ramsey, the senior officer); Charles Bronson (Danny, the Tunnel King); Donald Pleasence (the Forger); James Coburn (Sedgwick, the Manufacturer); David McCallum (Ashley-Pitts, Dispersal), Hannes Messemer (von Luger, the Commandant); John Leyton (the Tunnel King); Nigel Stock (Cavendish, the Surveyor); Robert Desmond (Griffith, the Tailor); **Running Time:** 168 minutes.

BACKGROUND: Prior to making *The Great Escape* director John Sturges was known for helming such popular films set in the American West as *Bad Day at Black Rock* (1955), *Gunfight at the O.K. Corral* (1957) and *The Magnificent Seven* (1960). What distinguishes *Great Escape* from its predecessors is its setting – a newly constructed POW camp in Germany especially designed for Allied prisoners who had a history of attempting to escape the German camps.

Sturges' film, which is based on a non-fiction book published in 1950, includes a plot that is not totally factual, since the screenwriters fabricated fictional character names. The cast list included above is a large-than-usual listing of actors that appear in this film, since there are so many individuals involved in the plan to construct a tunnel that would allow as many as 250 prisoners to escape. Another departure from reality is the fact that in Paul Brickhill's book all of the escapees are British soldiers, while in the film there are a few Americans and an Australian among those attempting to dig their way out of stalag Luft III.

PLOT: The film begins with the arrival at the new camp of several captured Allied soldiers who have been assigned there because of their previous escape attempts. One particular captive, Roger Bartlett, is known to many of the other prisoners because of his many previous escape attempts.

Almost as soon as he arrives, Bartlett secretly calls a meeting at which he unveils a new plan to escape the camp. Based on the special talents of some of the other men being held there, tasks are assigned for such things as forging papers, tailoring clothes, and the gathering of wood for use in the tunnel. Once the digging begins, three separate sites to be used for digging are labelled "Tom," Dick," and Harry."

An ingenious plan is devised in which some of the soldiers form a choir that sings Christmas carols out in the yard while other men inside one of the barracks starts hammering to make equipment needed for the escape. Other soldiers are assigned tasks such as knocking on walls to signal the diggers as to when it is safe to continue making noise.

When the night of the escape arrives, more than seventy men manage to escape through the tunnel before the guards discover men coming up through a hole in the ground not far from the woods that surround the camp.

The final part of the film details the various ways in which the escapees try to avoid capture. At the end of the film most of the men are apprehended, and fifty of them are shot, except for a select few who manage to avoid capture.

MEMORABLE MOMENTS: During the initial meeting, when Bartlett is addressing the other captives, he outlines what the men will be doing by saying, "We're going to devote our energies to sports and gardening, all the cultural pursuits, as far as they are concerned. In fact we're going to put the goons to sleep. Meanwhile, we DIG!"

When the digging begins, the work team has to be signalled when the guards come in for their routine inspections. In one such scene, a guard asks questions. When Danny, the principal digger, doffs his clothes and goes into a nearby shower, the guard asks him what he's doing. He answers in his Polish accent, "Shower. I need a vash." Standing nearby is Sedgwick, who is also asked what he is up to. His answer: "I'm watching him. I'm a lifeguard."

More humor occurs when Ramsey is observing Griffith, who is demonstrating his tailoring skills when he shows some of his new civilian coats and other apparel accessories. When Ramsey asks where the various fabrics have come from, Griffith says they're from Hendley, who has well earned his reputation as "the Scrounger." When Ramsey asks how Hendley got them Griffith responds, "Don't ask!"

The whole last section of the film is memorable, when the various escapees are shown getting away by various means. The scenes cut back and forth among six different escape scenarios. In the first, Barlett and his friend Mac board the same train with Ashley-Pitt and Hendley, who has to guide along his cellmate Blythe, who is almost totally blind.

Sedgwick steals a bicycle and pedals all the way to a French village, where he receives help from two members of the French resistance.

Hilts steals a motorcycle from a German soldier and manages to outpace a large unit of German soldiers until he is apprehended in a field after making some dangerous jumps over the hilly terrain.

Meanwhile, Danny and his friend Willie go across lots of waterways in a rowboat, until they manage to board a ship bound for Sweden.

Most of these escapees get caught, and most are killed, with the exception of Hendley and Hilts, the latter of whom winds up back in a solitary holding cell bouncing his baseball repeatedly off a wall.

SUMMATION: *The Great Escape* excels as a fine example of a potent historical drama laced with humor as the attempt to tunnel out of the stalag gets underway. The film includes a superlative cast, with special kudos going to Steve McQueen, James Coburn, and especially Charles Bronson, whose portrayal of a troubled young Polish-American soldier provides some of the film's best moments.

WHAT AWARDS SHOULD THIS FILM HAVE WON?: Ferris Webster's editing, especially in the final escape scenes, is a great asset, as is also Elmer Bernstein's dramatic music. Bernstein's score was snubbed by the Oscars, as was Charles Bronson, who truly deserved a supporting Oscar for his role.

In all, Sturges' film remains a classic portrayal of a lesser-known aspect of World War II.

OSCAR SNUB #32 – *IN COLD BLOOD* (1967)

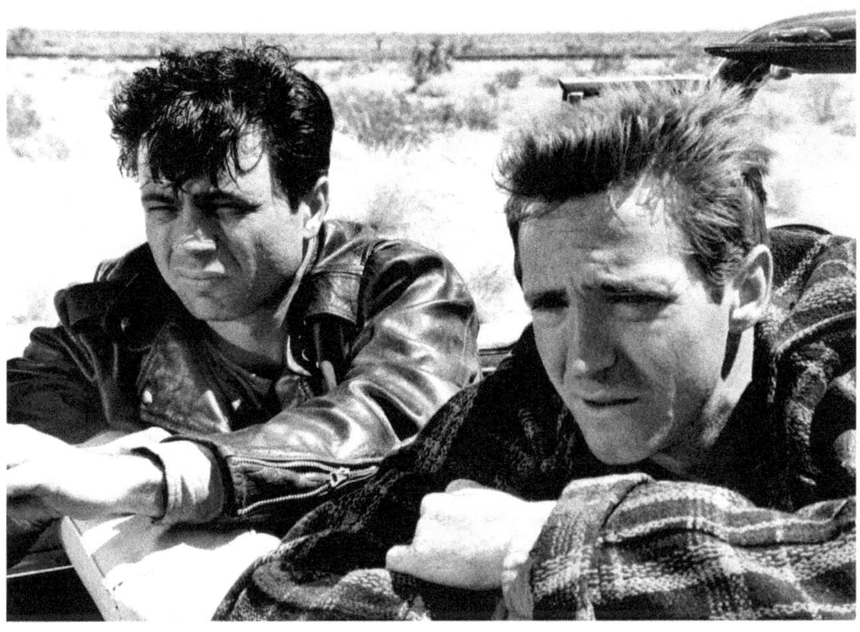

In Cold Blood (1967)
Directed by Richard Brooks
Shown from left: Robert Blake, Scott Wilson
Credit: Columbia Pictures/Photofest © Columbia Pictures

Director: Richard Brooks; **Producer:** Richard Brooks; **Studio:** Columbia; **Cinematography:** Conrad Hall; **Art Direction/ Interior Decoration:** Robert Boyle, Jack Ahern; **Costume Design:** Jack Martell; **Editing:** Peter Zinner; **Sound:** William Randall, Jr., Dick Tyler, and A. Pianatedosi; **Musical Score:** Quincy Jones; **Cast:** Robert Blake (Perry Smith); Scott Wilson (Dick Hickock); John Forsythe (Alvin Dewey); Paul Stewart (Bill Jensen); Gerald O'Loughlin (Harold Nye); Jeff Corey (Mr. Hickock); Charles McGraw (Tex Smith); John McLiam (Herbert Clutter); **Running Time:** 134 minutes.

BACKGROUND: In late 1959, Perry Smith and Dick Hickock, who had been cellmates at Kansas State Penitentiary until their release a few months earlier, met up in Kansas City and drove to the small town of Holcomb, Kansas, where they planned to rob a farmer named Herbert Clutter of money they were convinced he had hidden in a safe in his home.

Late on Saturday, November 14, they arrived at the house, and once they got in, they tied up Mr. Clutter, his wife, and their two teenage children. When they could not locate a safe, they wound up killing all four of the Clutters and absconding with the only cash they could find, which amounted to less than fifty dollars.

Kansas authorities spent lots of effort in identifying the killers, who were arrested for a lesser crime but eventually confessed to the murders, were tried and convicted, and in 1965, after losing several appeals, were hanged for the Clutter murders.

In Cold Blood is based on a 1965 book by Truman Capote, who became fascinated with the case, made several visits to Holcomb to interview local residents, and even was allowed to visit the convicts while they were in prison awaiting their execution.

Richard Brooks's film carefully details the events surrounding the killings, and also includes profiles of both killers and their family backgrounds. It was Perry's troubled relationship with his father that became Capote's principal interest, and that backstory is central to the film's narrative.

PLOT: The film begins with Perry meeting up with Dick, who has received a letter which includes information from another prisoner about a farmer named Clutter who has a secret stash of $10,000 hidden in a safe. Interspersed with the journey of the two parolees to Holcomb, Kansas, are scenes showing the Clutter family at home earlier on the day of the horrific murders.

When the two miscreants arrive at the River Valley Farm and are about to make their way into the Clutters' home, the film skips ahead to scenes involving Perry and Dick on the lam, which alternate with criminal search actions by agents of the Kansas Bureau of Investigation and their eventual arrest and trial of the two killers.

The last part of the film shows a confession that Perry makes to Agent Dewey that includes a graphic description of the murders. This leads to the moment when both convicts are hanged.

MEMORABLE MOMENTS: In an early scene, when Dick and Perry stop at a gas station on the way to Holcomb, Perry looks in a washroom mirror and imagines himself onstage at a Las Vegas casino singing and playing the guitar that he brings along on their fateful trip along with a large and heavy box of books and music. Although brief, this moment allows the viewer to understand Perry's dreaming of a better life.

In another flashback, Perry remembers his early childhood in which his father fantasizes about searching for "the sunken treasure of Captain Cortes" and the "Treasure of the Sierra Madre," in reference to the 1948 film that Perry has seen lots of times. Later in the film, Perry urges Dick to go with him to Mexico to search for these treasures.

Early in the criminal search, Agent Harold Nye keeps getting calls from people eager to collect reward money, and at one point amusingly says, "the only one who didn't do it is the butler."

Another memorable comment is later made by a reporter named Bill Jenson, who is writing commentary for a national news magazine. After a day of testimony in court Jensen turns to Agent Dewey and says, "They had to be crazy, no, maybe stupid but perfectly sane. How can a perfectly sane man commit a perfectly crazy act?"

During their attempt to elude capture, Perry, who is driving, stops the car to give a ride to a young boy and his ailing grandfather. When the boy says they have no money but collect discarded bottles for a three-cent refund, they stop at a roadside park and discover a trash container filled with bottles. Perry happily proclaims that they have found the treasure of Cortes.

The only time the convicts comment on their hideous killings comes right before Perry is hanged when he says, "I'd like to apologize, but who to?"

SUMMATION: *In Cold Blood* closely adheres to Capote's book except for the Jensen character, who fictionally adds commentary on the murder case. Otherwise, the film includes accurate portraits of both killers, with expert performance by both actors. This is especially true of Robert Blake, who vividly plays Perry as a deeply troubled man filled with painful memories and physical problems that play a significant role in his essentially wayward life.

The film reveals lots of character traits about both of its principal characters. Shortly before he is hanged, when Perry is asked about his relationship with his father, Perry says, "I hate him – and I love him."

The viewer may actually find some things to like about Perry, whose twisted relationship with his father helps to explain why Perry pulled the trigger to end the Clutters' lives. Meanwhile, the film's portrayal of Dick (Scott Wilson), as a punk with no moral compass gives the viewer little reason to lament his demise.

The film's candid portrayals of both killers is just one of the many virtues in this powerful drama that remains a vivid portrait of the criminal mind.

WHAT AWARDS SHOULD THIS FILM HAVE WON?: *In Cold Blood* had the misfortune of being released in the same year as two other acclaimed crime-related films, *In the Heat of The Night* and *Bonnie and Clyde.* Richard Brooks's film is as good as the other two, but the race-relations subplot of *Heat of the Night* may explain why Oscar voters preferred it to Brooks's film. *In Cold Blood* was also snubbed concerning its masterful masterful cinematography by Conrad Hall when that award went to Haskell Wexler for *Bonnie and Clyde.*

OSCAR SNUB #33 – *BADLANDS* (1973)

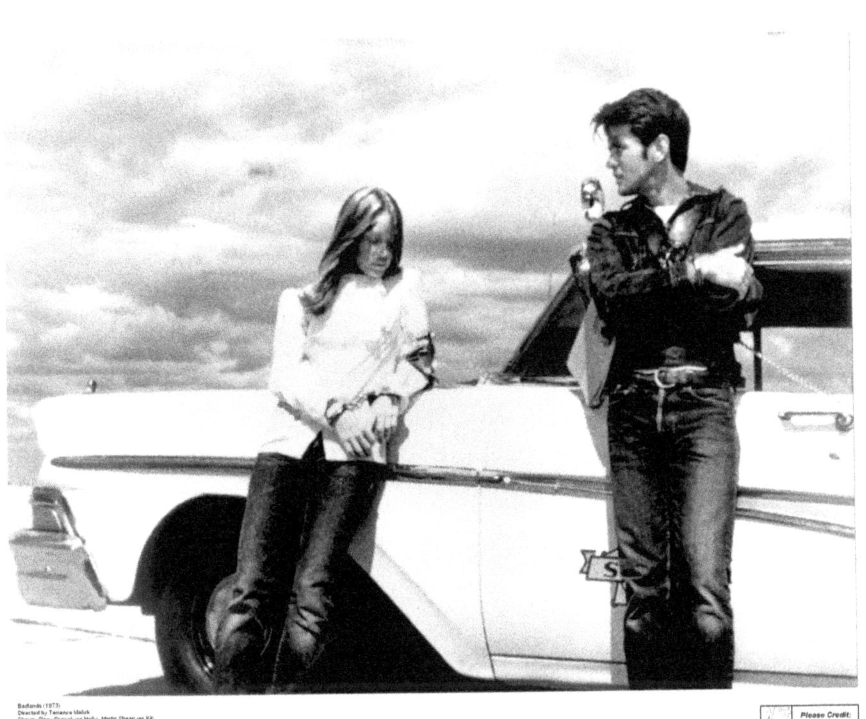

Director: Terrence Malick; **Producer:** Terrence Malick; **Studio:** Warner Bros.; **Screenplay:** Terrence Malick; **Cinematography:** Tak Fujimoto, Stevan Larner, and Brian Probyn; **Art Direction:** Jack Fisk; **Costume Design:** Rosanna Norton; **Editing:** Robert Estrin, Terrence Malick, and Billy Weber; **Sound:** Maury Harris; **Musical Score:** George Tipton, with music by Carl Orff, Erik Satie, and others; **Cast:** Martin Sheen (Kit Carruthers); Sissy Spacek (Holly Sargis); Warren Oates (Holly's father); Ramon Bieri

(Cato); Alan Vint (deputy); Gary Littlejohn (Sheriff); John Carter (rich man with Cadillac); **Running Time:** 93 minutes.

BACKGROUND: Terrence Malick has become one of the most highly regarded American filmmakers of all time. While his body of work is small compared to that of such directing contemporaries as Francis Ford Coppola, Martin Scorsese, and Steven Spielberg, Malick's works have left an indelible mark on the world of cinema.

Badlands deserves recognition as Malick's first film and was shot on a shoestring budget without big box-office stars.

Among the many unique aspects of *Badlands* is Malick's choice of factual material – a notorious crime spree by two youngsters in the American heartland. The killings by Charles Starkweather during a nine-day spree in the last days of 1956 and the beginning of 1957 made headlines in American newspapers everywhere. Starkweather's teenage girlfriend, Caril Ann Fugate, traveled with the killer and may have had little to do with the actual killings, but historians have disputed her role in the deaths of eleven people, including a two-year-old girl.

Malick used this series of events as the basis for his film, even though the film includes a disclaimer that the film's screenplay is a work of fiction. Malick used fictional names for the characters and altered the ages of the two refugees from justice, who in reality were both under the age of twenty. In Malick's film Kit is ten years older than Holly, who is fifteen.

PLOT: The film begins in a small town in South Dakota, where Kit works as a garbage collector. One day he meets Holly Sargis when his truck stops within a block of the house she shares with her widowed father. Soon thereafter he is fired from his job and starts seeing Holly on a regular basis, despite her father's objections.

After a confrontation with Holly's father, who tells Kit to stay away from Holly, Kit takes matters into his own hands and enters Holly's house with the intention of taking Holly with him. When Sargis tries to stop Kit from packing Holly's suitcase, Kit pulls a gun and shoots him twice. Kit then pours gasoline over the furnishings and sets the house on fire. Although Holly at first seems reluctant to go, she follows Kit on what turns out to be a murder spree.

Kit soon kills several other people, including two bounty hunters who find the couple hiding out in the woods in a makeshift shelter outside of town. Kit also kills Cato, his former co-worker in the trash-collection business, who Kit thinks is going to call the police when they arrive at his secluded home for a visit.

Holly is horrified by Kit's behavior, but decides to stay with him. At one point Kit breaks into a rather spacious home and holds a man and his deaf housekeeper hostage. When the fugitives leave, Kit hijack's the man's fancy Cadillac and they travel northward into Montana toward the Canadian border.

Holly finally decides to leave Kit, and she is soon taken into custody. Kit is soon thereafter pursued through the Badlands of Montana until he is finally arrested. After being handcuffed and put into the back of a police vehicle, Kit schmoozes with his captors but puts up no resistance as he faces the death penalty for his crimes.

MEMORABLE MOMENTS: One of the film's most impressively-shot moments occurs at the Sargis home after Kit kills Holly's father. Kit finds a gas can and unloads its contents upon the home's furnishings and sets the house ablaze. After Kit and Holly drive away the camerawork features closeups of various things as draperies and furniture when they catch fire, especially an old upright piano which becomes engulfed in flames. Throughout this scene there is no sound except the musical accompaniment of a lovely choral piece by Carl Orff, whose music is used frequently in the film to create a surprisingly lyrical mood.

Another impressive moment occurs in a nighttime scene with Kit and Holly getting out of the Cadillac when a late-night DJ radio show features Nat "King" Cole's 1957 hit "A Blossom Fell." This lyrical song provides an unusually romantic accompaniment as Kit and Holly dance slowly with only the car's headlights illuminating the scene.

The closing scenes include rather formulaic shots of Kit being chased across barren fields, but once he is arrested and put in the backseat of a police car he talks in friendly fashion with his captors, especially a young deputy, who seems to like Kit and even admits to the sheriff who is driving them to an airport that Kit reminds him of James Dean, the Hollywood actor who had died in 1955.

SUMMATION: Despite the film's rather violent premise, *Badlands* stands as a distinctive example of an unlikely type of film that uses visual imaging in a very poetical way. In many scenes there are closeup shots of various animals, including rabbits and deer, which create a curiously serene mood in the midst of the murderous acts that occur in the course of Kit and Holly's mis-begotten adventure.

There are also several beautifully filmed sky scenes, including shots of sunsets and lovely cloud formations, especially at the end of the film when the plane carrying Kit to meet his fate flies over the horizon.

Badlands includes impressive acting by its two leading players, Martin Sheen and Sissy Spacek both both of whom were at the time of the film's release at the beginning of their respective acting careers. Sheen often reflects a James Dean-type of persona, while Spacek excels in her role, which is greatly enhanced by her ongoing narration. Her vocal patter often reflects the content of articles in such period magazines as *True Confessions.*

Badlands remains a remarkable first film for Malick, whose small body of work includes some of the most memorable films of the past half century.

WHAT AWARDS SHOULD THIS FILM HAVE WON?: *Badlands* should have won for its stunning cinematography, and its lead performances should have at least earned acting nominations.

OSCAR SNUB #34 – *TAXI DRIVER* (1976)

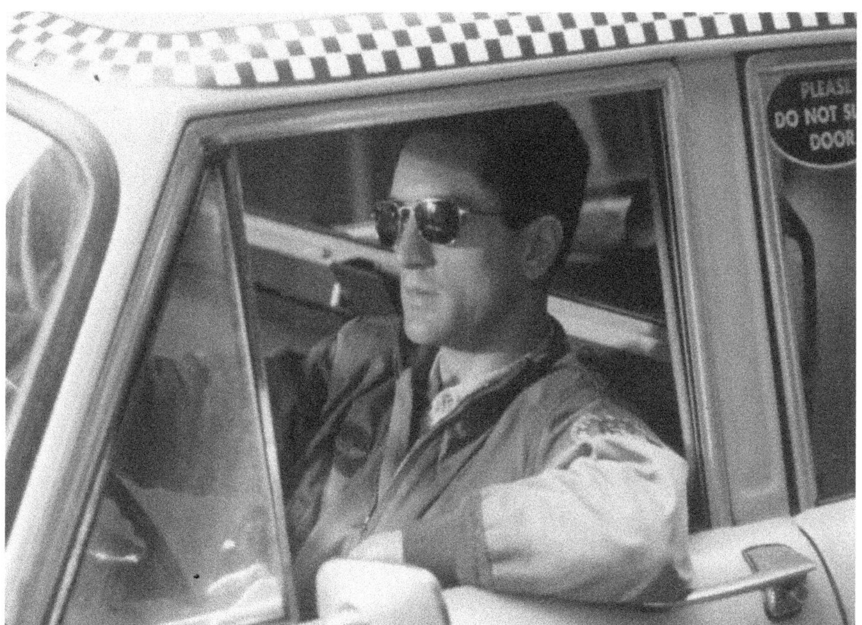

Taxi Driver (1976)
Directed by Martin Scorsese
Shown: Robert De Niro (as Travis Bickle)

Credit: ©Columbia Pictures Photographer: Josh Weiner

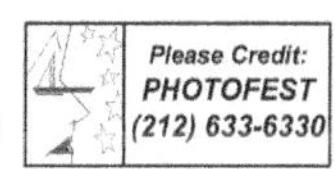

Director: Martin Scorsese; **Producer:** Julia and Michael Philips; **Studio:** Columbia; **Screenplay:** Paul Schrader; **Cinematography:** Michael Chapman; **Art Direction/Set Decoration:** Charles Rosen and Herbert Mulligan; **Costume Design:** Ruth Morley; **Editing:** Tom Rolfe and Melvin Shapiro; **Sound:** Rick Alexander; **Musical Score:** Bernard Herrmann; **Cast:** Robert de Niro (Travis Bickle); Jodie Foster (Iris); Harvey Keitel (Sport); Peter Doyle (Wizard); Albert Brooks (Tom); Leonard Harris (Charles Palantine); **Running Time:** 113 minutes.

BACKGROUND: With the 1970s arrival in Hollywood of such young directors as Francis Ford Coppola, Brian de Palma, and Martin Scorsese, films began taking on decidedly adult plot materials. This led to the first two *Godfather* films, which won the Best-Picture prizes in 1972 and 1974, respectively. In the wake of these films, Scorsese's violent drama *Taxi Driver* brought a thoroughly downbeat and dark-tinged story to the screen.

Paul Schrader's original screenplay was inspired by the writer's experiences as a nighttime cab driver whose motive for taking the job was his inability to sleep at night. In the film, the fictional character of Travis Bickle is a young man who has come back from a stint in the Marines during the war in Vietnam. Not much more is explained about him except his insomnia and his negative feelings about New York nightlife, which he observes is filled with pimps and prostitutes who have turned the city in his way of thinking into a disgustingly ugly place.

PLOT: Travis first appears as a rather decent guy, but one who seems awkward around others, especially women. Soon after beginning his cab-driving job, Travis becomes infatuated with a young lady named Betsy, who works at the campaign headquarters of a presidential candidate named Charles Palantine. At first Travis is spotted by Tom, one of Betsy's co-workers, when Travis is seen hanging out in his cab in front of the campaign building. Eventually Travis enters the headquarters to volunteer, but he is especially interested in meeting Betsy. At first Betsy seems annoyed by Travis, but he finally convinces her to go on a date with him.

Travis's lack of social skills are noticeable when he takes her to a porn film, and she quickly bolts from her seat and leaves the theater. Her subsequent avoidance of him only leads to the beginning of a series of snub that soon leads to his mental breakdown.

A second young woman with whom Travis becomes infatuated is Iris, a thirteen-year-old prostitute. After she agrees to meet him for lunch, he becomes increasingly aware that she should abandon her sordid lifestyle.

Travis's lack of sleep, together with pill-taking and increased drinking, drives him to contemplate doing violent acts. He purchases guns, practices his weapon skills at a shooting gallery, and then chooses Palantine as his target. When this fails, he decides to go after the men who control Iris.

In the last part of the film Travis shoots Iris's handlers and gets mortally wounded in the process. In the surprising final scene, he has recovered from his wounds and has also become a hero for rescuing Iris, who has returned to Pittsburgh to resume the life of a normal teenager.

MEMORABLE MOMENTS: Much of this film takes place after dark, when Travis observes the many low-life characters that people the New York streets from the vantage point of his cab. In an early scene the viewer can hear Travis's voice as he narrates the words he is writing into a journal, in which he inscribes as follows, "All the animals come out at night…someday a real rain will come and wash the scum away."

A much lighter tone occurs during a daytime scene when Travis enters the campaign headquarters in an attempt to meet Betsy. Travis's awkwardness has an appealing quality that causes Betsy to smile in a way that conveys her quickly growing interest in him.

After Travis starts to become obsessed with guns and displays the likelihood that he is going to do something harmful, he stands in front of a mirror, points a gun, and several times asks, "You talkin' to me?" In another disturbing moment he sits with his legs on a TV stand and rocks it until the TV topples backwards and explodes as it hits the floor.

The most disturbing scenes occur towards the latter part of the film, when Travis, sporting a Mohawk haircut, causes a disturbance at a political rally, and then shoots the men who have turned Iris into a young prostitute. After the shooting, Travis, who is now terribly wounded and out of bullets, sits on a couch, points a finger at his head, and repeatedly makes a shooting sound.

SUMMATION: *Taxi Driver* is not always easy to watch, but it has expert cinematography by Michael Chapman that make the nighttime scenes of Travis driving his cab fascinating to view.

The many moments of narration are also a key element in making this film memorable. Especially noticeable is Travis's vocal wording of an anniversary card that he is planning to send to his parents. The version of his life that he is describing in this card differs greatly from the one that the viewer has been watching.

A particularly memorable narration is that of Iris's father, whose voice is heard as the viewer sees a hand-written letter thanking Travis for rescuing Iris and helping her return to Pittsburgh.

On a first viewing *Taxi Driver* may seem terribly sordid, but as in the earlier Oscar-winning film *Midnight Cowboy,* there is a human element about Travis's need for connection with those around him that makes his journey into hell and back one that the patient viewer can strongly appreciate. The heroism of Travis's actions may seem ironic, considering that he commits multiple murders along the way, but his efforts to save Iris from a life tainted with sordidness make Travis Bickle a compelling character. The one question that the film does not answer is whether Travis will ever slip again into the type of insanity that he displays throughout much of the film.

WHAT AWARDS SHOULD THIS FILM SHOULD HAVE WON?: Both Robert De Niro and Jodie Foster deserved Oscars for this film. Cinematographer Michael Chapman was also snubbed. His superb views of New York after dark are truly memorable. Finally, *Taxi Driver's* memorable music represents the last film score by Bernard Herrmann, who died shortly after the recording sessions. His haunting blues theme for alto saxophone is a huge asset to this film.

OSCAR SNUB #35 – *RAGTIME* (1981)

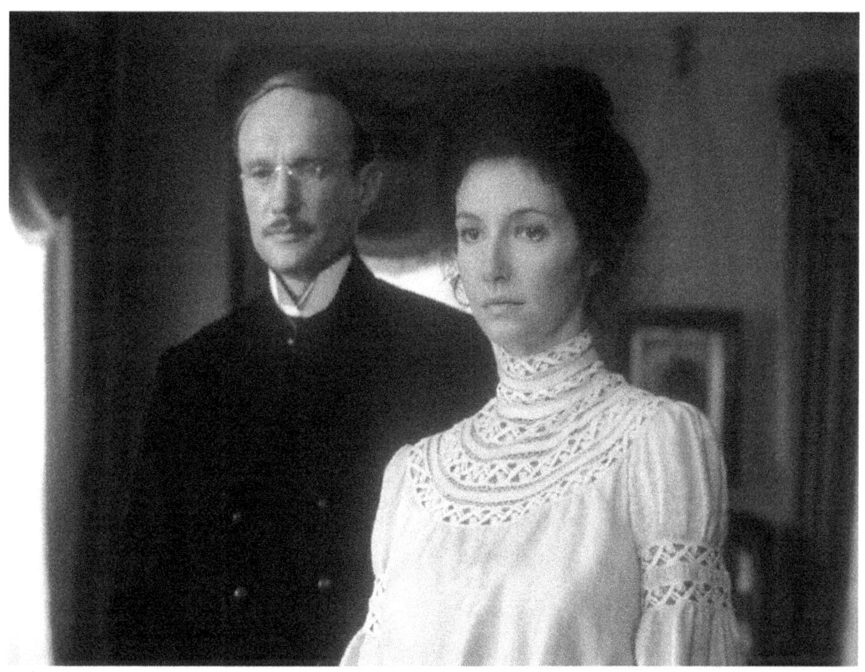

Director: Milos Forman; **Producer:** Dino De Delaurentiis; **Studio:** Paramount: **Screenplay:** Michael Weller, from the novel by E. L. Doctorow; **Cinematography:** Miroslav Ondricek; **Production Design:** John Graysmark; **Costume Design:** Anna Hill Johnstone; **Editing:** Anne Coates, Antony Gibbs, and Stanley Warnow; **Sound:** Chris Newman; **Musical Score:** Randy Newman; **Cast (in alphabetical order):** James Cagney (Rhinelander Waldo); Brad Dourif (Younger Brother); Moses Gunn (Booker T. Washington); Robert Joy (Harry Thaw); Norman Mailer (Stanford White); Elizabeth

McGovern (Evelyn Nesbitt); Mandy Patinkin (Tateh); Howard Rollins, Jr. (Coalhouse Walker, Jr.,); Mary Steenburgen (Mother); **Running Time:**155 minutes.

BACKGROUND: *Ragtime* is based on the best-selling 1975 novel by E. L. Doctorow that mixes real-life characters with fictional ones that live in or near New York City at the start of the 20th Century. The author cleverly incorporated into his book such factual real-life persons as Harry Houdini, Teddy Roosevelt, Booker T. Washington, Evelyn Nesbitt, and Evelyn's jealous husband, Harry Thaw, who in 1905 infamously shot architect Stanford White to death at the Madison Square Garden and went on trial for murder.

Intermixed with these real people is Doctorow's fictional plot, which includes three sets of characters that represent different social levels. The family from New Rochelle represents the upper class, while the black piano-playing musician and his girlfriend come from a much lower social level, and the immigrant sketch artist, his unfaithful wife, and their little daughter, are near the bottom of the social order.

The author cleverly brought these characters together by intermingling their lives with the facts of the Nesbitt/Thaw "Crime of the Century" case and having three members of the New Rochelle family becoming involved in the plight surrounding the black musician.

PLOT: The film begins with a collage of shots that feature newly filmed footage of a handsomely dressed couple dancing to a lilting waltz theme by the film's composer, Randy Newman. This opening segment also includes vintage newsreel footage of various historic figures, including Houdini doing one of his daring stunts, and newsreel shots of a nude statue (modelled by Evelyn Nesbitt) begin placed on the roof of Madison Square Garden. This scene also shows a fictitious black piano player named Coalhouse Walker, Jr. in a movie theater accompanying silent film footage.

In the next sequence the affluent family in New Rochelle is introduced as they gather for dinner. During this meal the wife (identified only as

Mother) is called to the garden where a newborn dark-skinned baby has been found. Soon the child's mother is located and the family decides to house both mother and child until they can locate the baby's father.

The father turns out to be Walker, the black piano player who is auditioning for a job in a band at a jazz club. Once he gets hired, he comes looking for the family he has abandoned. Interspersed with the story involving the New Rochelle family and Coalhouse Walker is the murder of Stanford White and its aftermath.

Throughout the film Evelyn appears as a naive young woman who wants success and attracts the attention of Mother's brother (referred to simply as Younger Brother), who resides with his sister and her husband (ID'd as simply Father). Brother disapproves when Evelyn starts taking dance lessons in the wake of her divorce.

The film also features the immigrant named Tateh, who discovers his wife's unfaithfulness and then takes their daughter to Philadelphia, where he attracts attention for a series of sketch books which, when the pages are rapidly flipped, resembles a primitive type of motion picture. Tateh eventually becomes a movie director, with Evelyn as his star.

Coalhouse Walker becomes a successful musician, but his career is upended when his Model T Ford is maliciously damaged by a group of volunteer workers at a fire station. After Walker's fiancée, Sarah, is mortally wounded by a cop when she tries to resolve their situation, Walker forms a gang that starts blowing up fire stations with bombs made by the company that Younger Brother works for.

In the film's last segment, Walker and his gang take possession of the J. P. Morgan library, but his plan to seek justice backfires when the police surround the building and police commissioner Rhinelander Waldo orders him to be shot.

MEMORABLE MOMENTS: The film's ending is memorably similar to that of the start, with shots of Houdini performing the same stunt as shown in the opening newsreel, and Evelyn once again dancing with the same partner. Then a newspaper headline announces the start of World War I.

The murder scene at the rooftop nightclub of the Madison Square Gardenly is vividly filmed, with a lavish musical performance taking place while Harry Thaw stalks Stanford White. After the shooting, Thaw's erratic behavior clearly indicates his contempt for the victim.

Another worthwhile moment occurs after Walker and his gang seize control of the Morgan Library. When Commissioner Waldo asks the library curator where his boss is and learns that J. Morgan is sailing down the Nile, Waldo slyly remarks, "Lucky him!"

The last moments are memorably similar to those at the start, with shots of Harry Houdini performing the same stunt shown in the opening newsreel and Evelyn Nesbitt once again dancing with the same male partner, while a newspaper headline announces the beginning of World War I. The film ends with a reprise of the lyrical opening music.

SUMMATION: *Ragtime* ambitiously combines actual history with a fictitious plot. The result is a film that is fascinating to watch, even though it dwells too long on the Morgan Library subplot.

The film's portrayal of the various social strata of New York society in the opening years of the 20th century gives a good idea of the treatment of black people at the hands of the mostly white population of the day.

The portrayal of the New Rochelle family reveals social complications, since Mother appears to be more liberal than does Father, who accepts his wife's concern for the welfare of Walker's fiancée and infant child but wants to maintain the cultural divide between the races.

Even with these reservations, *Ragtime* is a memorable social study about America at the dawn of the modern era.

WHAT AWARDS SHOULD THIS FILM SHOULD HAVE WON?: *Reds, Raiders of the Lost Ark,* and the Oscar-winning Best Picture *Chariots of Fire*, were 1991's big winners, but *Ragtime* deserved recognition for its impressive production design, costuming, cinematography, and Randy Newman's charming score. Howard Rollins, Jr. should have been awarded for his memorable acting. Sadly, his film career was very brief.

OSCAR SNUB #36 – *THE COLOR PURPLE* (1985)

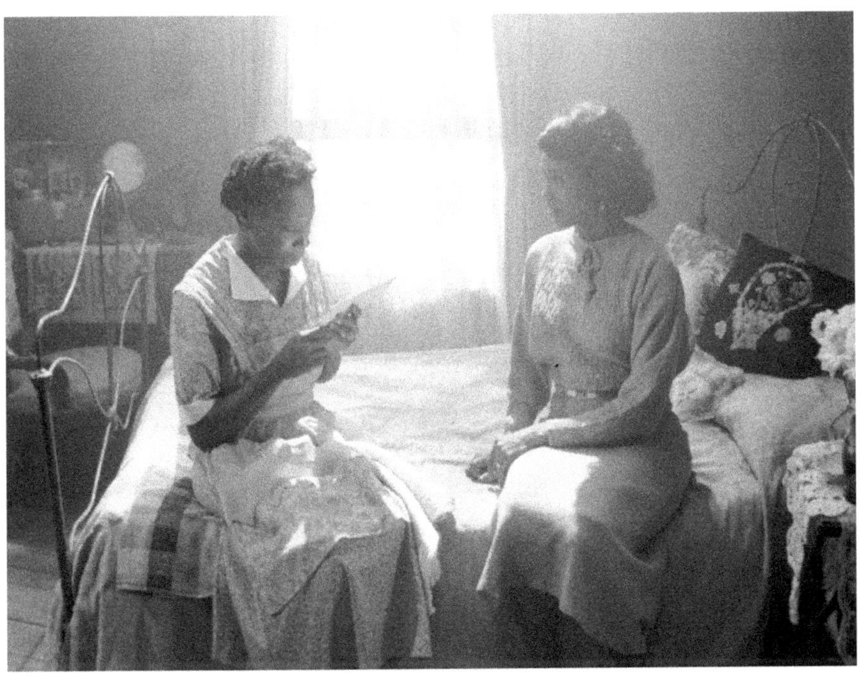

Director: Steven Spielberg; **Producer:** Steven Spielberg, Kathleen Kennedy, Frank Marshall, and Quincy Jones; **Studio:** Warner Bros.; **Screenplay:** Menno Mayjes, from the book by Alice Walker; **Cinematography:** Allen Daviau; **Art Direction/Interior Decoration:** Michael Riva and Robert W. Welch; Linda DeScenna; **Costume Design:** Aggie Guerard Rodgers; **Editing:** Michael Kahn; **Sound:** Richard L. Anderson; **Musical Score:** Quincy Jones; **Makeup:** Ken Chase; **Cast:** Whoopi Goldberg (adult Celie Johnson); Danny Glover (Albert Johnson); Margaret Avery (Shug Avery); Oprah Winfrey

(Sofia); Adolph Caesar (Old Mister Johnson); William Pugh (Harpo Johnson), Akosua Busia (adult Nettie); **Running Time:** 152 minutes.

BACKGROUND: *The Color Purple* is based on a 1982 novel by Alice Walker, who became the first Black woman to win the Pulitzer Prize for fiction. The book is unusual in that Walker conceived her work as a series of letters which the character named Celie writes to God because she believes no one else will listen to her plight about being a young girl in Georgia who has conceived two children from a man she thinks is her father. This man takes the children at birth and lies that he has killed them. He later sells Celie to a widower who wants a wife that can take care of him and his children.

The screenplay uses the novel's story for a series of narrations by Celie, but the screen version turns much of the book's content into a more conventional type of story-telling.

PLOT: The film begins in 1909 when Celie, who is fourteen and living with her younger sister, Nettie, in rural Georgia, is about to give birth. The baby's father, who is thought to be Celie's own parent, takes the baby away right after it is born.

Her "father" soon arranges for her to marry a farmer named Albert Johnson, whose wife has died and left him with several children. Celie is treated badly, and not long into the arranged marriage Albert forces Celie's sister off the property and tells her to never return. Celie anxiously awaits letters to come from Nettie, but Albert threatens Celie to never open the mailbox.

In 1916 Albert becomes excited when a former mistress and singer named Shug Avery comes for a visit. Shug at first scorns Celie but eventually becomes more than a good friend.

Meanwhile, Harpo, Albert's oldest offspring, marries a headstrong woman named Sofia. After giving birth to several children, Sofia leaves Harpo and takes her offspring with her. Harpo spends most of his time building a bar that attracts lots of local residents. It is in Harpo's juke joint that Shug entertains the crowd as a singer.

Meanwhile, Sofia is offered a job by the mayor's wife as a maid but she refuses the offer. In the ensuing tussle during which Sofia slugs the mayor, Sofia is violently arrested and spends several years in jail.

Celie remains afraid of Albert until she reaches the point where she refuses to tolerate his cruelty any longer. She moves away and opens a dress shop with the help of Shug and some other female friends. Sofia has come out of confinement to take the job that she had earlier refused to accept. She also becomes reunited with Harpo and with Shug's help Celie finds the letters from Nettie that Albert has stashed away.

When Celie reads the long-hidden letters, she finds that her sister has been living in Africa for many years. In a surprising act of atonement, Albert uses some hidden funds to file immigration papers that allow Nettie and members of her African family to come to Georgia so that Celie can be reunited with her sister and even meet her children that been given away.

MEMORABLE MOMENTS: In an early scene, when Nettie is on her way to school, Albert chases her on horseback with the assumption that he is going to rape here. After she fights him off he yells to her, I'll get you!" When Nettie is chased off Albert's land, Celie calls after her, "Write! Write!"

In a scene wherein Albert has received a letter from Shug announcing her impending arrival, Celie's voice is heard saying to God in one of her letters, "Nellie never writes." Shortly thereafter, when a drunken Shug arrives, she greets Celie by saying, "You sho is ugly!"

In an effort to serve Shug, Albert frantically tries to cook her breakfast. As Celie watches Albert deliver the tray to Shug's room, she witnesses the tray's contents being flung out the door. When Celie then prepares a well-cooked replacement, this time the tray is sent out the door of Shug's room, but the contents have been eaten.

When Harpo's opens for business, Shug appears in a flaming red dress to sing a song called "Miss Celie's Blues." The effect on the crowd is spontaneously electric, with wild dancing and general revelry. The only one unaffected by the music is Celie, who sits quietly at a table distant from the merrymaking. Not long thereafter Shug comes to realize that Albert has been consistently cruel to his wife. This leads to a mutual attraction between the two women and the real meaning of love which up to this point Celie has been totally denied.

The final scene, in which Celie meets her now-adult sister and the two grown children which Celie has long thought her stepfather had killed, brings the film to an emotionally satisfying end.

SUMMATION: *The Color Purple* came as a surprise to those who knew Spielberg's previous work as a director of thrillers (as in *Jaws*) and sci/fi fantasies (as in *Close Encounters of the Third Kind* and *E.T.) Color Purple* stands as an expertly filmed version of Alice Walker's story.

There is uniformly excellent acting by the entire cast, with Oprah Winfrey stealing every scene in which she appears. Whoopi Goldberg is also quite effective, although the shyness of her character is somewhat ponderous in the early part of the film.

Color Purple earned nominations in eleven categories but won no Oscars, thanks largely to the handsomely filmed but static *Out of Africa.* Incidentally, the 1977 film *The Turning Point* is the only other film to receive eleven nominations and win nothing.

WHAT AWARDS SHOULD THIS FILM SHOULD HAVE WON?: *Color Purple* deserved to win as Best Picture, and Spielberg should have at least won a nomination for his superb direction. Also, Oprah Winfrey was snubbed for her memorable supporting role.

OSCAR SNUB #37– *HOOSIERS* (1986)

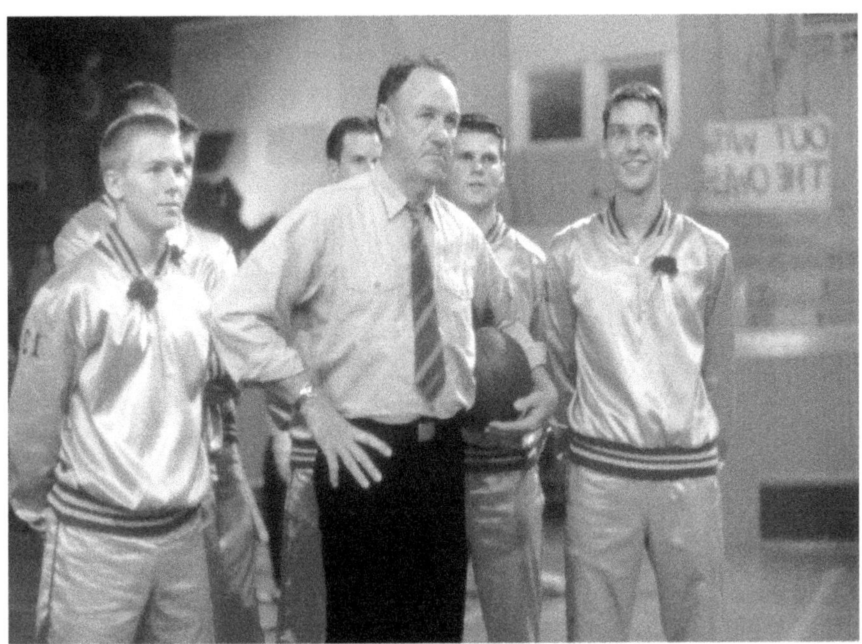

Hoosiers (1988)
Directed by David Anspaugh
Shown: (front) Gene Hackman, (back, l. to r., not obscured) Wade Schenck, Scott Summers, Steve Hollar
© Orion Credit: Orion / Photofest

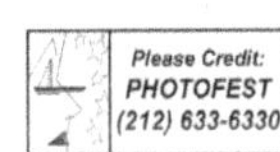

Director: David Anspaugh; **Producer:** Carter De Haven and Angelo Pizzo; **Studio:** Orion; **Screenplay:** Angelo Pizzo; **Cinematography:** Fred Murphy; **Production Design:** David Nichols; **Costume Design:** Jane Anderson; **Editing:** C. Timothy O'Meara; **Supervising Sound Editor:** Bill Phillips; **Musical Score:** Jerry Goldsmith; **Cast:** Gene Hackman (Coach Norman Dale); Barbara Hershey (Myra Fleener); Dennis Hopper (Shooter); Sheb Wooley (Cletus); Fern Persons (Opal Fleener); The Hickory Huskers: Brad Boyle (Whit); Steve Hollar (Rade); Brad Long (Buddy); David

Neidorf (Everett); Kent Poole (Merle); Wade Schenck (Ollie); Scott Summers (Strap); Maris Valainis (Jimmy Chitwood); **Running Time:** 113 minutes.

BACKGROUND: There have been lots of sports-themed films throughout the history of cinema, but few of them have been about high-school basketball. *Hoosiers* is set in the fictional town of Hickory, a small farming community in Indiana with a student enrollment so small that there are only eight players on the Hickory Huskers team.

As the 1951-1952 schoolyear begins, the team faces challenges due to the sudden death of their coach. A major difficulty is that Jimmy Chitwood, the team's best player, is grieving the loss of the coach and refuses to join the team. A third problem concerns Norman Dale, who hasn't coached in twelve years, ever since his banishment from college coaching for hitting one of his players.

With these challenges, the new season begins with a negative reaction by local citizens who passionately love basketball but have strong doubts about the newly hired coach's methods.

PLOT: When Norman Dale arrives in Hickory at the invitation of Cletus, the high school's principal and Dale's longtime friend, he knows this is his one chance to redeem himself as a basketball coach.

Dale's first day on the job does not go well. He first meets Myra Fleener, a faculty member who resents his presence before knowing anything about him. He is also insulted by a male faculty member who has been filling in as coach until Dale's arrival. Even the players seem resentful, including two whose vocal scorn leads to their being dismissed from the team until they can learn to behave properly. Additionally, Myra advises Dale to not force Jimmy to play because he is still in mourning.

Without Jimmy, however, everyone knows that the team has no chance of winning games. Dale persists in trying to make the best of the situation, even though he at this point has only six players to start with, one of whom is too small to me of much benefit to the team.

The season does not begin well, and at one point the townsfolk gather to vote Dale out as coach. But just as the vote takes place, Jimmy shows up to declare that he will agree to play, but only if Dale is retained as the team's coach. With Jimmy as the team's star and the roster now including eight players, the Huskers gradually become a winning team and reach the regional playoffs. With their final win the Huskers become the first Indiana team from such a small town to win the state championship.

MEMORABLE MOMENTS: Shooter, the father of Everett, one of the Huskers, helps to provide some of the film's more memorable moments. A seemingly hopeless drunk, Shooter turns out to be very knowledgeable about basketball and becomes a real asset as Dale's coaching assistant. To put Shooter to the test, Dale allows himself to be evicted during a game. Shooter is at first reluctant to take Dales's place, but he manages to maneuver a game-winning play that buoys Shooter's confidence. This is the first of many scenes in which the Huskers start becoming a winning team.

After Shooter returns to drinking a tender moment comes when Dale visits him in the hospital to assure him he will still have his job when he returns.

As the team progresses towards the postseason, Strap is the player who routinely prays on bended knee before games. When he is called upon at one point to replace an injured player, Dale says," "God wants you on the floor." After Strap sinks a two-pointer Dale asks, "What's gotten into you?" and Strap says, "It's the Lord. I can feel his strength." Dale's response is, "Keep his strength on the dribble."

The end of the season provides emotional excitement as the Huskers, led by Jimmy, win their final games. The pounding rhythms of Jerry Goldsmith's musical score are a huge asset to these scenes, especially in the regional championship game in which Dale inserts Ollie into the lineup during the final seconds. When Ollie, the team's shortest player, makes two free throws that clinch the victory, Ollie is hoisted onto his teammates' shoulders and becomes an instant hero.

Right before the state-championship game when Dale invites team members to make comments, one of the players says, "This is for all the small schools who never had the chance to get here." Dale then gathers his players into a tight embrace and says, "I love you guys."

Late in the film, when Dale and Myra are walking in the woods, he gently places his hands on her face, tenderly kisses her, and then says, "I've been wanting to do that ever since I first saw you." Hackman's sincerity makes this a memorable acting moment.

SUMMATION: *Hoosiers* was a real sleeper when it was first released. Its success with audiences was largely based on word-of-mouth raves that revealed this as an exceptional film that should appeal to anyone looking for a movie with a really involving story.

Gene Hackman's performance is enhanced throughout by the eight young actors who were chosen from a pool of 600 applicants to play the Huskers.

Viewers should be moved by the film's scenario about emotionally wounded people who get second chances. Shooter finds a way to redeem himself as a knowledgeable assistant, while Jimmy overcomes his grief to become the team's leading scorer. Myra gets a second chance with Dale, who she at first finds arrogant but later learns otherwise.

The ultimate second chance belongs to Norman Dale, who accepts his coaching position with the realization that this is perhaps his last opportunity to lead a team to victory.

WHAT AWARDS SHOULD THIS FILM SHOULD HAVE WON?: *Hoosiers* deserved awards for its screenplay and the acting by Gene Hackman and Dennis Hopper, but the film was really snubbed when Jerry Goldsmith's emotional and often exciting score was overlooked in favor Herbie Hancock's jazzy improvisations heard in *'Round Midnight.*

OSCAR SNUB #38 – *HOPE AND GLORY* (1987)

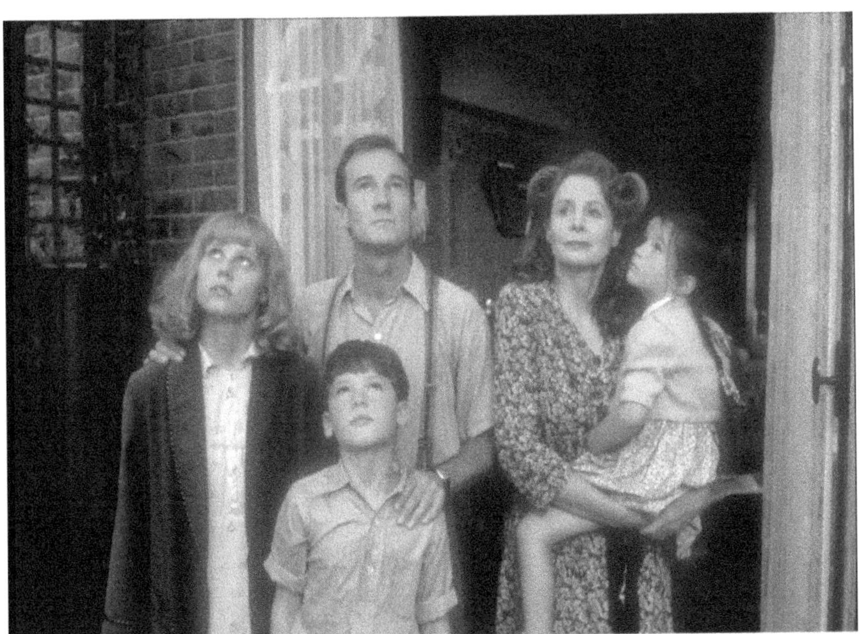

Hope and Glory (1987 British)
Directed by John Boorman
Shown from left: Sammi Davis (as Dawn Rowan), Sebastian Rice-Edwards (as Bill Rowan), David Hayman (as Clive Rowan), Sarah Miles (as Grace Rowan), Geraldine Muir (as Sue Rowan)

Credit: Columbia Pictures/Photofest © Columbia Pictures

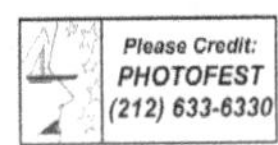

Director: John Boorman; **Producer:** John Boorman: **Studio:** Columbia; **Screenplay:** John Boorman; **Cinematography:** Philippe Rousselot; **Production Design:** Anthony Pratt; **Costume Design:** Shirley Mussen; **Editing:** Ian Crafford; **Sound:** Ron Davis; **Musical Score:** Peter Martin; **Cast:** Sarah Miles (Grace Rohan); Sebastian Rice-Edwards (Bill Rohan); David Hayman (Clive Rohan); Sammi Davis (Dawn Rohan); Geraldine Muir (Sue Rohan); Susan Woolridge(Molly); Jean-Marc Barr (Bruce); Derrick O'Connor (Mac); Ian Bannen (Grandfather); **Running time:** 113 minutes.

BACKGROUND: Several film directors have made movies based on their own lives; some classic examples are Barry Levinson's *Avalon* (1990), Kenneth Branagh's *Belfast* (2021), and Steven Spielberg's *The Fabelmans* (2022). In all of these films the plots revolve around thedirectors' childhoods and are based on screenplays that they themselves have written. In the case of *Hope and Glory,* John Boorman relates memories of his youth in England during the first part of World War II, when Hitler's Luftwaffe dropped bombs onto London on a nightly basis.

A much-earlier film that *Hope and Glory* resembles is William Wyler's 1942 Oscar-winning film about a fictional British family in World War II, *Mrs. Miniver* (which is written about in my previous book, *Best Picture,* published in 2024). The plots of both of these films concentrate on families and how the bombings affect them.

PLOT: Boorman's film concerns the Rohan family that lives on Rosehill Avenue on the outskirts of London. When the war begins, Clive enlists for active duty in the British army, while his wife, Grace, remains at home with their three children, teenager Dawn, the five-year-old Sue, and Bill. At about nine when the war begins, Bill is based on Boorman's own childhood experiences. What Bill witnesses after his father leaves for the war takes up much of the film. No battles are shown, but the film reveals the impact of German planes dropping bombs on the Rohans' neighborhood, which is greatly damaged in the course of the film.

Another element in Boorman's film is the role of the Rohan's oldest daughter, Dawn, who falls in love with Bruce, a Canadian soldier, when he is on leave. When the family learns that she is pregnant, a hurried wedding takes place.

Bill is often seen playing with his friends in the wreckage of homes in the neighborhood that have been destroyed in the bombing attacks. While the adults mourn the losses suffered by their friends, the children take advantage of the destruction by sifting through the wreckage for anything that can be played with.

In the latter part of the film, after the Rohans' home has burned to the ground, they move out of London and relocate to the country home of Grace's parents. It is here that Bill spends time with his grandfather, who makes his grandson both a fisherman and a googlie-throwing cricket player. Bill's adventures in this much different environment provide the film with its upbeat closing scenes.

MEMORABLE MOMENTS: A touching scene occurs early in the film when Grace brings her two younger children to a train station for transport to a safer environment. As the children are boarding the train, Grace becomes distraught at the idea of seeing her children going away and she excitedly runs to the train to reclaim them with the help of her good friend, Mac, a civilian who spends lots of time with the family when Clive is away.

During a bombing attack, Grace wants her children to stay away from the door and remain inside. But Bill and Dawn run outside and start jumping up and down when they view the colorful flames, which resemble fireworks to them. They seem completely oblivious to danger when the fires light up the skies.

Late in the film, when their grandfather tells Bill and little Sue to catch fish when they are in a small boat, a stray bomb explodes in the nearby waters and hundreds of dead fish start floating in the stream. When Bill gets out of the boat and starts loading dead fish onto the boat with his sister's help, their grandfather is simply amazed with the catch, since he had earlier deplored the lack of fish when he was trying to catch them earlier in the day.

In the film's last scene, Bill is being driven by his grandfather to Bill's hated school in London as the new school year begins. When they approach the school they see children running in all directions and yelling with delight. When one of Bill's friends comes up to him and yells, "It was a stray bomb; thank you, Adolph," Bill realizes that the school has been destructively bombed during the night. The subsequent celebrating by Bill and his grandpa brings *Hope and Glory* to a delightfully uplifting close.

SUMMATION: This film, with its many light-hearted scenes, is a viewing experience that portrays World War II in a way that is far different from films like *Mrs. Miniver.* Boorman's film, which relies heavily on the filmmaker's own memories of the war, is a refreshing film, with many scenes that portray Bill's excitement at witnessing such things as blimps that fly over the houses on Rosehill Avenue and planes that appear to be in the midst of bombing missions.

This film gives a very limited view of World War II, but Boorman's ingenious intention has been to present his personal impressions of the war. His point of view is that of a child who likes to play with military toys but is too young to fully appreciate the horrors happening around him. *Hope and Glory* is a vivid account of the impact that World War II had on families living in England at that time.

WHAT AWARDS SHOULD THIS FILM HAVE WON?: Ironically, *Hope and Glory* was released in the same year as Steven Spielberg's *Empire of the Sun* and Bernardo Bertolucci's Oscar-winning film, *The Last Emperor*, both of which involve the impact of World War II on children. The last-named film garnered nine Oscar wins, but the impact of both the Boorman and Spielberg films cannot go unappreciated. *Hope and Glory* should have won Oscars for its original screenplay and for its impressive production design of a badly bombed London neighborhood.

In some ways I prefer *Empire of the Sun* [see next entry] as an example of a child subjected to the horrors of war, but *Hope and Glory* is a memorable example of how children learn to survive during wartime.

OSCAR SNUB #39 – *EMPIRE OF THE SUN* (1987)

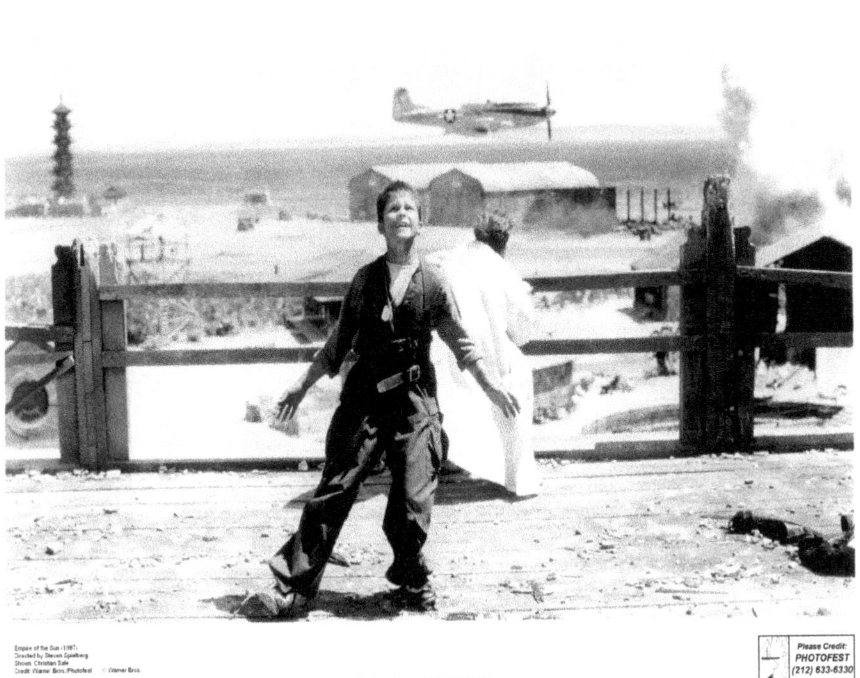

Director: Steven Spielberg; **Producer:** Steven Spielberg, Kathleen Kennedy, and Frank Marshall; **Studio:** Warner Bros.; **Screenplay:** Tom Stoppard, based on the novel by J. G. Ballard; **Cinematography:** Allen Daviau; **Production Design:** Norman Reynolds; **Costume Design:** Rob Ringwood; **Editing:** Michael Kahn; **Sound:** Robert Knudson, Don Digirolamo, John Boyd, and Tony Dawe; **Musical Score:** John Williams; **Cast:** Christian Bale (Jim Graham); John Malkovich (Basie); Miranda Richardson (Mrs. Victor); Nigel Havers (Dr. Rawlins); Joe Pantoliano (Frank); Masato Ibu (camp commander);

Takatoro Kataoka (Kamikaze boy pilot); Emily Richard (Jim's mother); Rupert Frazer (Jim's father); **Running Time:** 152 minutes.

BACKGROUND: British author J. G. Ballard is best known for his science-fiction writings, but in 1984 he turned to memories of his own youth in China to create *Empire of the Sun,* which is loosely based on his experiences in a Japanese internment camp during World War II.

Like Jim (Christian Bale) in Spielberg's film Ballard spent over three years in confinement. The major difference is that in reality Ballard did not live apart from his parents, while in the film based on Tom Stoppard's screenplay, young Jim and his parents become separated when Japanese troops invade Shanghai in the wake of Pearl Harbor and Jim winds up being transported to a camp at Soochow Creek, adjacent to a Japanese military airfield.

In the film, Jim learns to fend for himself and becomes a teenage huckster under the tutelage of Basie, a captured American sailor who shows Jim how to make profitable trades, especially with regards to food items which the prisoners badly need in order to survive.

PLOT: The film begins right before the Pearl Harbor attack, when Jim and his parents attend a costume-themed Christmas party in the upscale British Compound of Shanghai that is protected by a pact with the Chinese government. As soon as the attack in Hawaii occurs, Japanese troops invade and the Grahams frantically try to find ways to leave China. In the chaos that descends on Shanghai, Jim gets separated from his parents and is told to go to their home until they can rescue him.

Jim goes to their suburban residence, but his parents never show up and he leaves on his bicycle when the food runs out. He is eventually arrested, and together with many other British families and several Americans, he is transported to a Japanese internment camp.

After Jim's arrival, the film shifts forward to 1945, where an older Jim is surviving by trading goods for food. He is also schooled by a British physician who tends the health needs of the British prisoners in the Soochow camp.

The Japanese captors eventually abandon the place and force all of the camp survivors to travel with them. Jim is finally rescued by a troop of American soldiers and brought back to Shanghai and placed in an orphanage along with many other children until their parents can claim them. At first Jim does not recognize his parents but his mother finally sees him and they lovingly embrace each other.

MEMORABLE MOMENTS: While at the Christmas party Jim strays from the other guests and meanders into the countryside where he spots a vacated Japanese airplane. After he climbs into the cockpit and pretends to be a fearless pilot, he is spotted by Japanese soldiers. Jim hurriedly exits from the plane and his father, along with another party guest, manages to escort him back to the party. This scene provides an early example of Jim's fascination with airplanes.

When Jim first arrives at the camp he approaches a Japanese warplane that is being prepared for battle, with sparks flying everywhere. As he touches the plane three Jap pilots observe him. Jim salutes them and they return the gesture, with highly emotional music in the background.

As the film advances to 1945, Jim is seen running hastily around the camp and exchanging non-food items for such things as cabbages and potatoes, with the camp commander as the recipient of freshly shined boots. The playfulness of this scene is greatly enhanced by John Williams's rambunctious music.

A much darker moment occurs when P-51 bombers start dropping bombs on the nearby airfield. When Jim runs up to the roof of one of the camp's taller buildings to get a closer look, Dr. Rawlins hurriedly runs after him to bring him back down. When they embrace each other, Jim tearfully admits that he cannot remember what his parents look like.

Several times in the film Jim has friendly encounters with a Japanese boy who is being trained as a Kamikaze pilot. When the war ends Jim becomes deeply distraught when one of Basie's companions shoots the boy when Jim holds up a mango for the boy to cut with his sword. Jim then rebuffs Basie for teaching him to be a huckster.

The Welsh song "Suo Gan," which is beautifully introduced when Jim sings it as a choirboy in the Shanghai Cathedral in the opening scene, recurs as one of Jim's few childhood memories.

SUMMATION: *Empire of the Sun* includes many scenes that occur as life lessons for Jim, who seems to thrive despite the terrible living conditions that surround him. The viewer may not feel emotionally engaged with Jim as he witnesses the suffering of those around him, but he vividly exhibits the ways in which children can be affected by war.

Spielberg's film bears resemblance to John Boorman's *Hope and Glory*, which also came out in late 1987 [see previous entry]. Both films show war from a child's vantage point, but Ballard's story depicts the trauma of a boy's childhood due to his parents' absence.

Though not a box-office hit, *Empire of the Sun* remains a major film of the1980s.

WHAT AWARDS SHOULD THIS FILM HAVE WON?: *The Last Emperor* swept the Oscars for 1987 with awards in all nine categories in which it was nominated, including Best Picture, Director, and Screenplay, plus the six categories in which *Empire* was cited: Cinematography, Production Design, Costume Design, Editing, Sound, and Musical Score. I would have awarded those Oscars to *Empire of the Sun*, especially the scoring award, which should have gone to John Williams for his outstanding music that includes a recurring emotional theme with wordless voices, the fast-paced music for Jim's entrepreneurial escapades, and the memorable vocal piece "Exultate Justi," which is heard when Jim approaches an American military officer to surrender at the end of the war.

OSCAR SNUB #40 – *FIELD OF DREAMS* (1989)

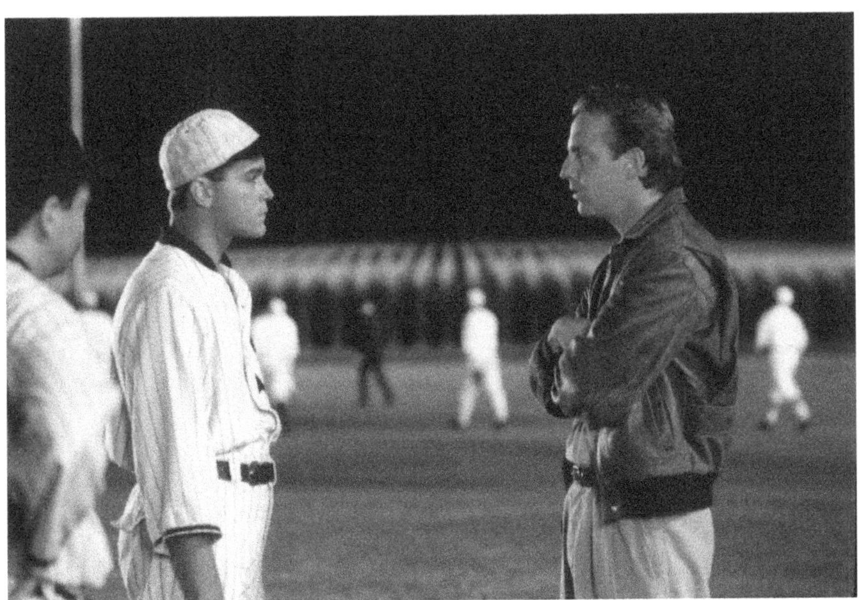

Field of Dreams
Directed by Phil Alden Robinson
Shown: Ray Liotta (as Shoeless Joe Jackson), Kevin Costner (as Ray Kinsella)
Credit: Universal Pictures/Photofest © Universal Pictures

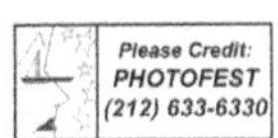

Director: Phil Alden Robinson; **Producer:** Lawrence Gordon and Charles Gordon; **Studio:** Universal; **Screenplay:** Phil Alden Robinson, based on the novel *Shoeless Joe* by W. P. Kinsella; **Cinematography:** John Lindley; **Production Design:** Dennis Gassner, **Costume Design:** Linda M. Bass; **Editing:** Ian Crafford; **Sound:** Sandy Gendler; **Musical Score:** James Horner; **Cast:** Kevin Costner (Ray Kinsella); Amy Madigan (Amy Kinsella); Gaby Hoffmann (Karin Kinsella); Ray Liotta (Shoeless Joe Jackson); James Earl Jones (Terrence Mann); Timothy Busfield (Mark); Burt Lancaster (Dr.

"Moonlight" Graham); Frank Whaley (Archie Graham); Dwier Brown (John Kinsella); **Running time:** 106 minutes.

BACKGROUND: Screenwriter and director Phil Alden Robinson started his film career by writing scripts. The first one of these to be filmed was the 1984 movie *In the Mood,* which starred Patrick Dempsey as the real-life Sonny Wisecarver, who became known as the "Woo-Woo Kid" in the 1940s. Robinson followed this film with *Field of Dreams,* an adaptation of W. P. Kinsella's fanciful novel *Shoeless Joe,* about the infamous "black sox scandal" that involves baseball players from the 1919 Chicago White Sox team who are banished from the sport but come back as ghosts to play on a cornfield in Iowa.

Kinsella's novel involves the writer J. P. Salinger, but Robinson rewrote the part as a fictional writer named Terrence Mann, whose love for baseball causes him to be coaxed by Iowa farmer Ray Kinsella into coming to Kinsella's farm where Ray has turned part of his cornfield into a baseball infield.

PLOT: The film begins with a narration by Ray about his late father's love for baseball and the Chicago White Sox, plus the scandal in 1919 in which eight players conspired to throw that year's World Series. This narration also includes Ray's regret that his relationship with his father ended badly.

The film advances to the scene in which Ray walks through his cornfield and hears an otherworldly voice that calls to him several times, "If you build it, he will come." His skepticism over this message is allayed when he has a vision of a baseball field complete with light poles.

He becomes the laughingstock of other farmers, but somehow he is compelled to construct the field with the loving support of his wife, Annie, and their young daughter, Karin. Ray believes that the reasons for his actions will eventually be explained to him.

After Shoeless Joe Jackson appears to play ball, seven other White Sox players show up, and Joe eventually invites other deceased players to participate in games. Ray then gets another message from the beyond that says, "Ease his pain." This message directs him to Boston and to Terrence Mann, who at first scorns Ray for bothering him, but eventually Mann gets messages himself and travels with Ray to the field in Iowa where still more players have begun to appear.

Ray finally realizes that the "Ease his pain" message refers to himself and to his deceased father, John Kinsella, who appears as a young baseball player and and gets introduced to Ray's wife and daughter. A reconciliation takes place between Ray and his father as they play catch on the field, which John Kinsella describes as "a place where dreams come true."

MEMORABLE MOMENTS: After the field is constructed, several months go by with nobody playing ball on the field until Karin asks her father one day about someone being there. Ray then realizes that the ghost of Joe Jackson has appeared. At one point Joe asks if this is heaven. When Ray answers that they are in Iowa, Joe responds by saying that it feels like heaven.

Later, when Ray and Terrence travel to Minnesota to find Dr. Graham, who long before had a very short-lived stint as a baseball player, Graham refuses to go with them, but when Ray and Terrence begin the trip to Iowa, a young player hitches a ride with them and this person turns out to be a much younger Archie Graham. Archie is welcomed by the other players and is given the chance to play that Doc Graham never had when he was young.

The final scenes are very memorable, especially the moment when Ray realizes that the young ball player who remains on the field after the others have disappeared into a crop of cornstalks is Ray's father. With James Horner's emotionally uplifting music, the film then ends as the camera moves away from the two Kinsellas tossing a baseball back and forth to an aerial shot of the field of dreams as seen from a distance with long lines of cars headed to the field, as earlier predicted by Terrence when he had said that people would come from all over to discover something treasurable that they lost but now have found.

SUMMATION: *Field of Dreams* is an enjoyable excursion into a world of fantasy, with some of the same elements that make Frank Capra's *It's a Wonderful Life* so memorable. Whereas Capra's film features an angel that comes to earth to rescue George Bailey when he is contemplating suicide, *Field of Dreams* asks the viewer to share Ray Kinsella's plight when he spends his life savings on making a ballfield with no clear understanding of the reason the ghostly voice has called to him.

Ray suffers some of the same difficulties that George Bailey faces, although the tone of *Field of Dreams* is much lighter than the often very downbeat *Wonderful Life.* Both films invite viewers to suspend disbelief and share in the experiences the films' central characters go through in finding meaning in their lives.

Not every viewer may see the value in the fantasy realm occupied by *Field of Dreams,* but this film has something to say about the love of baseball that once occupied the position as America's national sport. In a more personal sense, this film allows viewers to share a dream felt by many that they could somehow become reconciled with deceased family members after their deaths. The wishful thinking in *Field of Dreams* makes this an endearing film.

WHAT AWARDS SHOULD THIS FILM HAVE WON?: *Driving Miss Daisy* deserved the Oscar as 1989's best film, but I would have awarded *Field of Dreams* an Academy Award in the Adapted Screenplay category, and I would have given James Earl Jones a Supporting Actor award. Sadly, this beloved actor never won an acting Oscar in his long and distinguished career.

OSCAR SNUB #41 – *AWAKENINGS* (1990)

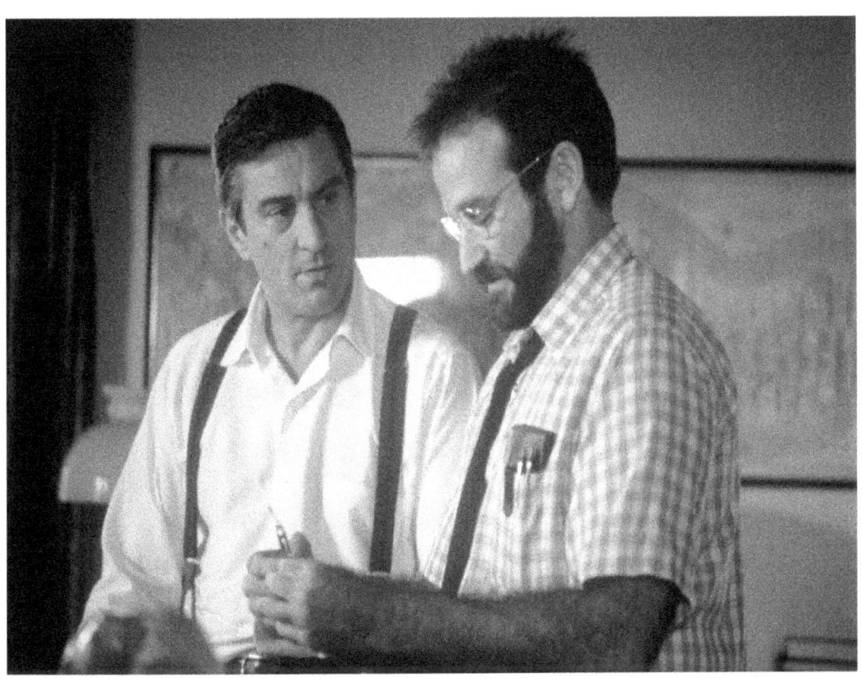

Awakenings (1990)
Directed by Penny Marshall
Shown from left: Robert De Niro (as Leonard Lowe), Robin Williams (as Dr. Malcolm Sayer)
Credit: Columbia/Photofest © Columbia Pictures

Director: Penny Marshall; **Producer:** Walter E. Parks and Lawrence Lasker; **Studio:** Columbia; **Screenplay:** Steven Zaillian, based on the book by Oliver Sacks, M.D.; **Cinematography:** Miroslav Ondricek; **Production Design:** Anton Furst; **Costume Design:** Cynthia Flynt; **Editing:** Jerry Greenberg and Battle Davis; **Sound:** Jerry Ross; **Musical Score:** Randy Newman; **Cast:** Robert De Niro (Leonard Lowe); Robin Williams (Malcolm Sayer, M. D.); Julie Kavner (Eleanor Costello); Ruth Nelson (Mrs. Lowe); John

Heard (Dr. Kaufman); Penelope Ann Miller (Paula); Alice Drummond (Lucy); Anne Meara (Miriam); **Running time:** 122 minutes.

BACKGROUND: Oliver Sacks, M.D. (1933-2015), was a well-known British neurologist who specialized in working with patients who had various mental and physical illnesses. His most famous treatments came while he worked at a chronic-illness facility in the Bronx during the late-1960s and diagnosed patients who had been afflicted with a type of sleeping sickness known as encephalitis lethargica. Those who were stricken with the disease became totally immobile and were largely placed in facilities that were designated for chronic patients.

Dr. Sacks discovered that a drug called levodopa (commonly referred to as L-dopa) could help patients become fully mobile again. His 1973 book *Awakenings* documents his work with L- Dopa during the summer of 1969, when he was able to reactivate several patients. The 1990 film directed by Penny Marshall is a slightly fictionalized version of Sacks's medical experiments.

PLOT: The film begins when Dr. Malcolm Thayer (the fictional name given to Dr. Sacks) applies for a research position at Bainbridge Hospital in the Bronx. He gets hired to treat patients, although he states to the medical staff that he doesn't work well with people. When he discovers that a group of patients is totally immobile, he does some extensive research and finds that an encephalitis epidemic had occurred during the 1920s, and several of the patients at this facility were infected with the disease. Thayer also learns that the L-dopa drug has been used successfully in treating patients in other facilities that have had symptoms similar to the ones that have afflicted many residents of Bainbridge.

Thayer becomes interested in one particular patient, Leonard Lowe, who contracted a paralyzing ailment at the age of eleven and has been a patient at Bainbridge for thirty years. When Thayer convinces Dr. Kaufman, the head of the medical staff, to experiment on a single patient, Leonard is chosen for the application of L-dopa.

After Leonard becomes mobile again, the staff is allowed to use the drug on the entire unit where Leonard is being treated. The awakening of these fifteen patients is a gradual process, but soon they all become fully functional and Thayer takes them out of the hospital on field trips. His interest centers primarily on Leonard, whose high degree of intelligence helps Thayer in studying the beneficent effects of the drug.

Unfortunately, Thayer learns the effects of the drug are not permanent and Leonard lapses gradually back into the condition that had afflicted him for thirty years.

MEMORABLE MOMENTS: In Thayer's first few days in his new job, he discovers that the catatonic patients in one particular ward can reflexively catch balls and fountain pens when these objects are being dropped or thrown. In one rather amusing scene he has the patients sitting in a circle and throwing a soccer ball back and forth without the ball ever falling on the floor.

After Leonard is selected for the trial use of L-Dopa, at first there is little result, but one night Thayer finds Leonard sitting at a table drawing his name on a writing pad. When Leonard says that it's quiet, Thayer responds by telling him everyone is asleep. Leonard's response is, "I'm awake," and then he smiles.

After this, the other patients in the ward are treated with the medicine. Again there is a moment when Thayer and the other staff members are astonished to find the ward residents fully awake and have to tell the patients what year it is. Lucy, one of the oldest patients, is shocked when she finds out that it is not 1926.

One of the film's funniest moments comes when Miriam, another activated patient, is told by one of the nurses that her husband has divorced her. Her response is, "Thank God!"

Late in the film, when Leonard begins to regress into his former incapacitated state, he tells Paula, a woman whose father has been a long-time stroke patient at Bainbridge, that she should not visit him anymore, despite the fact that he has grown very fond of her. She respects his wishes, but before she leaves she takes Leonard's hand and holds him while they dance to a slow piano piece played by one of the other reactivated patients. As she holds him, Leonard stops shaking and rests his head on her shoulder. This is one of the film's most tender scenes.

At the film's end, when the patients have regressed to their previous state of immobility, Thayer gets ready to leave the hospital when he sees Eleanor, a sympathetic nurse, also heading out. Whereas he had previously made excuses for not accompanying her for a cup of coffee, now he nervously tries to propose the same to her. When she agrees, they walk down the street in a way that contradicts his earlier pronouncement that he is not a "people person."

SUMMATION: *Awakenings* faced some strong competition for the 1990 Best-Picture award, especially from Kevin Costner's *Dances with Wolves,* which won seven Oscars, including Best Picture and six other awards. Still, Penny Marshall's film is the most heartwarming film of the year, and one that clearly invites the viewer to see it more than once.

WHAT AWARDS SHOULD THIS FILM HAVE WON?: Kevin Costner's epic Western *Dances with Wolves* dominated the 1990 Oscars, but the other four nominees have considerable merit, including *The Godfather Part III, Goodfellas, Ghost,* and especially *Awakenings.* While this last film may not have the Oscar type of presence that its competitors have, it remains an example of excellent filmmaking. Both of its stars, Robeert De Niro and Robin Williams, gave performances that can be considered among the best work of their respective acting careers, and Penny Marshall was really snubbed when she failed to get a nomination in the Best-Director race. Her work on this film and the baseball-themed *A League of Their Own,* which came out two years later, proved her to be a filmmaker of exceptional skill.

OSCAR SNUB #42 – *THE REMAINS OF THE DAY* (1993)

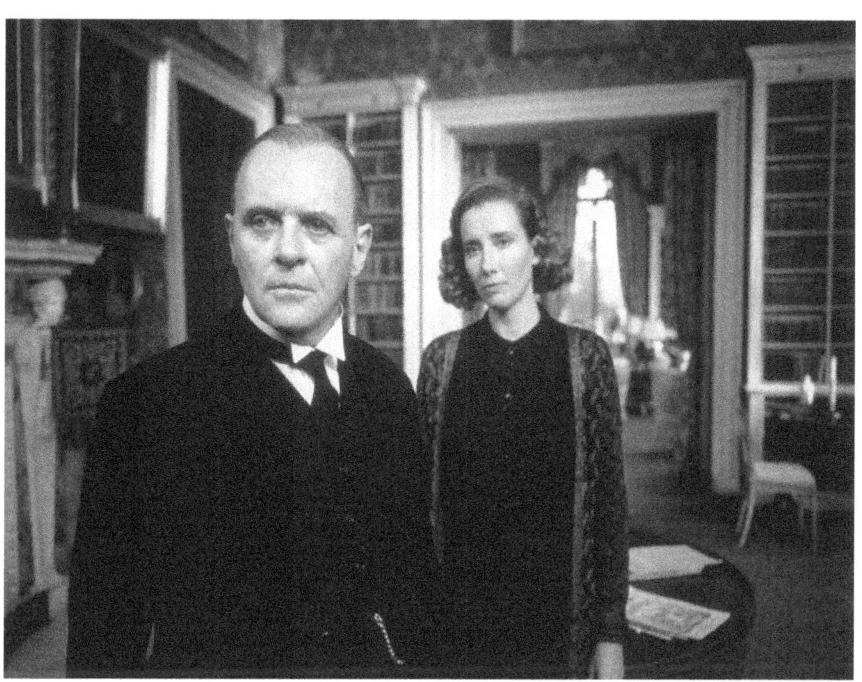

The Remains of the Day (1993)
Directed by James Ivory
Shown from left: Anthony Hopkins (as Stevens), Emma Thompson (as Miss Kenton)
Credit: Merchant Ivory Productions/Photofest © Merchant Ivory Productions

Director: James Ivory; **Producer:** Mike Nichols, James Ivory, and Ismael Merchant; **Studio:** Columbia; **Screenplay:** Ruth Prawer Jhabvala, from the novel by Kazuo Ishiguro; **Cinematography:** Tony Pierce-Roberts; **Production Design:** Luciana Arrighi; **Costume Design:** Jenny Beaven and John Bright; **Editing:** Andrew Marcus; **Sound:** Colin Miller; **Musical Score:** Richard Robbins; **Cast:** Anthony Hopkins (Stevens); Emma Thompson (Miss Kenton); James Fox (Lord Darlington); Christopher Reeve (Lewis); Peter Vaughan

(Stevens's father); Hugh Grant (Cardinal); Ben Chaplin (Charlie, head footman); **Running Time:** 134 minutes.

BACKGROUND: *The Remains of the Day* is a film adaptation of the Booker Prize-winning novel by Kazuo Ishiguro (b. 1954), a Japanese-born writer who grew up in England and has become one of the most respected authors of modern times. His body of work was awarded the Nobel Prize for Literature in 2017.

James Ivory's film adheres closely to the novel, in which an Englishman recalls his life as the head butler to an English aristocrat named Lord Darlington. Mr. Stevens recounts his relationship with Miss Kenton, who is the head housekeeper at Darlington Hall until she leaves her position to marry a small business owner in a distant part of England.

PLOT: The film portrays Stevens as a meticulously devoted butler whose primary goal always seems to be the best servant he can be, without taking sides in the growing tension between England and Germany during the 1930s. His loyalty to Lord Darlington conflicts with his relationship with Kenton, whose personal interest in Stevens is often compromised by his lack of civility towards her.

The film's plot unfolds in an unusual way since Stevens is first shown driving across the English countryside in 1958 to meet Kenton, who has corresponded with him and suggests that she has not had a happy life since leaving Darlington Hall before World War II began.

The film then goes back to 1935, when Kenton began working at Darlington. Her relationship with Stevens becomes frayed when Lord Darlington allows Stevens's father to come to the hall as an underbutler. It is obvious that Stevens, Sr. is becoming frail when he trips over patio stones and falls to the pavement while carrying a large tea set.

A major part of the film concerns a conference that takes place when a large international group of diplomats is invited to Darlington Hall to discuss the growing tension over the rise of the Nazi party in Germany. While Lord Darlington seems convinced that concessions need to be extended towards Germany, Jack Lewis, an American congressman, feels that the other guests attending this series of meetings should not be swayed by Darlington's pacifist beliefs.

Further tension between Stevens and Kenton occurs when Darlington orders two young German women who have been employed as part of the household staff to be dismissed because they are Jewish. Kenton strongly objects when she learns that Stevens has carried out the Lord's orders without any objection.

When Kenton tells Stevens that she has been offered a marriage proposal, he doesn't offer her any concern for her situation, even though it is rather obvious that she has feelings for Stevens.

At the end of the film they meet again when Stevens borrows a car from Lewis, who has now taken possession of Darlington Hall after the death of its former owner, to go on a holiday.

Although they seem friendly towards each other, Stevens still cannot bring himself to return the affection that Kenton has rather obviously held toward him over the years.

MEMORABLE MOMENTS: In a scene in which Lord Darlington implores Stevens to help his employer in introducing Darlington's godson, Cardinal, to "the birds and the bees," Stevens mistakenly thinks that he should educate the young man in the ways of nature pertaining to the raising of flowers in the hall's extensive gardens. When Stevens escorts Cardinal into the gardens, the young man seems amused and perplexed by Stevens's botany-based comments.

The lavish gathering of dignitaries during the years prior to World War II is a highlight of the film, especially when Lewis stands alone in objecting to Darlington's sympathetic approach in dealing with Germany. It is ironic that Lewis becomes the owner of the estate following Darlington's death.

The final part of the film includes a tender moment when Stevens and Kenton meet for the last time, and one of them says that the best part of the day comes in the evening, when lights come on and illuminate the surroundings. This seems to suggest that the regret for the mistakes from the past can be set aside by embracing the present moment.

SUMMATION: *Remains of the Day* is a beautifully designed film with few highly dramatic moments, but there are noteworthy scenes where Stevens seems to hide behind a veneer of stiff upper-lipped dignity when he is confronted with Miss Kenton's more outgoing persona.

An aura of tragedy hangs over the film, especially when Lord Darlington's pro-German sympathy clearly points in the direction of his ultimate disgrace. Even more tragic, perhaps, is Stevens's lack of involvement in the social concerns that surround him. His stance often seems regrettable when he cannot accept Kenton's attempts to draw him out of his stoic ways.

The ultimate worth of this film may be hard to fathom upon a first viewing, but patiently attentive viewers should find this to be a supreme example of highly artistic filmmaking.

WHAT AWARDS SHOULD THIS FILM HAVE WON?: The 1993 Oscar race was dominated by Steven Spielberg's excellent version of *Schindler's List,* which swept the Academy Awards with seven wins, including that of Best Picture. *Remains of the Day* was honored with eight nominations but came away with no wins. Ivory's film should have been awarded for its costuming and production design.

The performances by Anthony Hopkins and Emma Thompson were both Oscar-worthy, but both had received Oscars for films in the two preceding years, Hopkins for his stunning portrayal of Hannibal Lector in the 1991 film *The Silence of the Lambs,* and Thompson for her memorable role in James Ivory's 1992 film, *Howards End.*

OSCAR SNUB #43 – *NOBODY'S FOOL* (1994)

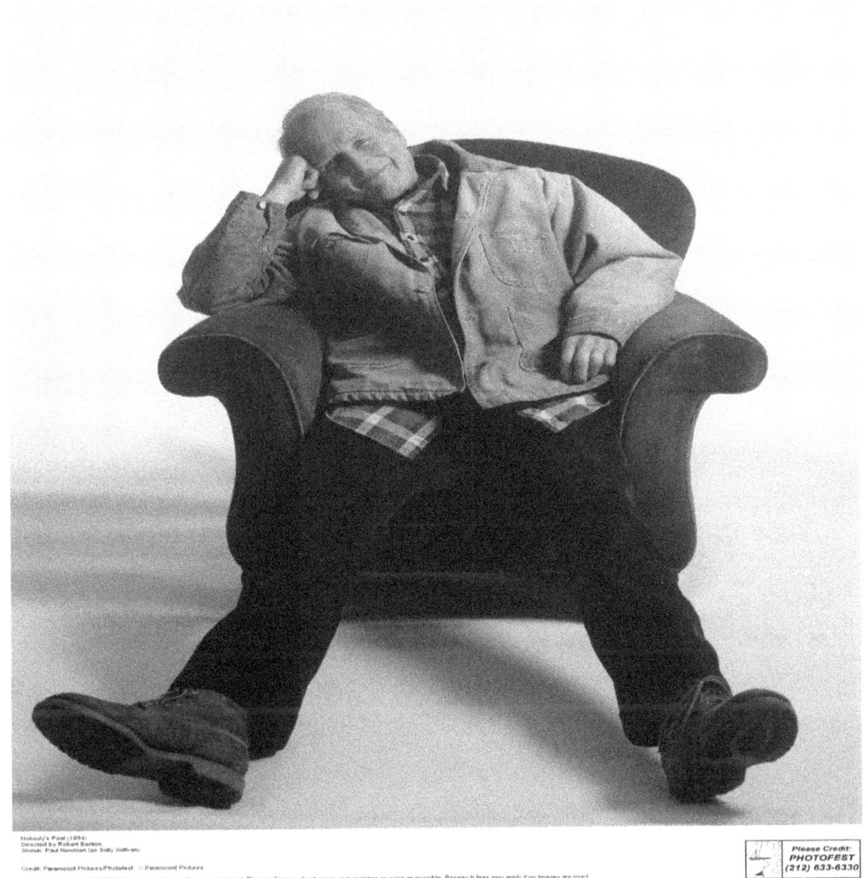

Director: Robert Benton; **Producer:** Scott Rudin and Arlene Donovan; **Studio:** Paramount; **Screenplay:** Robert Benton, from the novel by Richard Russo; **Cinematography:** John Bailey; **Production Design:** David Gropman; **Costume Design:** Joseph G. Aulisi; **Editing:** John Bloom; **Sound:** Maurice Schell; **Musical Score:**

Howard Shore; **Cast:** Paul Newman (Donald "Sully" Sullivan); Jessica Tandy (Miss Beryl Peoples); Bruce Willis (Carl Roebuck); Melanie Griffith (Toby Roebuck); Dylan Walsh (Peter Sullivan); Pruitt Taylor Vince (Rub Squeers); Gene Sax (Wirf); Phillip Seymour Hoffman (Officer Raymer); **Running Time:** 110 minutes.

BACKGROUND: Richard Russo is a reknowned American novelist who earned a Pulitzer Prize in 2002 for his novel *Empire Falls.* Nine years earlier filmmaker Robert Benton secured the film rights to Russo's 1993 novel *Nobody's Fool*, which is set in a fictional town in upstate New York, where the passage of time has witnessed both the decline of industry and the accompanying depletion of the area's financial stability.

Russo's characters are usually faced with personal problems that make their lives difficult. The story that Russo tells in *Nobody's Fool* is built around Donald "Sully" Sullivan, a sixty-year-old construction worker who has long been separated from his ex-wife and son, the latter of whom has a wife and two small children and seems headed in the same direction as his father. All the various people that Sully deals with have their own problems as they live from day to day.

PLOT: The film begins in North Bath, N.Y., on the day before Thanksgiving when Miss Beryl awakens her tenant (and former eighth-grade student) Sully with the news that a tree branch has fallen on a birdbath in a neighbor's yard and that God is zeroing in on her. After Sully refuses a cup of tea (which he seems to do every day), he departs for a court date to get compensated for a serious fall that occurred earlier while working for the Tip Top Construction Company.

Carl Roebuck, the company's owner, has refused to accept liability for the fall, but Sully's inept lawyer, known as Wirf, causes Sully to lose his case. Still, both Carl and Wirf later join Sully at their favorite hangout, the Iron Horse Café, where they play poker on a regular basis along with Sully's best friend, Rub Sweers, and also the local pharmacist and sheriff.

Despite Sully's spite for Carl, he agrees, as he has in the past, to work on a cash basis at one of Carl's properties. After Sully's truck breaks down, he surprisingly meets his son, Peter, whom Sully abandoned long ago when he left his wife, but stayed only a short distance from his family home. Peter and his wife and two sons have come to North Bath to have Thanksgiving dinner with Sully's ex-wife and her second husband. Sully shows up, but he only lasts long enough to witness his grandchildren getting into a chase that results in food dishes crashing on the floor.

A day later, Sully learns that his son's marriage is in peril when Peter says he and Will, the older boy, plan to stay around for a while. Soon Peter goes to work along with Sully in doing some demolition work on an old house. Peter also gets to see the house that Sully had grown up in and learns that Sully had a terrible upbringing because of his father's drinking.

Meanwhile, Miss Beryl's son, Clive, wants his mother to evict Sully, but Clive's financial difficulties over an amusement-park deal that would bring new jobs to the area goes under and Clive suddenly disappears.

Sully has a crush on Carl's wife, Toby, but when she finally decides to leave her unfaithful husband and go to Hawaii on a trip that Sully had earlier jokingly proposed, Sully declines the offer because of his newfound responsibilities in accepting the role of father and grandfather.

The film ends with Sully back at Miss Beryl's house, but he seems to have matured in some small ways, such as repairing the porch rail that Beryl has repeatedly been asking him to fix.

MEMORABLE MOMENTS: *Nobody's Fool* is filled with small moments that are infiltrated with clever dialogue, much of which comes out of Russo's novel. An early example comes when Miss Beryl asks Sully about having tea and he answers, "Not now, not ever." Later, when she finds out that Sully has stolen Carl's new snowblower out of spite, she says, "Donald, does it ever bother you that you haven't done more with the life God gave you," Sully answers, "Not often---now and then."

When Sully drops in on Toby when he's looking for her husband to get paid, she jokingly says that they should get some guns and rob banks like Bonnie and Clyde, Sully says that she would have to be Clyde because "I'm too tired."

One of the film's best scenes occurs when Toby breaks in on a poker game to announce that she has two tickets to Hawaii. Sully follows her to her car and kisses her as she prepares to drive away. The tears in her eyes speak volumes about their mutual feelings of regret when she understands why he can't go with her.

Despite Sully's seeming lack of responsibility, he does nice things for other people, such as confirming to Rub that, although Sully has developed feelings as a father and granddad, Rub is still his best friend. Sully also makes Peter call the latter's wife to patch up their relationship, and Sully also helps Will develop confidence by giving him an old stopwatch to count minutes during which Will must try to do something brave.

SUMMATION: The many small moments that involve Sully's interaction with the other characters in this often heartwarming story ultimately make *Nobody's Fool* a truly prizeworthy film. It includes one of the best roles in Paul Newman's long career and features notable supporting work by Melanie Griffith. Jessica Tancy's performance is memorable as the last in her long career. At the film's release shortly after her death in September, 1994, it was dedicated to her.

WHAT AWARDS SHOULD THIS FILM HAVE WON?: Despite Tom Hanks's win for Best Actor in *Forrest Gump,* I would have given the award to Paul Newman, who in many films gave performances in which he truly lived the characters he was playing. That aspect of his acting skill is never more visible than in *Nobody's Fool.*

OSCAR SNUB #44 – *THE SHAWSHANK REDEMPTION* (1994)

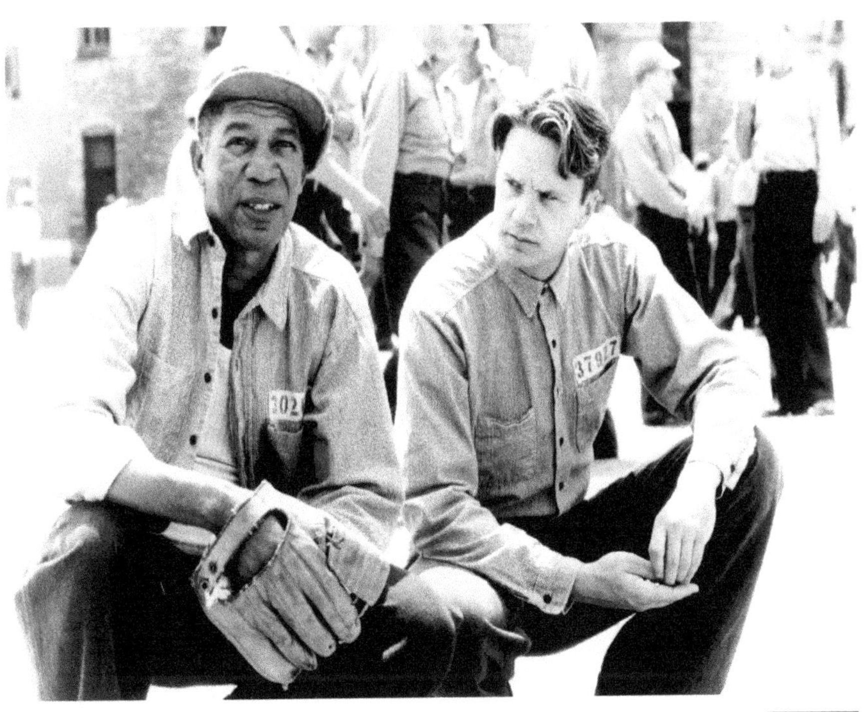

Director: Frank Darabont; **Producer:** Niki Marvin; **Studio:** Columbia; **Screenplay:** Frank Darabont, based on the story *Rita Hayworth and Shawshank Redemption* by Stephen King; **Cinematography:** Roger Deakins; **Production Design:** Terence Marsh; **Costume Design:** Elizabeth McBride; **Editing:** Richard Francis-Bruce; **Sound:** Robert J. Litt, Elliot Tyson, Michael Herbick, and Willie Burton; **Musical Score:** Thomas Newman; **Cast:** Tim Robbins (Andy Dufresne); Morgan Freeman (Ellis "Red" Redding); Bob Gunton (Warden Norton); William Sadler (Heywood); Clancy Brown (Captain

Hadley); Gil Bellows (Tommy); James Whitmore (Brooks Hatlen); **Running time:** 142 minutes.

BACKGROUND: For the past five decades Stephen King has been one of America's most popular writers. His thrillers, many of which are laced with supernatural elements, have routinely been on best-seller lists and have been adapted into movie box-office hits.

Shawshank Redemption is based on a story that first appeared in a collection of short novellas called *Different Seasons*, published in 1982. In King's story, which is set in Maine, a young bank employee is falsely accused of murdering his wife and her lover. After his conviction he is sent to Shawshank Prison, where he is able to use his financial skills in a variety of ways that includes helping prison officials and even the warden in filling out tax forms and setting up trust funds. His best friend is Red, a longtime inmate, con man, and convicted murderer.

PLOT: Andy arrives at Shawshank in 1947 and faces lots of brutality at the hands of other inmates. He also suffers beatings carried out by Captain Hadley, a guard whose violent behavior results at one point in the death of an inmate. Andy also has to deal with Warden Norton, who not only allows the beatings but manipulates Andy into supporting Norton's corrupt money laundering.

Andy's ally, Red Redding, helps Andy by getting him provisions through Red's secret trade deals that provide inmates with things they want. Through Red, Andy gets a large poster of Rita Hayworth to adorn a wall in his cell. More significantly, Andy also gets a small rock hammer for making chess pieces out of rock. Over a period of many years the hammer also becomes a valuable aid in Andy's escape from Shawshank in 1966.

MEMORABLE MOMENTS: The first part of the film includes scenes that may seem familiar to viewers who have watched earlier Hollywood films about prison life. But midway through *Shawshank* there are many scenes that are out of the ordinary. Some of these involve an elderly inmate named Brooks, who runs the prison's library and also pushes a book cart through the corridors to deliver books and also contraband.

When Andy gets moved out of the laundry and gets assigned as an assistant in the library he starts soliciting contributions by writing an endless stream of letters to get government grants and also charitable funding to expand the prison's library collection. At one point he receives a box of books and is told to stop soliciting, but Andy decides to double the number of letters.

According to Red, Brooks has become "institutionalized." After fifty years of incarceration Brooks is finally paroled, but life outside the prison has no meaning for him and he ultimately hangs himself in his small apartment. The last shot of the scene focuses on a support beam above which Brooks is sadly hanging that has words carved into it that read, "Brooks was here."

In a scene where Andy locks doors and broadcasts a recording of a duet from Mozart's opera *The Marriage of Figaro,* everyone gets to hear this lovely music. There is a memorable shot of the entire prison population standing transfixed in the yard as they listen to the recording.

Later, when Andy helps a young inmate named Tommy in getting a high-school diploma, there is an emotionally wrenching scene in which Warden Norton inquires about Tommy's knowledge concerning Andy's wrongful conviction. After Tommy reveals what he knows concerning the deaths of Andy's wife and her lover, Norton gives a signal for Hadley to shoot Tommy to death.

After Andy's escape there is a noteworthy scene in which a string of cop cars comes speeding to the prison to arrest the warden, whose corrupt financial dealings have been revealed in documents that Andy has mailed to the proper authorities. When Norton hears the sirens he takes a loaded gun and fatally shoots himself.

Andy escape scene is revealed after Norton's suicide, when Red, who has been narrating his relationship with Andy throughout the film, describes what he calls the "longest night of my life." Here the viewer gets to see Andy crawling through a hole in the wall of his cell that he made with his small rock hammer and going through the prison sanitation system. It is especially moving when Andy splashes through a creek, strips off his shirts, and stands with arms stretched out to feel the rain pouring down during a nighttime thunderstorm as he experiences his first taste of freedom in almost twenty years.

The last scenes are also memorable, when a year later Red gets paroled after forty years and finds Andy on a beach in Mexico.

SUMMATION: During its theatrical run in 1994 *Shawshank Redemption* was not a huge success with audiences, despite many favorable reviews. In the Oscar voting in early 1995 the film won six nominations, including citations for Best Picture and for Morgan Freeman's performance in the Best Actor category, but the film's makers came away empty-handed.

Through sales of copies of the film on videodiscs plus frequent showings on various TV channels, *Shawshank* began to gain a huge following, and today this film remains one of the most highly acclaimed films of the past thirty years.

WHAT AWARDS SHOULD THIS FILM HAVE WON?: In the 1994 Oscar race *Shawshank Redemption* lost in four categories to that year's big winner, *Forrest Gump.* Tom Hanks won over Morgan Freeman in the Best-Actor Category, while *Forrest Gump* also walked off with awards for Best Picture, Writing: Based on Material from Another Medium, and Film Editing.

I would definitely have awarded Oscars to *Shawshank Redemption* in the writing, editing, and musical-score categories. I would also have given Tim Robbins an acting nomination for his stellar work alongside Morgan Freeman, plus a belated supporting bid to James Whitmore, whose only nominations came in 1949 and 1974. His skillful playing of Brooks is a real asset to this film.

OSCAR SNUB #45 – *THE SIXTH SENSE* (1999)

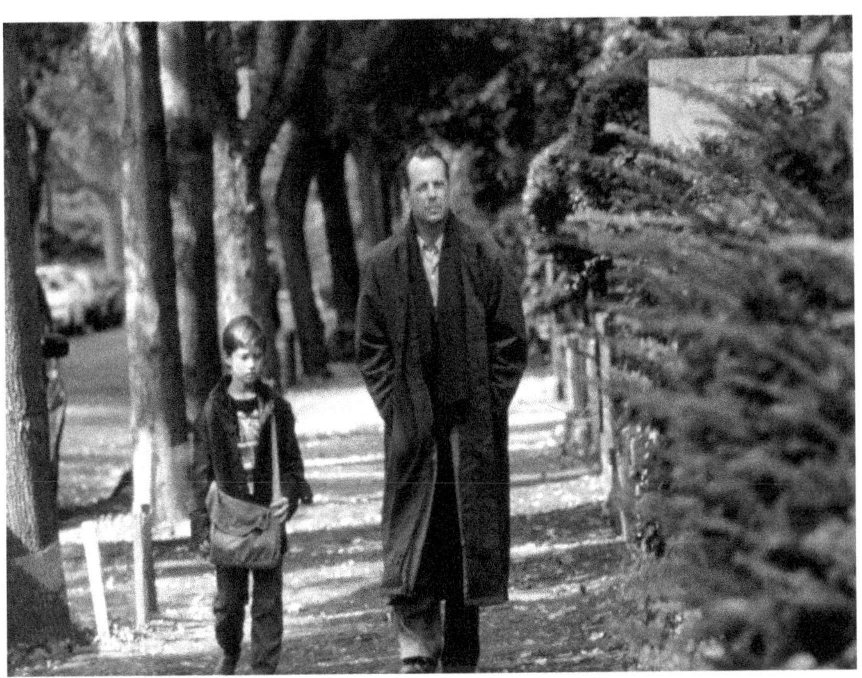

Director: M. Night Shyamalan; **Producer:** Frank Marshall, Kathleen Kennedy, and Barry Mendel; **Studio:** Buena Vista (through Disney); **Screenplay:** M. Night Shyamalan; **Cinematography:** Tak Fujimoto; **Production Design:** Larry Fulton; **Costume Design:** Joanna Johnston; **Editor:** Andrew Mondschein; **Sound Mixing:** Allen Byer; **Musical Score:** James Newton Howard; **Cast:** Bruce Willis (Malcolm Crowe); Haley Joel Osment (Cole Sear); Toni Collette (Lynn Sear); Olivia Williams (Anna Crowe); Trevor

Morgan (Tommy Tammissimo); Donnie Wahlberg (Vincent Gray); M. Night Shyamalan (Dr. Hill); **Running Time:** 107 minutes.

BACKGROUND: For much of the past three decades India-born director and screenwriter M. Night Shyamalan has been a major filmmaker. His parents, both of whom are doctors, moved to the U.S. when Shyamalan was an infant. As a teenager in the 1980s he used a Super 8 camera to make over forty short films. In 1992, the year he graduated from New York University, he made his first professional movie, *Praying with Anger* followed a few years later by *Wide Awake.*

Shyamalan would soon become a major force in filmmaking when the Disney company financially backed a supernatural thriller named *The Sixth Sense* that he both wrote and directed. This film became the second-biggest box-office hit of 1999 and earned six Oscar nominations, including nods for Best Picture, Best Director, and Shyamalan's original screenplay. Although he was snubbed in all of these categories, he went on to make several more successful psychological thrillers, including *Unbreakable* (2000), *Signs* (1002), and *The Village* (2004).

Shyamalan's subsequent career has had its ups and downs, but in 2024 his cleverly scripted film *Trap* showed signs of a critical and box-office resurgence.

PLOT: Dr. Malcolm Crowe is a successful child psychologist who has just won a major award from the city of Philadelphia for his work. Following the award ceremony, while he and wife Anna are celebrating at their home, they find that Vincent Gray, one of Crowe's former patients, has broken in and appears to be in a very distressed state of mind. Before Crowe can stop him, Vincent points a gun at him, fires once, and then turns the gun on himself. Anna comforts her husband, who appears to be seriously wounded but still alive.

In subsequent scenes Crowe, in a possible attempt to atone for his failure to sense Vincent's suicidal behavior, visits Cole Sear, a troubled boy around the age of nine who lives with his single mother. Crowe's efforts to help Cole are at first of little value, but after Cole is abused by

Tommy, a fellow classmate at the school they both attend, Crowe learns the reason for Cole's state of mind when the boy tells him that he sees dead people that do not know they are dead and seem to wander around aimlessly.

Crowe helps Cole in dealing with his ghostly visitations by helping the boy to realize these apparitions are possible attempts by the deceased to resolve issues associated with their deaths. Crowe's friendly intercession also helps Cole's mother in dealing with her son's troubles.

MEMORABLE MOMENTS: The opening scene is quite shocking, since Vincent's sudden appearance comes without warning and his hysterical ranting is truly upsetting, especially when he yells at Malcolm, "You failed me!" The subsequent shooting is even more shocking.

A later scene in which Cole and his mother are invited to a friend's birthday party includes a highly dramatic moment when Tommy, who likes to bully other kids, drags Cole to a walk-in closet and locks him in. When Lynn hears her son's screaming she runs up the stairs and frantically tries to break into the closet to rescue her son.

In the following scene, when Crowe visits Cole in a hospital room where the boy has been placed for observation, Cole whispers to Crowe, "I see dead people." He also indicates that he sees them all the time and that they often appear angry. Crowe suggests that they might be trying to undo some grievous wrong committed against them.

In a later scene Crowe finds a way to help Cole by accompanying him to the home of Kyra, a little girl who has just passed away. Through Crowe's encouragement Cole visits the spirit of Kyra in her bedroom and then receives a box from her to take to her grieving father who is downstairs at a post-funeral reception. Through video footage that Kyra has secretly taken, the father learns that his wife had repeatedly added a potentially harmful liquid to the milk that Kyra was given on her food tray. When the truth comes out and the wife stands accused, Cole is comforted by the awareness that Kyra's death has been explained.

For much of the film Cole's mother suffers from her suspicion that Cole has a mental disorder, but while the two of them are stuck in her car due to a traffic accident that has blocked the road ahead of them, Cole tells her about his ghostly apparitions, and that her deceased mother has visited him to relay the message that grandma was always proud of her daughter. This revelation leads to a tender embrace between mother and child.

Crowe also finds a peaceful reconciliation with his wife, who has been distraught ever since the night that her husband was shot. Viewers need to be aware that Shyamalan's script contains a surprise twist that should startle those that see this film for the first time.

SUMMATION: Shyamalan's film includes shock moments that are greatly enhanced by the scoring of James Newton Howard, whose musical punctuations accompany the visions that Cole experiences and add tension that should keep viewers on edge.

Sixth Sense can seem like a throwback to horror films of the 1950s in which scary moments appear without warning. Yet Shyamalan's skillful use of these moments increases the impact of *Sixth Sense* from the start. Viewers might dismiss the plot of this film as contrived, yet there is something about its overall impact that makes *Sixth Sense* one of the most memorable horror films ever made.

WHAT AWARDS SHOULD THIS FILM HAVE WON?: Horror films have almost never won Academy Awards. The only exception is Jonathan Demme's masterfully directed 1991 film *Silence of the Lambs.* Yet *The Sixth Sense* includes such an ingeniously conceived story, with a memorably understated performance by Bruce Willis and fine acting by Haley Joel Osment, that the film should have won Oscars for its screenplay and Osment's nominated performance.

OSCAR SNUB #46 – *GOOD NIGHT, AND GOOD LUCK.* (2005)

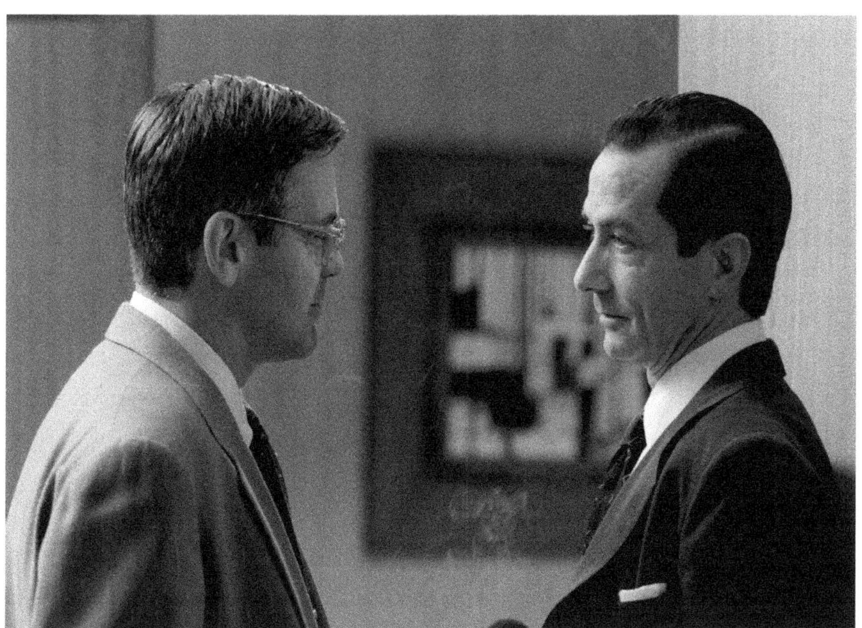

Good Night, And, Good Luck (2005)
Written & Directed by George Clooney
Shown from left: George Clooney (as Fred Friendly), David Strathairn (as Edward R. Murrow)
Credit: Warner Bros./Photofest © Warner Bros. Photographer: Melinda Sue Gordon

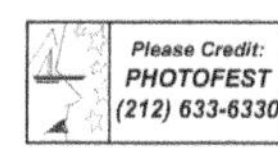

Director: George Clooney; **Producer:** Grant Heslov; **Studio:** Warner Independent Pictures; **Screenplay:** George Clooney and Grant Heslov; **Cinematography:** Robert Elswit; **Production Design:** Jim Bissell; **Costume Design:** Louise Frogley; **Editing:** Steven Mirrione; **Sound Editing:** Aaron Glasscock and Curt Schulkey; **Musical Score:** Jim Papoulis; **Cast:** David Straithairn (Edward R. Murrow); George Clooney (Fred Friendly); Jeff Daniels (Sam Mickelson); Patricia Clarkson (Shirley Wershba); Robert Downey, Jr, (Joe Wershba); Frank Langella (William S. Paley); **Running time:** 93 minutes.

BACKGROUND: By the time he co-wrote and directed *Good Night, and Good Luck.,* George Clooney had come a long way from being the young actor who had appeared in countless TV shows in the 1980s and 1990s. His breakthrough role came when he was cast as Dr. Doug Ross in the NBC hit series *ER*, which made its debut in the fall of 1994.

Following his departure from the show after the first five of its fourteen seasons, he soon became a major film star with such successful movies as *Three Kings* (1999), *O Brother, Where Art Thou?* (2000), the remake of *Oceans Eleven* (2001), plus sequels to this last film in 2004 and 2007. In 2002 he made his directing debut with *Confessions of a Dangerous Mind,* which led to *Good Night, and Good Luck.,* for which he won nominations as director and co-screenwriter in 2005. That same year, he also won an Oscar for his supporting role in *Syriana.*

The screenplay of *Good Night, and Good Luck* takes an unusual approach as a biographical film about the renowned CBS reporter and TV host Edward R. Murrow. It focuses on just a few months, from late 1953 into early 1954, during which time Murrow used his weekly show *See It Now* to counter the accusations of communism made by Joseph McCarthy.

The Wisconsin senator became notoriously known for his attempts to expose supposed infiltration by Communist sympathizers in the U.S. military and in the entertainment media. Murrow was at the forefront of those who resented McCarthy's blatant attempts to ruin the careers of people he recklessly accused of being members of the Communist Party.

PLOT: *Good Night, and Good Luck.,* the title of which is taken from Murrow's signature sign-off words from his radio and TV programs, is framed by a speech that Murrow gave on October 25, 1958, when he was presented with a prestigious award by an organization of radio and TV dignitaries during a banquet held in Chicago.

The film then goes back to October 14, 1953, when Murrow and his production team discuss topics for upcoming segments of *See It Now.* During their meeting they discuss a disturbing report about an Air Force lieutenant named Milo Radulovich who has been relieved of military duty because his father and sister have been accused of being communist sympathizers. Murrow uses his program as a means of refuting the accusations brought by McCarthy.

Much of the film concerns Murrow's meetings with members of the CBS staff, including producer Fred Friendly, news director Sam Mickelson, and CBS president William S. Paley, and others, in dealing with McCarthy's ruthless methods used in exposing supposed communists.

Following the announcement that Radulovich has been reinstated in his military position, Murrow hosts a segment of *See It Now* focused on McCarthy and announces that the senator will have a chance to respond to Murrow's statements on a later telecast.

After this program airs on April 6, 1954, Murrow spends the next segment of his show giving damning evidence that McCarthy's anti-communist crusade is deeply flawed by its blatantly untrue statements about those the senator has targeted.

The film ends with Murrow concluding the speech he gave in Chicago in 1958.

MEMORABLE MOMENTS: In an early scene, when Murrow and Friendly are planning the program that aims to defend Lt. Radulovich against McCarthy's accusations, the two newsmen agree to work together, even though Friendly has misgivings. Murrow kiddingly calls him a coward, and then Friendly responds by saying "better yellow than red."

At the end of the *See It Now* program that focuses on Radulovich's plight, after Murrow signs off with his signature words, "Good night, and Good luck," he says to a staff member, "No one should be condemned for the sins of the father."

When McCarthy is offered the opportunity to respond to this program, the film uses archival footage of the senator for his rebuttal. It is distressing to watch the real McCarthy making so many outrageous comments that form his presentation. No actor could have played the role of McCarthy in this film as vividly as the senator himself.

When cuts to the news staff are announced by CBS President Paley, Joe and Shirley Wershba, who realize that their marriage violates company rules, discuss at home whether he should resign. She quips that someone may be listening to her phone calls behind her back. When Joe asks who that is Shirley says, "Chairman Mao."

At the end of the film, when Murrow is back in Chicago making his speech, he concludes with these memorable words about television: "This instrument can teach, it can illuminate, and yes it can even inspire. But it can do so only to the extent that humans are determined to use it towards those ends. Otherwise it is merely wires and lights in a box. Good night, and good luck."

SUMMATION: George Clooney's film is a perceptive look at the McCarthy era as reflected in the efforts by Edward R. Murrow in countering McCarthy's persecution of so many people in the early 1950s.

This film promotes the moral responsibility of people in public life, whether government officials or those working in radio, TV, and movies, in seeking truth, rather than accepting false and potentially harmful information without the use of proper background checking.

Good Night, and Good Luck is extremely well-made, with an intriguing series of performances by singer Dianne Reeves and a small jazz combo of such standards as "How High the Moon" and "When I Fall in Love" that punctuate the film at various times.

WHAT AWARDS SHOULD THIS FILM HAVE WON?: 2005 was a strong movie year, with *Brokeback Mountain* and *Crash*, the winner, competing for Best Picture. *Good Night* should have been awarded for its excellent cinematography and production design, while Clooney and Heslov deserved Oscars for their screenplay. Additionally, Straithairn was snubbed for his performance. He truly brought Murrow's persona to life onscreen.

OSCAR SNUB #47 – *INTO THE WILD* (2007)

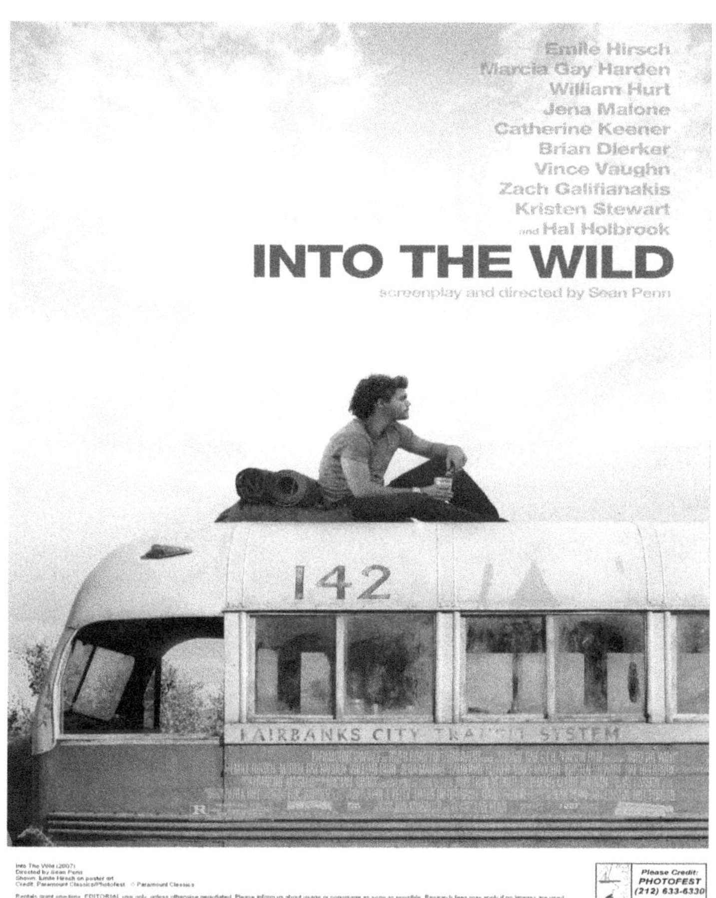

Director: Sean Penn; **Producer:** Art Linson, Bill Pohlad, and Sean Penn; **Studio:** Paramount Advantage; **Screenplay:** Sean Penn, based on the book by Jon Krakauer; **Cinematography:** Eric Gautier; **Production Design:** Derek R. Hill; **Costume Design:** Mary Claire Hannan; **Editing:** Jay Cassidy; **Sound Design:** Martin

Hernandez; **Musical Score:** Michael Brook, Kaki King, and Eddie Vetter; **Cast:** Emile Hirsch (Chris McCandless); Marcia Gay Harden (Billie McCandless); William Hurt (Walt McCandless); Jena Malone (Carine McCandless); Brian Dierker (Rainey); Catherine Keeler (Jan Burres); Vince Vaughn (Wayne Westerberg); Kristen Stewart (Tracy Tatro); Hal Holbrook (Ron Franz); **Running Time:** 148 minutes.

BACKGROUND: Sean Penn has had a very successful career as both an actor and a director. From his hilarious early role in *Fast Times at Ridgemont High* in 1982, Penn quickly earned respect for his acting skills and won Oscars for his leading roles in *Mystic River* (2003) and *Milk* (2008), in the latter of which he played the gay San Francisco city supervisor Harvey Milk.

Penn has also received recognition for directing, with *Into the Wild* being the most lauded example of his directing career.

In 1996 author Jon Krakauer wrote a fascinating book about Chris McCandless, a young man who, upon graduating in 1990 from Emory University in Atlanta, disposed of all his ID and credit cards, gave his life savings to charity, and took off from Atlanta in his used Datsun to explore Alaska. Two years later, his body was discovered in a discarded school bus in a remote region of the 50th state where he had been living for several months.

Penn's film is a meticulously produced version of McCandless's adventures in the wild.

PLOT: The film, as narrated by Chris's devoted younger sister, Carine, begins with Chris being dropped off at the end of a remote road west of Fairbanks. Chris continues on foot until he finds the bus that becomes his temporary home.

The film then goes back two years to Chris's graduation from Emory, and his subsequent actions in abandoning his family and setting out on a cross-country journey in his old car.

After a flash flood makes the Datsun undriveable, Chris continues his trek by hitching a ride with a hippie couple, Jan and Rainey, with whom Chris spends time before setting out again.

Chris then works as a harvester in Carthage, South Dakota, and later paddles a kayak down the Colorado River, has a short stay south of the Mexican border, and then hops on northbound trains in order to move closer to Alaska.

Along his journey he makes friends, including Jan and Rainey in California, Wayne Westerberg, who owns the harvesting company in South Dakota, and especially Ron Franz, an elderly man in Northern California whose fondness for Chris leads him to drive Chris to the Canadian border. Chris then hitches rides to reach his destination.

Chris adapts well to living alone in the wild, but when he mistakenly eats from a plant that he later learns is considered inedible, his error leads to a tragic end to his Alaskan adventure.

MEMORABLE MOMENTS: When Chris (now calling himself Alexander Supertramp) spends time with Jan and Rainey along the California coast, Chris says some insightful things that help Rainey improve his relationship with Jan, who has been wandering alone in the surf. Chris then chases after her, and although he has admitted his fear of water, he strips off his clothes and joyfully splashes in the ocean with Jan. The big smile on his face insightfully suggests that he has found meaning in leaving behind the life that his parents had planned for him.

During one of Carine's narrations, she reveals that a possible reason for Chris's abandonment of his family stems from his belated awareness that their father was still married to his first wife when they were born. In a distressing flashback, Walt and Billie, their biological mother, are fighting, with Walt physically abusing her. According to Carine, Chris never told his parents that he knew the truth about Walt's first marriage.

There is a joyful moment when Chris is kayaking in the Colorado River and survives a perilous stretch of rapids. When the waters become calm, he raises his arms and breaks out in a huge smile after battling with the wild for the first time.

A similar moment occurs later when Chris stands on top of the abandoned bus and happily stretches out his arms.

When Chris spends time in a nomad camp called Slab City, he meets a teenage girl who sings at a gathering while he accompanies her on a keyboard. Afterwards, she offers herself to him, but he declines and then gives her some friendly advice by saying, "Just remember, if you want something in life, just reach out and grab it." At this point he leaves her teary-eyed.

When Chris gets Ron to climb a huge hill, they sit together and Ron tries to mollify Chris's anger about his parents by saying, "When you forgive, you love, and when you love, God's light shines on you."

SUMMATION: Even though the story of *Into the Wild* moves in a non-chronological way, the adventures that Chris experiences and the people he befriends along his journey make for a truly memorable film. Penn's screenplay is faithful to Krakauer's book, and most viewers by the end of the film should reach the conclusion that Chris's abandonment of family, although selfish in many ways, may be seen as a reckless but heroic attempt to live by simple means without being pinned down by society's conventional rules. Not everyone will agree with Chris McCandless's choices, but he deserves credit for trying to find himself through his journey into the wild.

WHAT AWARDS SHOULD THIS FILM HAVE WON?: In my estimation, *Into the Wild* is a better film than the five nominees for 2007's Best Picture. It surpasses *Atonement, Juno, Michael Clayton, There Will Be Blood*, and especially the winner, *No Country for Old Men*, the Coen Brothers' violent tale of stolen drug money and a cold-blooded revenge killer. Sean Penn deserved awards for both his direction and screenplay, and *Into the Wild* should have received a nomination for Best Picture along with a nod to Emile Hirsh for his star-making performance.

OSCAR SNUB #48 – *DOUBT* (2008)

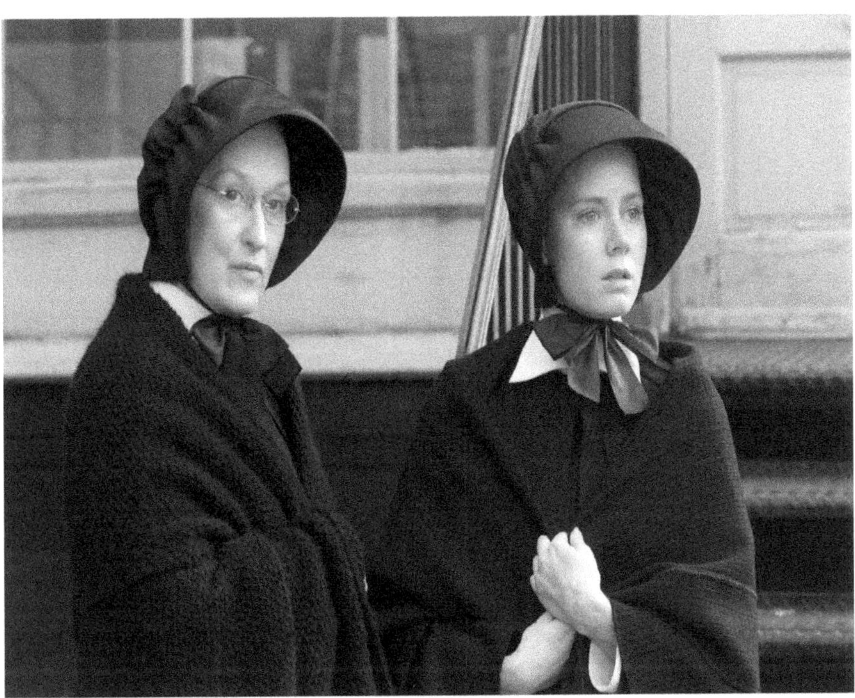

Director: John Patrick Shanley; **Producer:** Scott Rudin and Mark Roybal; **Studio:** Miramax Films; **Screenplay:** John Patrick Shanley, based on his stage play; **Cinematography:** Roger Deakins; **Production Design:** David Gropman; **Costume Design:** Ann Roth; **Editing:** Dylan Tichenor; **Sound Mixing:** Danny Michael; **Musical Score:** Howard Shore; **Cast:** Meryl Streep (Sr. Aloysius Beauvier); Phillip Seymour Hoffman (Fr. Brendan Flynn); Amy Adams (Sr. James); Viola Davis (Mrs. Miller); Joseph Foster (Donald Miller);

Mike Roukis (William London); Lloyd Clay Brown (Jimmy Hurley); **Running Time:** 103 minutes

BACKGROUND: John Patrick Shanley, an award-winning writer, playwright, and director, became known in 1987 for his Oscar-winning screenplay of Norman Jewison's *Moonstruck.* Since then, Shanley has written scripts for several other films, plus over twenty plays for the New York stage. The most celebrated of these plays is *Doubt: A Parable,* which won Shanley both a Tony Award and the Pulitzer Prize in 2005. The film version, which Shanley also directed, was released in 2008.

For *Doubt,* Shanley created a story based on memories of his own Catholic upbringing. Both the play and the film adaptation take place at St. Nicholas, a Catholic parish in the Bronx in the months following the John F. Kennedy assassination in November of 1963. The church's pastor, Fr. Flynn, wants to make changes inspired by the Vatican Council that was going on at that time, while the school's principal, Sr. Aloysius, is an old-school nun who uses scare tactics to maintain her authority. It is not surprising that these two very different people will clash and that the nun will try anything to get the priest removed from his post.

PLOT: Donald Miller is an eighth-grader and the first Black student to attend St Nicholas Parish school. In the film's opening scene, after Donald performs his assigned duties as an altar server for the morning Mass, a janitor reports to Fr. Flynn that Donald has been drinking altar wine. Flynn tries to keep this news private because it could cause the boy to be excluded from the alter-boy roster.

Due to Donald being picked on by some of the other students, Flynn has been friendly toward him. However, when news of the altar wine gets to Sr. Aloysius, the school's principal, she starts spreading rumors that Flynn is molesting the boy. Sr. James, a young nun newly assigned to the parish as a teacher, becomes a ploy in Sr. Aloysius's plot to have Flynn removed from the parish.

MEMORABLE MOMENTS: During the morning Mass that occurs in the opening scene, while Fr. Flynn is giving his sermon, the viewer gets the first glimpse of Sr. Aloysius in her black habit and head covering as she slowly moves along an outer aisle of the church to discipline children who are not paying attention or are asleep. With whispers and hand gestures she makes them sit up straight.

During the homily, which addresses the issue of doubt, Flynn uses a hypothetical situation to convey his message. He refers to a cargo ship that founders and leaves one lone sailor to navigate his way in a small lifeboat back to dry land. Flynn questions whether the sailor will survive by saying, "Doubt can be a bond as powerful and sustaining as certainty. When you are lost, you are not alone." With this enigmatic statement the sermon ends.

A sign that there is a big difference between the priests and the nuns at St. Nicholas comes during an evening meal when Flynn is eating with two other clergymen and laughing as they share raucous jokes. The film then shifts to the convent where Sr. Aloysius sits at the head of a dinner table while the other nuns, most of them of advanced age, eat in total silence and without smiling. Sr. Aloysius finally starts questioning the sermon Flynn had given that morning. Her displeasure with Flynn's sailor story is evident.

When Donald's mother is invited to St. Nicholas to talk with Sr. Aloysius, the conversation quickly turns to Fr. Flynn's supposed fondness for Donald. Mrs. Miller's pleas on behalf of her son fall on deaf ears, even though Donald is described as troubled, and frequently beaten by his father for behaving in a possibly effeminate manner.

Mrs. Miller's emotional distress is quite moving when she emphasizes the need to keep Donald in the parish school and get good enough grades that he can attend a decent high school. Sr. Aloysius's failure to get Mrs. Miller to support her plan against Flynn is troubling to view.

The confrontational scene in the principal's office is highly dramatic, especially when Flynn realizes there is nothing he can do to stop Sr. Aloysius from pursuing her plot against him. The shouting match in this scene is especially disturbing since these two people represent religious leaders who ostensibly should be devoted to extending kindness to others rather than resentment.

SUMMATION: *Doubt* needs to be watched attentively, especially in scenes where bursts of wind scatter leaves in ways that symbolize the spread of rumors.

The film's setting in the winter months keeps the visual style of the film very bleak and lacking color. This starkness plays visually into the film's central story of personal conflict.

One of *Doubt*'s greatest assets is the acting that drives the story forward. The female players are all outstanding, with Streep giving a chilling portrait of a nun who wants control at any price and resents the pastor of the parish for daring to challenge his congregation with moral questions that demand people to think for themselves.

Amy Adams is also excellent as the young nun who acts as a bridge between Flynn and Sr. Aloysius but doesn't have the power to effectively interfere with Sr. Aloysius's eviction plan.

The film's most outstanding performance is that of Viola Davis in one extended scene, where her painful reaction to Sr. Aloysius's determined effort to convince her that Flynn is molesting her son brings her to tears.

Hoffman handles his scenes with Streep in excellent fashion, although the selection of this actor seems curious since the priest is very Irish in Shanley's original play. Despite this concern, *Doubt* is still a truly memorable viewing experience.

WHAT AWARDS SHOULD THIS FILM HAVE WON?: *Doubt* should have won an Oscar for Shanley's adaptation of his play, and Viola Davis was unfairly snubbed as a Supporting-Actress nominee. The film itself should have been among the five Best-Picture nominees.

OSCAR SNUB #49 – *NEBRASKA* (2013)

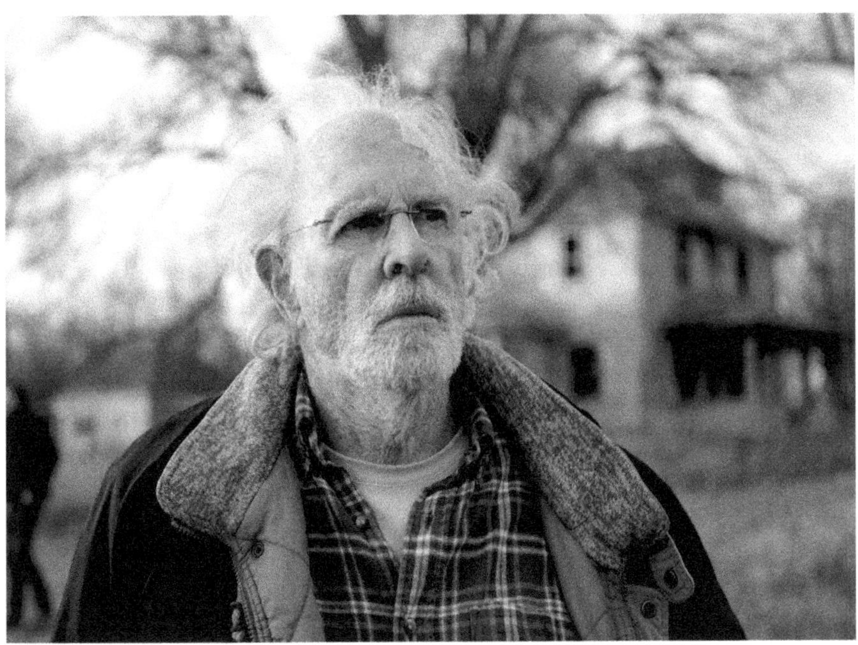

Nebraska (2013)
Directed by Alexander Payne
Shown: Bruce Dern
Credit: Paramount Pictures/Photofest © Paramount Pictures

Director: Alexander Payne; **Producer:** Albert Berger and Ron Yerxa; **Studio:** Paramount Vantage; **Screenplay:** Bob Nelson; **Cinematography:** Phedon Papamichael; **Production Design:** Dennis Washington; **Costume Design:** Wendy Chuck; **Editing:** Kevin Tent; **Sound Editor:** Joe Lemola; **Musical Score:** Mark Orton; **Cast:** Bruce Dern (Woody Grant); Will Forte (David Grant); June Squib (Kate Grant); Bob Odenkirk (Ross Grant); Stacey Keach (Ed Pegram); Mary Louise Wilson (Aunt Martha); Tim Driscoll (Bart); Devin Ratray (Cole); **Running Time:** 115 minutes.

BACKGROUND: Since graduating from UCLA with a Master of Arts degree in 1990, Alexander Payne has gradually earned a place of distinction among Hollywood filmmakers. Beginning in 1996 with *Citizen Ruth*, a scathing satire about abortion issues, Payne has made such prominent works as *Election* (1999), *About Schmidt* (2002), *Sideways* (2004), and *The Descendants* (2011). By 2013, when he directed *Nebraska,* he had already won an Academy Award for the screenplay of *Sideways* and was on his way towards his third nomination as a director.

The characters in Payne's films often face problems in their lives, as in *About Schmidt,* in which Jack Nicholson plays a man who has just lost his wife, or in *Descendants,* in which George Clooney stars as a man whose wife lies in a coma. In *Nebraska*, Bruce Dern's character, Woody Grant, is an elderly retired auto mechanic who is in the beginning stages of Alzheimers. His long-suffering wife, Kate, and his older son, Ross, want to put Woody in a nursing home, but his younger son, Will, feels that his father should be allowed to remain in the home he has lived in for most of his married life.

PLOT: As in several other Payne films, *Nebraska* is set in and around the Midwestern state that provides the film's title. In this case, the family that is portrayed actually lives in Billings, Montana, but travels East towards Lincoln, Nebraska, where Woody is determined to collect a million-dollar prize that he thinks he has been awarded by a certificate he has received from a company that deals in magazine subscriptions.

Neither Will nor Kate can convince Woody that this letter is not an actual prize-winning document, and Woody makes more than one attempt to leave the house and walk all the way to Lincoln. Will finally agrees to humor his father by saying that he will drive Woody to the address in Lincoln where he can collect his presumed award.

While they are on route, Will decides to stop along the way because the office in Lincoln won't be open until the next Monday morning. They make arrangements to stop in the town of Hawthorne (a fictionally named town about 200 miles west of Lincoln. which is where Woody was born and where his brother, Albert, and Will's Aunt Martha live.

During their stay, in which they are joined by several other members of Woody's extended family, including several of his brothers, the entire family finds out about Woody's supposed good fortune and the entire town thinks of Woody as a celebrity. Things get further complicated when some of Woody's relatives and old friends think he should share his fortune with them.

When Woody finally accepts the truth about his award letter, Will arranges to trade in his car for a well-maintained five-year-old truck and gives his father ownership of it.

MEMORABLE MOMENTS: After leaving Montana on the way to Nebraska, Will stops near Rapid City, South Dakota, so he and Woody can have a look at Mount Rushmore. When Woody sees the stone carvings he exclaims, "Washington is the only with any clothes; they are just kinda roughed in. Lincoln doesn't even have an ear."

While staying in Hawthorne they go into a bar, and after several beers Will argues that Woody is having too much to drink. Woody's response is, "You would too if you were married to your mother."

After Kate arrives by bus, they go to a cemetery where several of their kin are buried. At one point Kate views the various plots of her Catholic relatives and ponders their proximity to those of Woody's family and says, "I wouldn't be caught dead around all those damn Lutherans."

While at his sister's home, Woody says he wants to go to Lincoln right away. Will tries to convince him to stay and visit with relatives that he hasn't seen in ages by saying that all his brothers will be there. When Woody says that some of them are dead, Will encouragingly says, "The dead ones won't be here."

When they visit the house in Hawthorne where Woody grew up and look into the bedroom that Woody's parents had occupied, Woody remembers his father saying he would whip him if he ever went in. Woody then looks around and says, "Well I guess nobody's gonna whip me now."

After will and Ross steal an air compressor they mistakenly think was stolen by Woody's business partner and nemesis, Ed Pegram, Kate says, "What do you want to do now? Bust into a silo and steal some corn?"

The closing scene is very touching, when Will lets his father drive the new truck past the people in Hawthorne who have wanted some of Woody's prize money. As they reach the edge of town, Will trades places with Woody and drives them back to Billings. The film ends with the truck moving down the road until it is almost out of sight.

SUMMATION: *Nebraska* is a film filled with special moments. Despite Kate's endless stream of complaints about Woody and almost everybody else in the film, there is a basic air of tenderness, especially with Will, who claims that Woody is not crazy and volunteers to drive him to Lincoln.

The attempted bonding between Will and his dad may seem like a small thing, but it is a reminder that kindness among family members should not be undervalued. Will has failed in a personal relationship with a woman he has been living with for two years, and now he has a chance to mend fences with his father. This bonding makes *Nebraska* a memorable family portrait.

WHAT AWARDS SHOULD THIS FILM HAVE WON?: Among the ten nominees for Best Picture, *Nebraska* stands out as one of the very best films of 2013. At the very least it should have won awards for its cleverly-worded screenplay and insightful direction, and should have also received a richly-deserved award for Phedon Papamichael's brilliant black-and white cinematography.

OSCAR SNUB #50 – *HIDDEN FIGURES* (2016)

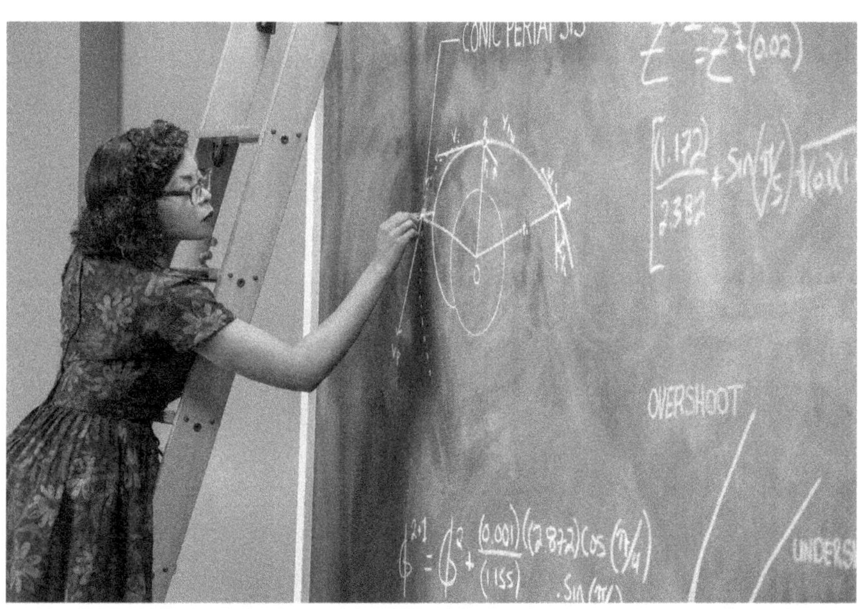

Hidden Figures (2016)
Directed by Theodore Melfi
Shown: Taraji P. Henson (as Katherine Johnson)
Credit: Twentieth Century Fox Film Corporation/Photofest © Twentieth Century Fox Film Corporation

Director: Theodore Melfi; **Producer:** Donna Gigliotti, Peter Chernin, Jenno Topping, Pharrell Williams, and Theodore Melfi; **Studio:** Fox 2000 Pictures; **Screenplay:** Allison Schroeder and Theodore Melfi, based on the book by Margot Lee Shetterly; **Cinematography:** Mandy Walker; **Production Design:** Wynn Thomas; **Costume Design:** Renée Ehrlich Kalfus; **Editing:** Peter Teschner; **Sound Editing:** Derek Vanderhorst and Wayne Lemmer; **Musical Score:** Hans Zimmer, Pharrell Williams, and Benjamin Wallfisch; **Cast:** Taraji P. Henson (Katherine Johnson); Octavia Spencer (Dorothy Vaughan), Janelle Monáe (Mary Jackson); Kevin Costner (Al

Harrison); Kirsten Dunst (Vivian Mitchell); Mahershala Ali (Colonel Jim Johnson); Jim Parsons (Paul Stafford); Glenn Powell (Colonel John Glenn); **Running time: 127** minutes.

BACKGROUND: On May 25, 1961, just four months into his presidency, John Kennedy announced in a speech before Congress that there would be an American on the moon by the end of the decade. The subsequent "race for space" was one of the top stories of the decade as the Russians had already succeeded in getting a Soviet astronaut named Yuri Gagarin into space on April 12, 1961.

The story of how America gained the lead in this unauthorized race was well told in a 1979 non-fiction book by Tom Wolfe named *The Right Stuff*. Four years later Warner Bros. released a brilliant film adaptation of Wolfe's book that won four Academy Awards but was snubbed in the Best Picture category.

The 2016 film *Hidden Figures* covers much of the same story as the earlier book and film, but with one major difference. Whereas *The Right Stuff* focuses primarily on the seven young American pilots who were selected as the Mercury-program astronauts, *Hidden Figures* is a behind-the-scenes version of the space race that is centered around the work of three brilliantly talented mathematics wizards who happen to all be black woman who work for the National Aeronautics and Space Administration through the Langley Memorial Aeronautical Laboratory in Langley, Virginia. The film insightfully shows the ways in which these three brave women endure prejudice because of both their gender and their color in getting Americans into space.

PLOT: The film begins with a prelude set in 1926 featuring Katherine Goble as a sixth grader at an all-Black elementary school who shows an extraordinary skill with math. In the very next scene, which takes place in 1961, Katherine is on route to Langley with her two best friends, Dorothy Vaughan and Mary Jackson, who are also math wizards. When their car breaks down on the way to work, a white police officer skeptically makes them identify themselves, but he winds up obligingly leading them to Langley at break-neck speed.

Hidden Figures portrays the difficulties these three women face when they are placed in an otherwise all-white work environment. Dorothy is doing the work of a supervisor of her work group without being officially named as head of her department. Meanwhile, Mary is praised by her peers as a talented engineer, but she can't get the courses she needs in order to join the engineering group because they are offered only at an all-white school. Katherine is invited to join an advanced mathematical team, but as the only woman in the room – and black woman as well, she feels the awkwardness in being among male employees who resent her very presence.

Hidden Figures revolves around these three women who collectively made an outstanding contribution to the NASA space program.

MEMORABLE MOMENTS: In an early scene, When Katherine first arrives at her new workspace, Al Harrison, her supervisor, is unhappy that their new IBM computer has not been installed yet. He angrily comments, "Space is a business. I need a mathematician. When are we going to find such a person before the Russians put a damn flag on the moon?" The irony here is that Katherine is standing right next to Al when he spouts off.

When Al hears that the Russian cosmonaut Yuri Gagarin has just gone into space he lashes out, "How the hell did we find ourself [sic] in second place in a two-man race?"

Later, when Dorothy starts privately studying the manual that came with the new IBM machine, she looks directly at the machine and says," "You have a brain. That I can work with."

Another noteworthy moment comes when Al scolds Katherine for taking forty-minute breaks so she can use the bathroom. She then yells in front of the entire room by telling him that the nearest bathroom for colored girls is on another campus a half-mile away. In her words," I work like a dog day and night, living off coffee from a pot none of you want to touch." She then rails against having to go such a long distance to get to the colored bathrooms.

After her outburst, Al uses a crowbar to take down a wall sign indicating "Colored Ladies Room." He then announces, "No more colored restrooms, no more white restrooms, just plain old toilets. Go where you damn well please, preferably closer to your desk."

When John Glenn's flight is delayed by uncertainty about where the space capsule will land, staff members wonder who they should get to recalculate the math. Glenn refers to Katherine when he says, "Let's get the girl to check the numbers, the smart one. I mean, she says they're good, I'm ready to go." After Katherine gets a corrected set of numbers, just before Glenn is enclosed in the capsule he says to those around him, "Thank her for me."

SUMMATION: *Hidden Figures* has an absorbing storyline that highlights the unsung efforts by three extraordinary women in advancing the Mercury project. The three lead actresses are all excellent in their roles and have fine support from everyone else in the cast. Costner is effective in a fictional role that is presumably a composite of NASA employees whose collective work resulted in the ultimate success of the Mercury program.

WHAT AWARDS SHOULD THIS FILM HAVE WON?: Of the ten nominees for Best Picture of 2016, *Hidden Figures* stands above all the other nominees, including such excellent films as *Fences, Manchester by the Sea, Lion,* and *Hell or High Water.* The year's big winners were *La La Land* with six Oscars, and *Moonlight,* which won Best Picture (although at the ceremony a misreading of the printed citation led to *La La Land* getting brief possession of the award).

Despite the mixup, *Hidden Figures* should have won, along with the Best-Actress award, which should have gone to Taraji P. Henson for her marvelous portrayal of Katherine.

PRELIMINARY NOTE FOR OSCAR SNUBS #51-52

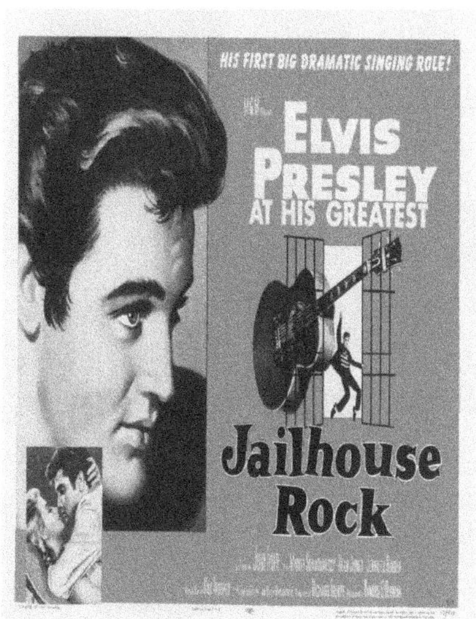

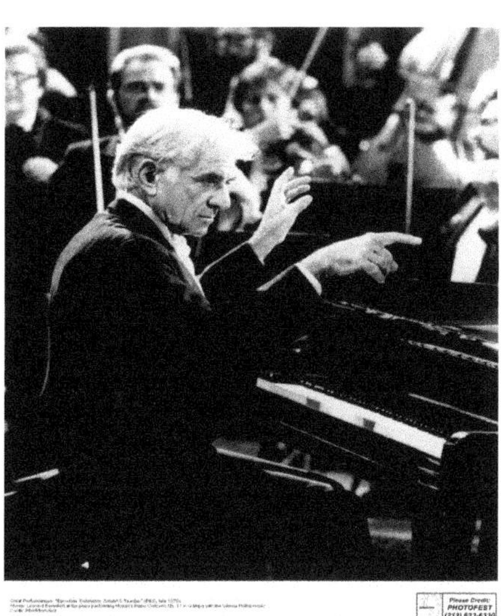

When I began this book I originally envisioned the inclusion of fifty films that exemplify the extraordinary qualities of films that over the years have been overlooked (that is to say, snubbed) in the annual Oscar race by the members of the Academy of Motion Picture Arts and Sciences. As I prepared the list, I began to realize that there are many more films worthy of being written about than just fifty. I finally decided that I would add two additional films of recent vintage that received lots of nominations but didn't win any awards on Oscar night.

One of the most interesting things about these two extra films is the fact that they are both biographical studies of famous musicians, and that these two publicly acclaimed personalities, although they were born and raised in America during the first half of the 20th century, were as different as any two people could possibly be.

I found it interesting that these two films, *Elvis* and *Maestro*, represent two opposite sides of the American music scene between World War II and the end of the war in Vietnam. The amazing career of Elvis Presley began suddenly in 1955, with a succession of number-one rock-and-roll hits recorded on the RCA Victor label, followed by a movie contract that led to such film hits as *Jailhouse Rock* in 1957. Leonard Bernstein's rise to prominence.

Leonard Bernstein's rise to prominence as a composer, pianist, conductor, writer, and TV personality took a lot longer. It began with his overnight celebrity as a replacement conductor of the New York Philharmonic in 1943 and led to his tremendous success as composer of the Broadway musical *West Side Story* in 1957 and the contract he signed in 1958 which made him the first American to ever be hired as music director of the New York Philharmonic.

No films could possibly hope to encompass all the facets in the careers of these two famous musicians, but both *Elvis* and *Maestro* take advantage of remarkable performances by the actors who portray them.

I hope that through these last two film profiles readers will gain a better appreciation of the film medium in its attempts to capture the essence of extraordinarily gifted men.

OSCAR SNUB #51 – *ELVIS* (2022)

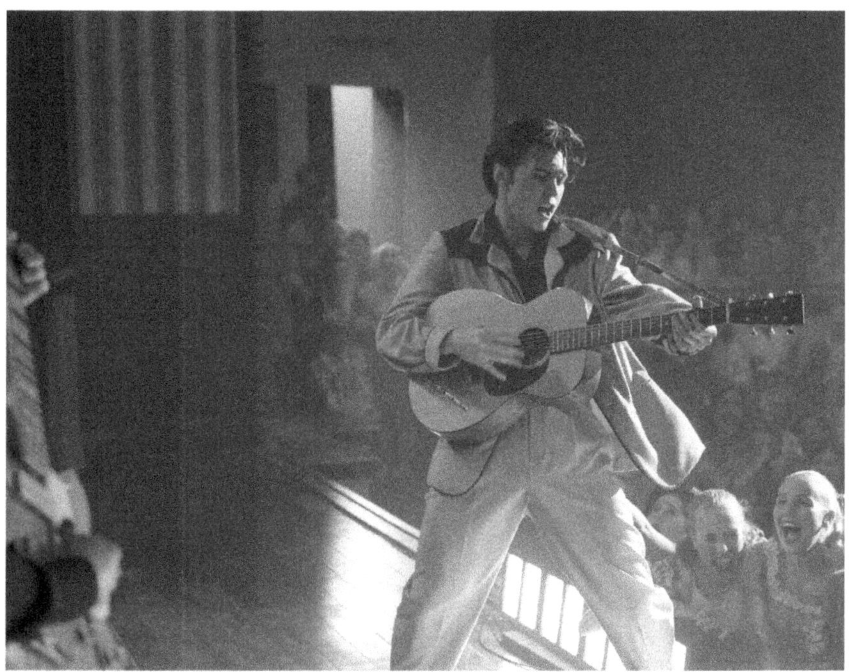

Photofest

Director: Baz Luhrmann; **Producer:** Baz Luhrmann, Catherine Martin, Gail Berman, Patrick McCormick, and Schuyler Weiss; **Studio:** Warner Bros.; **Screenplay:** Baz Luhrmann, Sam Bromell, Craig Pearce, and Jeremy Doner; **Cinematography:** Mandy Walker; **Production Design:** Catherine Martin and Karen Murphy; **Costume Design:** Catherine Martin; **Editing:** Matt Villa and Jonathan Remond; **Sound:** David Lee, Wayne Pashley, Andy Nelson, and Michael Keller; **Music:** Elliott Wheeler; **Makeup and Hairstyling:** Mark Coulier, Jason Baird, and Aldo Signoretti; **Cast:** Austin Butler

(Elvis Presley); Tom Hanks (Colonel Tom Parker); Olivia DeJonge (Priscilla Presley); Helen Thomson (Gladys Presley); Richard Roxburgh (Vernon Presley); David Wenham (Hank Snow); Kodi Smit-McPhee (Jimmie Rodgers Snow); **Running Time:** 159 minutes.

BACKGROUND: Several attempts have been made to make film biographies of Elvis's life. The most memorable is John Carpenter's 1979 made-for-TV movie that helped make a star of Kurt Russell. The most recent film is Baz Luhrmann's 2022 film, which is unlike the earlier film in that it not only vividly shows the "King of Rock and Roll" at his flashy best," but it also includes an historically correct portrayal of Colonel Tom Parker, the man largely responsible for making Presley one of the 20th century's most famous performers.

Only in recent years has it been revealed that not only was Parker not a colonel, but his real name was Andreas van Kujik, an undocumented immigrant in the U.S. who came from the Netherlands. Luhrmann's film explains that Parker first met Elvis Presley when the young singer lived in Tennessee and Parker started manipulating Elvis's career.

The film was first planned in 2014, but the project didn't begin to come together until Tom Hanks agreed to play Tom Parker in 2019. Later that year several actors were approached about playing Elvis, with Austin Butler, an unknown actor with little experience under his belt, winning the role. Covid-19 held up production in early 2020, with the film being completed in 2021.

PLOT: The film begins with the elderly Parker narrating Elvis's beginnings as a Mississippi-born youth who likes to hear Black gospel music performed in tent revivals. After the Presley family relocates to Memphis, Elvis is seen as a guitar-playing teenager attending Black clubs on Beale Street where he becomes infatuated with with upbeat rhythm-and-blues songs performed by such charismatic singers as Little Richard.

The film progresses to Elvis being discovered by Parker, who most recently has been managing country singer Hank Snow and Hank's teenage son. Once Elvis is invited to join one of Hank's country shows, the gyrating and swivel-hipped moves Elvis adds to his performance have a sensational impact, especially on teenage girls in the audience who react to Elvis's sexually provocative swiveling by loudly screaming.

Once Elvis becomes Parker's client, Elvis's fame rises rapidly, with a lucrative recording contract with RCA Victor. Elvis's records become huge sellers and soon Parker negotiates a movie contract for the 21-year old phenomenon with the Paramount studio in Hollywood.

Parker then relates Elvis's induction into the U.S. Army in 1958 and the singer's romance with 14-year-old Priscilla Beaulieu, whom Elvis first meets while stationed in Germany.

Parker's narration continues with Elvis's marriage in 1967, his daughter Lisa Marie's birth, and the controversial Christmas program in 1968 wherein Elvis defies Parker by exchanging familiar Christmas songs for some of Elvis's rock hits and a protest song inspired by the recent deaths of Martin Luther King, Jr. and Bobby Kennedy.

Late in the film Parker arranges Elvis's lavish shows in Las Vegas and maneuvers to keep Elvis from planning an international tour, which would force Parker to reveal his status as a U.S. non-citizen. Elvis's drinking and pill-taking are revealed, along with the failure of his marriage.

When Elvis learns that Parker has gambled away Elvis's entire fortune, the singer is forced to keep on performing until his premature death at age 42. Parker lives on for another 20 years.

MEMORABLE MOMENTS: When Parker observes the young Elvis on stage, the singer wears a pink costume and dances with gyrating leg moves that cause young girls in the audience to scream. the Colonel calls this appeal to female fans a "taste of forbidden fruit" and says that this was "the greatest carnival attraction I'd ever seen. He was my destiny."

In one scene Elvis's gyrating performance on an outdoor stage in Memphis is disrupted by local authorities who think Elvis's shows are indecent. The ensuing riot is a vivid depiction of the impact that Elvis Presley has on audiences (and local police) during his early years.

Some of the most impressive moments in the film come when Elvis defies Parker by doing his rock songs "Hound Dog" and "Blue Suede Shoes" instead of the traditional holiday songs that the TV producers want for Elvis's Christmas special. An added bonus comes when Elvis again defies Parker by singing "If I Can Dream" instead of "Here Comes Santa Claus."

Once Elvis starts performing in Las Vegas he amazes his audience by performing some of his songs in a gospel style, but with a rock beat. Especially memorable is Elvis's electric rendition of "It's All Right." The use of big-band orchestrations is a highlight of this scene.

At the end of the film the real Elvis appears in footage of one of his last performances sitting at a piano and impressing a Las Vegas audience with his emotional rendition of "Unchained Melody." This is especially moving because the viewer can sense that the end is near.

SUMMATION: As with such earlier Luhrmann films as the modern version of Shakespeare's *Romeo and Juliet* (1996) and the dazzling *Moulin Rouge* (2001), *Elvis* is a visually stunning film, with lots of split-screen imagery that helps to convey the excitement surrounding one of the 20th century's most unforgettable performers.

Butler is tremendous as Elvis, while Hanks effectively captures the complexity of a man who was a sly villain that exploited Elvis mercilessly. Elvis's life is seen as a circus, with Luhrmann vividly capturing the magical spell that Elvis cast on those around him.

WHAT AWARDS SHOULD THIS FILM HAVE WON?: There was stiff competition for the Best-Picture prize in 2022, especially from *The Banshees of Inisherin, The Fabelmans, Top Gun: Maverick,* and the overpraised winner, *Everything Everywhere All at Once. Elvis* deserved awards for production design and cinematography, and especially for Austin Butler's portrayal.

OSCAR SNUB #52 – *MAESTRO* (2023)

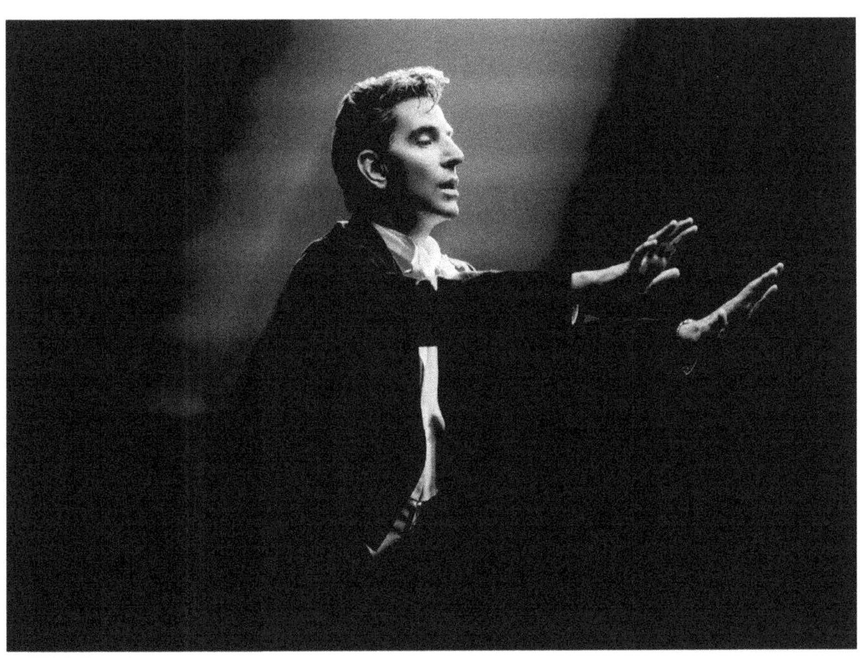

Maestro (2023)
Directed by Bradley Cooper
Shown: Bradley Cooper (as Leonard Bernstein)
Netflix/Photofest © Netflix

Director: Bradley Cooper: **Producer:** Martin Scorsese; Bradley Cooper; Steven Spielberg; Fred Berner; Amy Durning; Kristie Macosko Krieger; **Studio:** Netflix; **Screenplay:** Bradley Cooper and Josh Singer; **Cinematography:** Matthew Libatique; **Production Design:** Kevin Thompson; **Costume Design:** Mark Bridges; **Editing:** Michelle Tesoro; **Sound:** Richard King: **Music:** Leonard Bernstein and Gustav Mahler; **Conducting Consultant:** Yannick Nezet-**Seguin Cast:** Carey Mulligan (Felicia Montealegre); Bradley Cooper (Leonard Bernstein); Matt Bomer (David Oppenheim); Michael Urie (Jerome Robbins); Brian Klugman (Aaron Copland); Sarah Silverman (Shirley

Bernstein); Gideon Glick (Tommy Cochran); **Running Time:** 129 minutes.

BACKGROUND: Leonard Bernstein was one of the 20th century's most celebrated musicians, but in a genre far removed from that of Elvis Presley. Bernstein's theatrical works, symphonies, and other instrumental and choral music, have earned him lasting fame. Additionally, Bernstein's many years of conducting major orchestras and appearing on CBS TV programs added greatly to his celebrity during his lifetime. However, little is known about his personal life.

In 2008 a group of filmmakers began a project that evolved into *Maestro.* Both Martin Scorsese and Steven Spielberg expressed interest in the project, but after Bernstein's three adult offspring endorsed the project, Bradley Cooper came on board not only as the actor who would portray the famous musician but also the film's co-writer and director.

PLOT: The film begins around 1988, when the 70-year-old Bernstein is being filmed at his home by a camera crew. After he plays a piano sketch of one of his new composition, he pauses and admits how much he misses his wife, who died ten years earlier.

The film then moves back to 1943, when Bernstein gets a morning phone call that confirms he will conduct that day's Sunday matinee concert with the New York Philharmonic. After literally jumping for joy he arrives in a business suit on the stage of Carnegie Hall and begins the concert.

The film then shifts ahead a couple of years to a party at which he firsts meets Felicia. When he introduces himself while seated at a piano he simply says "I'm Lenny." Shortly thereafter they become engaged in a conversation which clearly suggests a mutual infatuation.

Not long after their first meeting it becomes clear to Felicia that Bernstein has had intimate relationships with gay men, especially with David Oppenheim, with whom he has been living, but she later decides to accept Lenny as he is and they get married.

The film then moves into the mid-1950s when the Bernsteins, now a family with three small children, are being interviewed by Edward R. Murrow for the live *Person to Person* TV show.

More time elapses as Bernstein continues to have relationships with men, especially an actor named Tommy Cochran, who seems to become a regular visitor at the Bernstein home in Connecticut. After a performance of a Bernstein work that shows Lenny and Tommy holding hands while sitting together in the audience next to Felicia, she walks out on their marriage.

Late in the film they are reunited when Felicia is diagnosed with lung cancer. After her death Bernstein continues his conducting career and also leads conducting classes at Tanglewood, but he clearly never gets over the loss of his wife.

MEMORABLE MOMENTS: The first part of the film, which is in black-and-white, features a romantic scene in which Lenny and Felicia are sitting back-to-back on the grass in Central Park and she admits that she's never seen him sitting down so long. She then says she knows who Lenny is, but they mutually consider to give marriage a try.

The TV interview is a fascinating scene, with the actual recorded voice of Murrow heard from an unseen TV set. During the conversation with Murrow, Bernstein admits that being both a composer and a conductor is like having an inner and an outer life, but in a schizophrenic way.

In the latter scenes, which are shown in color, a moment takes place in their New York apartment on Thanksgiving Day when the Bernsteins engage in a heated conversation in which Felicia says that her husband is going to die a lonely old queen. While their voices rise in tone the floats in the Macy's parade pass by the windows of the room. Especially memorable is the fact that the actors perform in this scene without any editor's cuts.

One of the film's finest moments occurs when Bernstein is conducting Mahler's Second Symphony in Ely Cathedral in England in 1973. With few cuts, Cooper conducts with such spirited animation that the viewer may believe that Bernstein himself is conducting.

SUMMATION: For viewers who are not well acquainted with Leonard Bernstein's career, much of *Maestro* may seem like a patchwork of meandering scenes. But others should find this a film of tremendous merit. Bradley Cooper is so visually transformed into the composer that viewers may easily forget that this is an actor's portrayal. Especially in the Mahler performance Cooper's grand gestures and wild gyrating, while vastly different from those of Elvis, expertly convey Bernstein's passionate involvement in the music. Few other conductors have ever been so visibly caught up in the music they are performing.

Beyond Cooper's dedicated performance is that of Carey Mulligan, who is the heart and soul of this film as a woman who shows an initial infatuation with Bernstein, but has to take a back seat to him throughout their marriage. The film often shows Mulligan in a corner of the shot, where she is the observer of Bernstein as a musician and as a man who visibly expresses affection to those around him, regardless of their gender.

A special moment occurs when, during the Mahler concert, the camera slowly moves around to reveal the orchestra members, and then backs away from the players until Felicia comes into view as she witnesses the magnificence of her husband's performance from a spot that is out of the audience's view. This image of Felicia as a shadow figure permeates much of the film and lets the viewer realize what a real asset Felicia was to her husband's career.

WHAT AWARDS SHOULD THIS FILM HAVE WON?: *Maestro* is an expertly crafted film, with superlative performances by its two stars. Both Mulligan and Cooper were equally worthy of Oscars for their roles. Additional awards should have been given for the film's expert cinematography, sound, editing, and especially for the makeup that helped physically transform Cooper into the esteemed musician. It's a real shame that this film was snubbed on Oscar night!!

APPENDIX: ALTERNATE LIST OF 52 SNUBBED FILMS

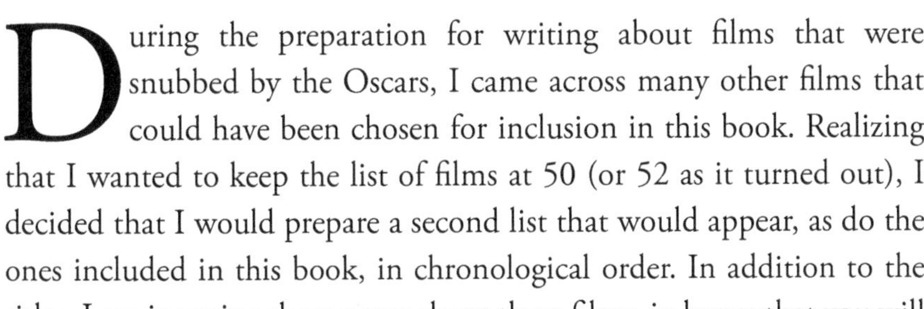

During the preparation for writing about films that were snubbed by the Oscars, I came across many other films that could have been chosen for inclusion in this book. Realizing that I wanted to keep the list of films at 50 (or 52 as it turned out), I decided that I would prepare a second list that would appear, as do the ones included in this book, in chronological order. In addition to the titles, I am inserting short notes about these films, in hopes that you will also appreciate them as worthy of being awarded Oscars.

1. *The Front Page* (1931). First filming of Broadway play is filled with rapid dialogue and fluid camera movement. Great acting by Adolph Menjou and Pat O'Brien. 3 noms.

2. *King Kong* (1933). First version of the giant ape story still holds up. Should have won for special effects and musical score, except those categories did not yet exist. O noms.

3. *The Thin Man* (1934). First of six films with William Powell and Myrna Loy as Nick and Nora Charles. An early detective story classic. Even Asta the dog is good. 4 noms.

4. *Top Hat* (1935). Fred Astairs and Ginger Rogers' third film together, with classic Irving Berlin songs. A great follow-up to *The Gay Divorcée* (1933). 3 noms.

5. *My Man Godfrey* (1936). Good comedy film, the first with four Oscar nominations in acting categories. Carole Lombard's only acting nod (a real snub!!) 6 noms.

6. *Four Daughters* (1938). Great debut for John Garfield, snub in supporting role. 5 noms.

7. *The Letter* (1940), Good William Wyler film, one of Bette Davis's many snubs. 7 noms.

8. *The Little Foxes* (1941). Strong Lilllian Hellman story. Great acting. Both Davis and Patricia Collinge were snubbed. Herbert Marshall not even nominated. 9 noms.

9. *Madame Curie* (1943). Great bio film. Greer Garson is good but won in '42. Walter Pidgeon's best role. He received a nomination but no win. 7 noms.

10. *Henry V* (1946). Olivier's best Shakespearean film. He was awarded honorary Oscar but was snubbed in acting category. *Hamlet* (1948) = consolation prize. William Walton's musical score also snubbed. 4 noms.

11. *I Remember Mama* (1948). Lovely sentimental drama. Four acting nods. 5 noms.

12. *Caged* (1950). Engrossing women's prison film. Eleanor Parker and Hope Emerson both nominated for their roles and both got snubbed. 3 noms.

13. *Death of a Salesman* (1951). Good version of play, fine acting, three acting nods. 5 noms.

14. *Quo Vadis* (1951). Spectacular Roman historical drama. Peter Ustinov nominated for playing Nero, but was snubbed. Great Miklós Rózsa musical score also snubbed. 6 noms.

15. *Ivanhoe* (1952). Colorful medieval saga. Another snub for Rózsa's music. 3 noms.

16. *The Band Wagon* (1953). Great Fred Astaire and Cyd Charisse dance numbers, especially "Dancing in the Dark." 3 noms.

17. *The Caine Mutiny* (1954). Fine WWII drama, Bogart snubbed as Captain Queeg. 7 noms.

18. *Rebel without a Cause* (1955). Dated but still potent drama. James Dean is terrific but not nominated (he received acting nod for *East of Eden* - another snub!). 3 noms.

19. *Friendly Persuasion* (1956). Fine Civil War-era story. Gary Cooper is good, Anthony Perkins was snubbed for his fine supporting role. 6 noms.

20. *Peyton Place* (1957). Good film from racy book. 5 acting nods, no wins. Russ Tamblyn's only nomination (a real snub). 9 noms.

21. *Witness for the Prosecution* (1957). Engrossing Agatha Christie murder drama. Charles Laughton was snubbed, as was Elsa Lanchester. 6 noms.

22. *Cat on a Hot Tin Roof* (1958). Good Tennessee Williams drama. Elizabeth Taylor and Paul Newman were snubbed. Burl Ives was not nominated (but won for *The Big Country*). 5 noms.

23. *Some Came Running* (1958). Fine drama, beautifully filmed. Shirley MacLaine is marvelous in first nominated role. Lost to Susan Hayward in *I Want to Live.* 4 noms.

24. *The Nun's Story* (1959). Compelling drama, with Audrey Hepburn nominated for playing a troubled nun. 8 noms.

25. *The Sundowners* (1960). Australian-set drama, fine acting by Robert Mitchum and Deborah Kerr, her sixth nomination, her sixth snub. 5 noms.

26. *Fanny* (1961). Beautifully filmed version of Broadway musical, minus the songs. Charles Boyer was snubbed for his role, Leslie Caron did not get nominated. 5 noms.

27. *The Sand Pebbles* 1966). Long but fascinating drama set in China. Steve McQueen's best film role and only nomination. Lost to Paul Scofield in *Man for All Seasons.* 8 noms.

28. *Five Easy Pieces* (1970). Jack Nicholson's first starring role and second nomination. Lost to George C. Scott as *Patton.* 4 noms.

29. *American Grafitti* (1973). George Lucas's first hit film, with great young cast. 5 noms.

30. *The Turning Point* (1977). Absorbing drama about ballet. 11 noms.

31. *The Elephant Man* (1980). David Lynch's masterpiece, with John Hurt as deformed Englishman John Merrick. Beautifully filmed in black-and-white. 8 noms.

32. *Somewhere in Time* (1980). Beguiling romantic drama involving time travel. Jane Seamour is enchanting. John Barry's lovely score got snubbed. 1 nom.

33. *The Verdict* (1982). Potent legal drama, Paul Newman's best role. 5 noms.

34. *The Dresser* (1983). Well-made adaptation of Ronald Harwood's play. Great performances by Albert Finney and Tom Courtenay. Both were snubbed. 5 noms.

35. *Silkwood* (1983). Good drama about Karen Silkwood. Fine work by Meryl Streep and Cher. Both were snubbed. 5 noms.

36. *Broadcast News* (1986). Excellent drama. Fine performances by William Hurt, Holly Hunter, and Albert Brooks. All were snubbed. 6 noms.

37. *Gorillas in the Mist* (1988). Compelling drama about Dian Fossey. Sigourney Weaver snubbed for her nominated role. 6 noms.

38. *The Godfather Part III* (1990). Last, and in some ways least, of the trilogy, but still highly recommended. Al Pacino deserved nomination but was snubbed. 7 noms.

39. *The Prince of Tides* (1991). Barbara Steisand's engrossing film of Pat Conroy novel. Nick Nolte was nominated for his role, but got snubbed. 6 noms.

40. *A Few Good Men* (1992). Good story, good film, fine performances. Tom Cruise failed to get nominated, while Jack Nicholson was nominated but snubbed. 4 noms.

41. *The Thin Red Line* (1998). Terrence Malick's beautifully filmed story about WWII in the Pacific. 7 noms.

42. *The Insider* (1999). Michael Mann's compelling film about a whistle blower. Russell Crowe in good form as title character, but was snubbed. His turn came in 2000. 7 noms.

43. *The Green Mile* (1999). Frank Darabont version of Stephen King novel, with fine performances by Tom Hanks and Michael Clarke Duncan. Not as compelling as *Shawshank Redemption*, but very worthwhile. 3 noms.

44. *In the Bedroom* (2001). A modern tragedy of a death in the family. Great work by Tom Wilkinson and Sissy Spacek. Both were snubbed. 5 noms.

45. *Gangs of New York* (2002). Martin Scorsese period drama set during the Civil War. Compelling acting by Daniel Day Lewis, but a snub. 10 noms.

46. *True Grit* (2010). Fine Coen Brothers remake of 1969 film. Good acting by Jeff Bridges in the John Wayne role, but he won in 2009. 10 noms.

47. *American Hustle* (2013). David O. Russell film about con artists pulling scams. Good acting, with nominations in all four acting categories. 10 noms.

48. *The Irishman* (2020). Martin Scorsese film about Jimmy Hoffa. Long and foul-mouthed but compelling drama. 10 noms.

49. *The Fabelmans* (2023). Steven Spielberg film about his own childhood. Fine acting by the two young actors that play the filmmaker at different ages. 7 noms.

50. *Killers of the Flower Moon* (2023). Martin Scorsese's epic film about Indian women in Oklahoma and the men that want to steal their oil-rich land. Fine performance by Lily Gladstone, but she was snubbed. 10 noms.

51. *A Complete Unknown (*2024). Highly entertaining film about young Bob Dylan. Fine performances by Timothée Chalamet and Edward Norton. Both were snubbed. 8 noms.

52. *Sing Sing (*2024). Very engaging look at prisoners putting on a show. Colman Domingo received second consecutive acting nod and second snub (his first nom was for 2023's *Rustin*). A gem and my pick for 2024's Best Picture. 3 noms.

BIBLIOGRAPHY

ONLINE SOURCES:

IMDb. This database was helpful in gathering names of movie actors and film crew members.

Wikipedia. This online source was helpful in gathering information about film plots, background on the films, and names of actors and film crew members.

REFERENCE WORKS ON THE OSCARS:

Holden, Anthony. *Behind the Oscar: The Secret History of the Academy Awards.* New York: Penguin Books USA, 1993.

Osborne, Robert. *75 Years of Oscar: The Official History of the Academy Awards.* New York: Abbeville Publishers, 1989.

Piazza, Jim, and Gail Kinn. *The Academy Awards: The Complete Unofficial History,* Revised ed. New York: Black Dog and Leventhal, 2014.

Wiley, Mason, and Damien Bona. *Inside Oscar: The Unofficial History of the Academy Awards,* Tenth anniversary ed. New York: Ballantine Books, 1996.

GENERAL REFERENCE WORKS ON FILM:

Brode, Douglas. *The Films of the Fifties.* Secaucus, NJ: Citadel Press, 1976.

Duncan, Paul. *Alfred Hitchcock: Architect of Anxiety 1899-1980.* Köln: Taschen, 2003.

Frankel, Glenn. *The Searchers: The Making of an American Legend.* New York: Bloomsbury, 2013.

Katz, Ephraim, with Roland Dean Nolan, *The Film Encyclopedia,* 7th ed. New York: Collins Reference, 2012.

Larson, Matt, and Laurence E. MacDonald. *100 Greatest Film Scores.* Lanham, MD: Rowman & Littlefield, 2018.

Maltin, Leonard, ed. *Leonard Maltin's 2015 Movie Guide.* New York: Signet, 2014.

Sennett, Ted. *Lunatics and Lovers: A Tribute to the Giddy and Glittering Era of the Screen's "Screwball" and Romantic Comedies.* New Rochelle, NY: Arlington House, 1973.

Silver, Alain, and James Ursini. *From the Moment They Met It Was Murder: Double Indemnity and the Birth of Film Noir.* Philadelphia: Running Press, 2024

Spoto, Donald. *Madcap: The Life of Preston Sturges.* Boston: Little, Brown, and Co., 1990.

Vermilye, Jerry. *The Films of the Thirties.* New York: Citadel Press, 1992.

INDEX 1: TITLES

INDEX 2: PERSONAL NAMES

www.ingramcontent.com/pod-product-compliance
Ingram Content Group UK Ltd.
Pitfield, Milton Keynes, MK11 3LW, UK
UKHW062259290726
14090UKWH00017B/778